BENTON MENNONITE
CHURCH LIBRARY
15350 CR 44
GOSHEN, IN 46526

W9-DEC-053

The Hammer Rings Hope

Photos and Stories from Fifty Years of Mennonite Disaster Service

Lowell Detweiler

Herald
Press

Scottdale, Pennsylvania
Waterloo, Ontario

To all the people who have served with

Mennonite Disaster Service during its first fifty years,

and to those who have allowed us to walk with them

and thus have become part of our story,

our faith, and our friends

Library of Congress Cataloging-in-Publication Data

Detweiler, Lowell, 1936-
    The hammer rings hope : photos and stories from fifty years of Mennonite Disaster
  Service / Lowell Detweiler.
       p. cm.
    Includes bibliographical references
    ISBN 0-8361-9110-2 (hardcover : alk. paper)
       1. Mennonite Disaster Service. 2. Disaster relief. I. Title.

BX8128.W4 D48 2000
361.7'5'088287—dc21

                                                    99-087272

The paper in this publication is recycled and meets the minimum requirements of
American National Standard for Information Sciences—Permanence of Paper for Printed
Library Materials, ANSI Z39.48-1948.

To order or request information, please call 1-800-759-4447 (individuals);
1-800-245-7894 (trade). Website: www.mph.org

Credits for cover photos, with page numbers: Front: tornado, by R. Wade Balzar, courtesy
of *Mennonite Weekly Review,* 8; rebuilding at Birmingham, by Carl Hiebert. Back: Flood,
courtesy of Marj Heinrichs, 89; barn raising, MCC photo, by Pearl Sensenig, 30; quake-
wracked house in California, MDS photo, 52; roofing, courtesy of Dan Yutzy, 125; burn
pile, MDS photo, 110; MDS sign, by Carl Hiebert.

Unless otherwise noted, Scripture is from the *Holy Bible, New International Version* ®,
copyright © 1973, 1978, 1984 by International Bible Society, and used by permission of
Zondervan Publishing House, all rights reserved. KJV, from the *King James Version, The
Holy Bible,* adapted. NLT, from the *Holy Bible, New Living Translation,* copyright ©
1996, used by permission of Tyndale House Publishers, Inc., Wheaton, IL 60189, USA, all
rights reserved. NRSV, from the *New Revised Standard Version Bible,* copyright 1989 by
the Division of Christian Education of the National Council of the Churches of Christ in
the USA, and used by permission.

THE HAMMER RINGS HOPE
Copyright © 2000 by Herald Press, Scottdale, Pa. 15683
      Published simultaneously in Canada by Herald Press,
      Waterloo, Ont. N2L 6H7. All rights reserved
Library of Congress Catalog Card Number: 99-087272
International Standard Book Number: 0-8361-9110-2
Printed in Canada by Friesens
Book design by Merrill R. Miller

09 08 07 06 05 04 03 02 01 00 10 9 8 7 6 5 4 3 2 1

Contents

Foreword

From 1950, Peter J. Dyck as pastor of Eden Mennonite Church, Moundridge, Kansas, promoted the vision of all Mennonites in the MCC constituency cooperating in disaster service. The Mennonite Service Organization was organized January 1951. Dyck recruited flood-control workers in spring 1951 and chaired the March 1952 inter-Mennonite meeting that formed a Disaster Committee, with Dyck as chair and John Diller as secretary-treasurer. By 1954, people called it "Mennonite Disaster Service."

MDS volunteers often face a key question: Why are you doing this? People have a right to know our motivation. Is it money? Does the church require it? Do we have a hidden agenda? It is also good for us to know why we give time, effort, and money to help people hit by natural disasters. Here are three reasons for doing good:

First, for the sake of the needy. We find it difficult to respond to many overwhelming needs in the world because they are too far away, too big, too intractable, or controlled by "principalities and powers" that are hard to deal with. But in MDS, there is good news: we can do hands-on work that makes a difference, brings hope to others, and adds meaning to our own lives.

When we want to aid people, we need to ask: Is it an urgent situation the party cannot handle alone? Can I really help? Is it biblically justified? For MDS following a natural disaster, the answers are *yes, yes, yes.* When a storm or flood wrecks a house, people urgently need outside help. Helping is something we can do. The Bible teaches us to follow the example of Jesus, who "went about doing good" (Acts 10:38).

Second, for the sake of God. With few exceptions, the thousands of MDS volunteers serve because of their personal relationship with God. They take Paul's words to heart: "Whatever you do, in word or deed, do everything in the name of the Lord Jesus, giving thanks to God the Father through him" (Col. 3:17, NRSV). Without this inner relationship, their service would still promote human welfare but not be called Christian. Christians blend their love for God and love for others.

This book abounds with testimonies about volunteering because of experiencing God's love. Volunteers then report that serving strengthened their faith. They say, "MDS is more than bricks and mortar!" "We need to keep focusing on our faith and why we are serving." After helping cope with 10 or 11 disasters, one admits, "If I were doing this for pay, I likely wouldn't be here. I need a channel for serving the Lord."

Third, for the sake of self. If eyebrows go up at this, I am not surprised. It is unworthy for us to serve with a hidden agenda of "what's in it for me?" As T. S. Eliot says, "There is no greater treason than to do the right thing for the wrong reason."

On the other hand, I believe we are so created that unless we reach out to others in need, we will bring damage to our souls. The story of Scrooge is legendary because it touches on that basic truth of human nature. We need each other to help us remain human. Too often people pursue their own pleasure and miss the satisfaction of living for others.

To help others is as necessary for our psychological and spiritual well-being as food and exercise are for physical health. I once told a friend that if we refuse to help a person in need when we can do so, we'll go to the dogs. He said, "Not only to the dogs, but to hell." That sounds like Jesus (Matt. 25:45-46) and Jonathan Edwards (1741).

Robert Kreider agrees that for our spiritual health we need to help people in need. He goes a step further: "MDS is fun. It's exhilarating. You drive through the night. You enjoy meeting people. It's great to tell stories when you come back."

A natural disaster destroys property and can also destroy reason and faith, relationships and hope. That is why it is so urgent for those who have been spared to assist disaster survivors, with saws and hammers, *and* with love and compassion. MDS presents a golden opportunity. As one volunteer says, "Lives were changed because of this trip, changed in Alabama, in our church, and in our family."

MDS is God's gift to the church. Jesus encourages us all, including those who may not yet have discovered the joy of helping someone in need: "Whatever you did for these members of my family, you did for me" (Matt. 25:40, adapted).

—Peter J. Dyck, Scottdale, Pennsylvania

Preface

As executive coordinator of Mennonite Disaster Service (MDS) from 1986 to 1998, my knowledge of and respect for this grassroots organization of committed volunteers has increased tremendously. On behalf of the organization, I had the privilege of receiving the thanks of many people for the services offered by our thousands of workers, including personal thanks from former President Jimmy Carter. At each visit to a project site and at each all-unit or regional meeting, I heard additional stories of our bearing "each other's burdens," adding to the oral history of MDS.

Some suggest MDS stands for "Mennonites Doing Something." We are a doing organization: we shovel mud, we remove debris, we repair and rebuild homes, we listen, we eat, we tell stories, and we hammer out hope. But we do not write and record our activity. Over these fifty years, many of our stories have been lost as early founders and volunteers have left us to hear the words, "Well done, good and faithful servants." In 1975, Katie Funk Wiebe gathered stories from the first twenty-five years of MDS activity for *Day of Disaster*. We appreciate permission to use significant material from her book in composing this record.

The last twenty-five years have brought increased numbers of disasters and have challenged MDS in new and different ways. Since 1989 the United States has seen the five largest disasters ever, measured by the value of property damaged or destroyed. In a changing world, MDS has been called upon to find new and creative ways to meet the needs of people facing the crisis of disaster, natural or human-made.

As we approached the year 2000 and the fiftieth anniversary of MDS, several factors combined that led to the proposal for this book. Since Hurricane Hugo hit the Caribbean and South Carolina in 1989, MDS has never had a quiet time, without major project activity. After twelve years of "chasing disasters," I was not sure at age sixty-two if I had the energy for another term as coordinator, a job that never ends. Yet I was not ready to retire. I was also aware of the coming fiftieth anniversary date and felt strongly that we needed to share more of the MDS story and thus challenge future generations to carry on the vision of caring service so wonderfully created and pursued during these first fifty years.

The MDS board enthusiastically supported a proposal simply called MDS 2000. It included writing this book and planning a major celebration at Hesston, Kansas, in the year 2000. The board's support of this two-year venture, with faith that I could write a book, has been the chief reason it has happened. Many others have joined in making this truly a team effort, as we intend for all MDS projects to be.

I have been asked whether I am writer, editor, or compiler. The answer is yes. I have written much of the book from interviews with dozens of persons and extensive research in MDS files. I have asked others to write or have used stories written by others. Because of limited space, their excellent contributions suffered difficult editing. I offer special thanks for contributions from John A. Lapp for chapter 3, Marj Heinrichs for chapter 7, Paul Unruh for chapter 9, and Edgar Stoesz for chapter 11. Many others have shared stories, poems, photos, and materials compiled in these pages. I extend appreciation to the many who shared materials we did not have room to use.

Though I cannot list everyone who has added to this story, let me recognize and thank the following:

• The MDS board, whose vision leads MDS daily and whose personal support kept me going during twelve years as coordinator and two years in this special assignment.

• The MDS 2000 Advisory Committee: Eldon King, Abe Ens, Syd Reimer, and Katie Funk Wiebe gave direct supervision and wise counsel for this effort.

• The MDS Akron staff, who provided encouragement along with logistical support and special counsel to many aspects of this book and the larger MDS 2000 project.

• Project assistants Ginny Sauder and Delphine Martin, who transcribed interviews, worked on special research and projects, sorted hundreds of photos, and performed many other tasks, without which I would never have completed this book. Glenda Hollinger and Dana Hess also transcribed many interviews.

• MDS network leaders, regional directors, unit leaders, project directors, and others who shared their stories and helped arrange interviews to gather others' stories. A special note of appreciation to MDS Kansas for the use of their facilities and their support of this project in many ways. Thanks also to the many MDS units who provided financial support for the MDS 2000 project.

• All who agreed to be interviewed or sent in stories or photos, while knowing that only a small percent of the gathered material could be included.

• The staff of the MCC records department and the Mennonite Archives in Goshen, Indiana, who gave patient and invaluable help in helping track down elusive historical information.

• Special thanks to Carl Hiebert, who volunteered his professional photographic skills and enriched this book with excellent photographs.

• Michael King, who served as personal editor and has made this book much better for your reading pleasure.

• Paul Schrock, David Garber, Merrill Miller, and their publishing team at Herald Press, who saw the promise of this book despite an untested author and who joined in the creative planning and publishing of *The Hammer Rings Hope*.

• Friesens of Altoona, Manitoba, whose offer to print the book at a subsidized price made the pictorial version a valid option.

• MDS Region V leaders, who found financial support to subsidize the printing costs so we could offer this book at a "blue collar MDS price." Thanks to sponsors Barkman Concrete, Loewen Windows, Mennonite Foundation (Ontario), Mennonite Savings and Credit Union (Ontario), Triple E Canada, and all others who contributed.

• Everyone who provided financial support for the MDS 2000 project, led by several sponsors whose generous contributions made it possible: Alfred G. Zook, Mrs. Amos J. Miller, The Dutch Corporation, Sauder Woodworking, Noah Zimmerly Jr., The Wichita Foundation, Levi and Lillis Troyer, and Mennonite Indemnity. Moser Motor Sales supplied the vehicle used for traveling, and K-Z Incorporated donated the trailer that served as office and traveling home.

Goodville Mutual Casualty Company, the Oak Grove Mennonite Church Foundation, and Schowalter Foundation provided the sponsorship for the special anniversary display.

• My wife, Ruth, for her support over the many years when MDS work required extensive travel, and especially during the long days of research, reading, and writing for this book.

• My dad, Oren Detweiler, who over many years taught me what servanthood was all about, and in September 1999, at age 101, listened with interest to many stories from this book, then one week later went to his heavenly reward.

Given the incomplete nature of many MDS records, it has been difficult to verify all the information in the book and identify some photo records. Thanks to those whose materials have been used without proper acknowledgments. We welcome any corrections for our files and for future printings.

"To God be the glory, great things he has done."

—*Lowell Detweiler*

Introduction

To understand this book, readers first need to grasp the structure and language of Mennonites and disaster agencies. Combining the complex worlds of Mennonites and of disaster services can be confusing to the uninitiated.

Mennonite Disaster Service (MDS) is the binational (Canada-United States) organization that responds to disasters in these two countries on behalf of many Mennonite and related groups. The Mennonite Central Committee (MCC) is the worldwide relief and service organization of these same groups. MDS was a section (department) of MCC until 1993, when it was separately incorporated (see chap. 11).

Almost all of the many varieties of Mennonites, Amish, Old Order Mennonites, and Brethren in Christ support MDS. The appendix offers a chart of supporting organizations and their representatives. Chapters 3 and 13 explain "who we are," "what we believe," and "how we work together."

Except for a few staff people at MDS headquarters in Akron, Pennsylvania, volunteers make up the entire grassroots network. The local unit is the building block of the MDS network, usually in a state or provincial area. These local units are grouped into regions, illustrated by shaded areas of the map on page 181. Each region also has its volunteer leadership. This book often refers to the unit-regional structure, as shown by the unit history chart with the appendixes.

Since beginning in 1950, MDS has cooperated with other church and disaster-response groups in coping with disasters. We have valued our partnerships with the American Red Cross and The Salvation Army, and we were founding members of the National Voluntary Organizations Active in Disaster (NVOAD), now with over thirty national members. We work in close cooperation with the Federal Emergency Management Agency (FEMA) and its state counterparts, and the Emergency Measures Organization (EMO) in Canada. These and other acronyms are listed below to assist in understanding the Mennonite and disaster language of this book. Enjoy the puzzle!

Mennonite and Disaster Service Language (Acronyms)

ACS	Adventist Community Services	FEMA	Federal Emergency Management Agency (U.S.)
ARC	American Red Cross		
BA	Beachy Amish (or Amish-Mennonites)	GC	General Conference (of the Mennonites)
BIC	Brethren in Christ	MB	Mennonite Brethren
CAM	Christian Aid Ministries	MC	Mennonite Church
CHPC	Conference of Historic Peace Churches	MCC	Mennonite Central Committee
CM	Conservative Mennonite	MDS	Mennonite Disaster Service
COs	conscientious objectors	MDR	Mennonite Disaster Relief (forerunner of MDS, in Manitoba)
COB	Church of the Brethren		
CPS	Civilian Public Service	MSO	Mennonite Service Organization (forerunner of MDS)
CRWRC	Christian Reformed World Relief Committee		
		NOA	New Order Amish
CWS	Church World Service	NVOAD	National Voluntary Organizations Active in Disaster
EMC	Evangelical Mennonite Church		
EMO	Emergency Measures Organization (Canada)	OOA	Old Order Amish
		OOM	Old Order Mennonite
FDS	Friends Disaster Service	TSA	The Salvation Army

R. Wade Balzat, courtesy of Mennonite Weekly Review

CHAPTER ONE

In the Eye of the storm

*The wind blows over it
and it is gone,*

*and its place remembers
it no more.*

Psalm 103:16

*Cast your bread upon
the waters,*

*for after many days you
will find it again.*

Ecclesiastes 11:1

Mennonite Disaster Service began in 1950 in Hesston, Kansas, as sincere followers of Christ asked what it means to live their faith and love their neighbors as themselves. During those first 40 years, the founders, as well as the thousands of their sisters and brothers who followed, used MDS to share the cup of cold water (Matt. 10:42) with neighbors all over North America and beyond. *Then on March 13, 1990, devastation threatened Kansas.*

BULLETIN

IMMEDIATE BROADCAST REQUESTED
NATIONAL WEATHER SERVICE WICHITA KS
4:20 PM CST TUE MAR 13 1990
THE NATIONAL WEATHER SERVICE HAS ISSUED A SEVERE THUNDERSTORM WARNING IN
THE FOLLOWING COUNTY: RENO
AT 3:18 PM A SEVERE THUNDERSTORM WAS IN THE RENO COUNTY AREA.
THIS THUNDERSTORM IS PRODUCING GOLF-BALL SIZE HAIL AND IS MOVING NORTHEAST AT
40 MPH. IT IS LOCATED NEAR PRETTY PRAIRIE
REMEMBER . . . SEVERE THUNDERSTORMS CAN AND OCCASIONALLY DO PRODUCE TORNA-
DOES WITH LITTLE OR NO ADVANCE WARNING. BE ON THE LOOKOUT.

Our Story Kirk and Jean Alliman

Kirk and Jean Alliman lived in Hesston, Kansas, 1981-93. Kirk was president of Hesston College and Jean a professor there. They lived at 103 Erb Street, on the west edge of Hesston. The Allimans share their memories of March 13, 1990, and the days that followed.

Kirk: I usually left the office close to five, so I was home by then. The weather was ominous. I even thought I could smell something in the air. Our daughter, Sarah, age eight, was

Photo, page 8: On March 13, 1990, a powerful tornado took dead aim at Hesston, Kan., the birthplace of MDS. Despite widespread devastation, no lives were lost in Hesston. Two fatalities occurred along its 100-mile path.

home from school. On TV we heard non-stop warnings that there was serious weather around. I'm not sure if the first announcement included Hesston, but it didn't take long to figure out that something terrible was in the making.

Jean: I was at Hesston Mennonite Church getting ready for a mother-daughter banquet. When the first sirens went off, we went to the basement. I didn't know Kirk was home but thought Sarah was home alone. When the sirens stopped, I jumped in the car and drove home.

I found Kirk and Sarah watching TV in

R. Wade Balzer, courtesy of *Mennonite Weekly Review*

Above: Looking southwest over Kropf Lumber Yard at the tornado seven minutes away.

the basement. The first thing I heard was "Hesston, you are in the direct line." Sarah and I took refuge in the windowless laundry room in the basement; Kirk scouted the storm from the backyard.

Kirk: From our deck on the west, I watched the storm approaching. I've heard that tornadoes can bounce, so I wasn't

convinced it was going to hit us. When it got to the Mennonite Brethren Church a block away, I realized this was for real. Jean says that when I ran to the basement, I was trembling. I remember seeing an enormously turbulent sky. It was something quite different and much uglier than I thought a funnel would be. I knew we were in trouble, so I joined Jean and Sarah between the washer and dryer, under blankets and pillows. We began to pray.

I guess that's when the clattering began. Jean said the funniest thing. She heard glass breaking and exclaimed, "Oh, no! I think a window is broken."

Jean: The first two weeks of March had been mild. I had already put houseplants on the deck. As I heard the clattering, I thought the plants had come through the French doors. Well, the deck had come through too!

Kirk: When it grew quiet, I went up to the first floor. Debris was everywhere. I hollered down, "There's no roof." Straight northeast from our house was one incredible picture of devastation. All the buildings had been blown away. Jean and Sarah joined me; we saw neighbors emerging from basements. It was a special feeling to see everyone alive. Soon we were surrounded by concerned friends and colleagues.

Soon after we emerged from the basement, our telephone rang. I crawled through the debris. The phone had been knocked off the desk and was covered by the collapsed roof. I remember thinking, Should I answer this? It was my mother in Iowa City. She had heard there were tornadoes in Kansas but didn't know we'd been hit. She was just wondering how things

were for us. I told Mother we'd had a unique experience. It was neat to have my folks know immediately that we were okay.

Jean: Soon it was dark, with rain threatening. Jim Mininger and others helped carry some of our things to the still-intact basement. They took the computers and whatever else they could. Along with the rain came another tornado warning, so the

Duane Graham

three of us went to Mininger's. We stayed several nights.

Kirk: I remember the meal conversation around the table and our total disbelief at what had happened. Then Jim and I started walking the town to get a feel of the larger situation. We discovered that a whole segment of town had been struck.

Jean: Later we decided, "We've got a big job ahead of us. Let's get a good night's sleep, get up in the morning, and get going." In fact, we didn't sleep a bit. We talked about what needed doing and how we'd do it. We thought we would have to get up, go over to the house, and pick up our mess. Little did we know what would happen. It was a remarkable experience.

At 7:30 the next morning, we went back to what was left of the house. Fortunately, two couples from MDS arrived, introduced themselves, and took charge of the cleanup. They provided wonderful support, especially in convincing us that much of what we wanted to salvage actually belonged in the dump. They helped us let go.

Kirk: That morning we were still under the naive impression that everything could be repaired and put back in place. I remember standing in the middle of the street with our insurance agent. I wasn't yet convinced that our house had been totally destroyed. I asked him what portion of our coverage we would get. He said, "Well, what part would you like to keep?" He made it clear, without any hassle, that we were entitled to maximum coverage on the house and contents.

MDS has a lot to offer disaster victims. Since MDS people have been through it so many times, they prioritize what needs to happen. As we sat in the wreckage, they helped identify what needed to be addressed. MDS workers were enormously helpful, so calm and caring. We assumed everybody in town was being treated the same way—with an unending series of wonderful acts of compassion and help.

I was surprised at how good it felt to hear from people near and far. People learned about the tornado through TV, newspaper, or by word of mouth. They called, e-mailed, faxed, and wrote. Many sent money, even people who knew we didn't need it. It felt wonderful to receive gifts from people who basically told us, "Go out and buy whatever you need to get back on your feet."

Left: Cleanup time at the Alliman home, 103 Erb Street, Hesston, the day after the tornado. Standing, from left: Kirk, Christopher, and Jean, with Sarah in front. Christopher was on a school band trip when the tornado hit.

The Storm

Most Kansans will not soon forget 1990. Unusually warm spring weather brought the first tornado sighting of the year on March 11. On Monday the 12th, came 17 reports of hail and windstorms in northeast Kansas.

By 9:30 a.m. on Tuesday, the weather service issued a rare morning tornado watch for much of central Kansas. Tornado warnings came after the first sighting at 4:34 p.m., when a tornado touched down two miles east of Pretty Prairie and headed northeast at 40 miles per hour. Gaining strength, it narrowly missed Haven, Yoder, and Burrton. Farm after farm was devastated. Homes, barns, sheds, fences, and trees in its half-mile-wide path were torn apart. The recently remodeled home of Toby and Wilma Yoder, a young Amish couple with two small children, was completely plucked off them as they knelt in the basement, sheltering their children beneath them.

Near Burrton the tornado claimed the first of its two victims, six-year-old Lucas Fisher, huddled in the basement with his mother, two brothers, and great-grandparents. He was crushed by falling bricks when a large tree was hurled against their chimney.

Right: An aerial view of downtown Hesston soon after the tornado passed through.

Hesston: In the Eye of the Storm

The tornado struck the west edge of Hesston at 5:37 p.m. At that point 100-200 yards wide, it blasted through town just north of the business center. The tornado damaged or destroyed more than 30 businesses and over 100 homes with winds up to 250 miles per hour. After ravaging Hesston, it exited on the northeast corner of town and headed again for rural Harvey County.

As this tornado left Hesston, the storm system spawned a second, more violent tornado one mile north. The twins traveled in parallel destructive paths for about two miles. Then their tails merged into one ferocious beast, with winds of nearly 350 miles per hour, rated at F-5, the highest wind-force number on Tetsuya Theodore Fujita's tornado intensity scale.

Near Goessel it claimed its second victim, Ruth Voth, who had just returned from visiting her husband, Harold, at the Newton hospital. No one knows if she saw the twister coming. Her body was found along the road, surrounded by debris from their home.

The tornado continued its devastating course northeast, finally lifting about 25 miles from Manhattan. Some reports:

• Seventeen tornadoes touched down in Kansas on March 13.

Fujita Tornado Scale

F-0	40-72 mph	gale
F-1	73-112 mph	moderate
F-2	113-157 mph	significant
F-3	158-206 mph	severe
F-4	207-260 mph	devastating
F-5	261-318+? mph	incredible

Ken Mantyla, courtesy of the *Wichita Eagle*

- At about 7:00 p.m., another tornado originated near Burrton, took a northerly path near Inman and on toward McPherson, and damaged 20 homes.
- Harvey County sustained $25 million in damages, $22 million of that in Hesston.
- An average Kansas tornado is on the ground 10 minutes and travels 6 miles. This one was on the ground nearly 2½ hours and traveled 100 miles.
- These two March 13 tornado deaths were the earliest tornado-related deaths of any year in Kansas history.
- The F-4 tornado that passed through Hesston ranks in the top 2 percent of most-severe tornadoes. The F-5 tornado northeast of Hesston was one of the most intense recorded.

Next Came a Flood . . . of Volunteers

The overwhelming volunteer response to the Hesston tornado began immediately. Neighbors checked on neighbors, helped them move valuable items out of the rain, and invited them to stay the night. The National Guard and emergency personnel arrived in Hesston to help with traffic control and to check for dead or injured. Less then 20 persons were taken to hospitals; four were admitted. The Red Cross set up a hundred cots in an emergency shelter at Hesston High School, but less than 10 local residents used them.

Murray Bandy, whose home was totally destroyed, was one of the few at the shelter that night. "It was almost midnight when I arrived at the Red Cross shelter. Irvin Harms was there with his little pad. He asked, 'Did you lose anything?' I said I

Duane Graham

lost everything. He asked where I lived and said he'd have someone there at 8:00 in the morning. There he was at midnight, trying to arrange help."

Irvin Harms (MDS Kansas leader), Homer Wedel, and Marvin Toews were the MDS Kansas committee members assigned to work in Hesston while others covered rural areas. They remember that night well. Irvin and Evelyn Harms had listened to storm reports as they drove toward home near Moundridge, and watched the storm from about two miles away as it headed straight for Hesston.

After the tornado passed, they left immediately for Irvin and Edna Reimer's home in Hesston. Irvin Reimer was Region III MDS director in 1990. Their house was intact but heavily damaged. The house next door was gone. They boarded up the shattered windows on the Reimer house,

then began a long evening of planning the intense days of work to follow.

Marvin Toews, with two others from the Inman area, headed for Hesston later that evening and drove right into the path of the later tornado heading north from Buhler toward McPherson. They took shelter in a farmhouse, waited for it to go by, then checked out numerous devastated farms in that area. Marvin arrived in Hesston later that night, ready to staff the MDS project office the next morning.

Homer Wedel received a late evening phone call from Irv Harms saying he was needed in Hesston to organize the next day's volunteers. They spent most of the night surveying the area and getting the MDS "office bus" out of storage in Newton. After an hour or two of sleep, they returned early to find 300-400 volunteers awaiting their directions!

The Mel Martin family home on Weaver Street, Hesston, caught fire right after the tornado.

The community of Hesston, where the goodness in every situation is attributed to the grace of God rather than to luck, put its deeply held religious convictions into practice. Families, friends, and acquaintances opened their doors to their homeless neighbors. Mennonite Disaster Service (MDS) seemed to materialize out of nowhere. That came as no surprise to Hesston, the community where the organization had been born 40 years earlier.
—Howard Inglish[1]

Road to Recovery

On Wednesday morning, March 14, more than 1,000 volunteers arrived in Hesston. Hundreds more helped in the rural areas from Pretty Prairie to Hillsboro. Hesston College dismissed classes for the day and sent 500 students and faculty to help. Nearby Bethel College and Tabor College also sent students.

Above: Replacing roofs to prevent further damage was an immediate priority. Volunteers and contractors were extremely busy during the next weeks.

As people returned home next morning, they found massive destruction and overwhelming response. Murray Bandy remembers standing on the floor of what was left of his house, looking around the neighborhood, and seeing 200-300 people picking up debris. The tremendous community response included help from surrounding towns, which sent loaders and trucks, emergency services, and security personnel. There was strong action from other disaster organizations, including the American Red Cross, Salvation Army, Seventh-Day Adventists, Methodists, Church of God in Christ (Mennonite), and many more.

Hesston mayor John Waltner recalls the response with a touch of community pride: "It was inspiring and really, really overwhelming. The first night already, people were here, wanting to help. The outpouring of care and concern and generosity came from everyone. It just seemed that people said, 'Let's see what it takes to get the job done,' and they were not concerned about protecting their turf and having their particular organizations look good. It was an awesome experience.

"One amazing story left me with a special image. On Tuesday night the B-1 bomber pilots and support personnel from nearby McConnell Air Force Base were watching TV reports on our disaster. Several said, 'We have the day off. Why don't we go to Hesston? Those people need help.' They arrived, reported in, were given MDS identification stickers to wear, and pitched in side by side with the MDS people.

"At lunchtime, the Red Cross served sandwiches at the high school. It was amazing, the symbolism of bomber pilots wearing MDS stickers, sitting with MDS people, talking about what they'd done. One can make too much of stuff like that, but I think it's powerful!"

Along the Storm's Trail

Although this storm is often called the Hesston tornado, the devastation, pain, and outpouring of concern spread the length of the 100-mile tornado path. The Old Order Amish made a major contribution to recovery in the Yoder area. Amish volunteers from as far away as Oklahoma came to help with the quick rebuilding of the Toby and Wilma Yoder home, as well as many others.

Near Goessel, the Schmidt family farm, Iris Lane Dairy, took a devastating blow. The Fred and Jim Schmidt families took refuge in their basements one-eighth mile apart, then emerged with gratitude and disbelief. The big farmhouse was badly battered and full of debris. The second house stood undamaged. The dairy barn was gone; all but one cow had survived. The next morning hundreds of volunteers arrived to begin the massive cleanup. Many of the Schmidts were active MDS members and had volunteered elsewhere. Now they found themselves on the receiving end, grateful for MDS.

In a project spread out over such a wide area, MDS leaders could not accurately

14

track how many volunteers worked under MDS, in addition to the hundreds who just pitched in and helped neighbors in need. At least 10,000 volunteers were involved in the first week of massive cleanup. Offers of help came from Goshen College in Indiana, from Pennsylvania, and many other areas. Most offers were turned down, with thanks, because of the tremendous local response. Led by local businesses, banks, many other organizations, and thousands of generous individual donors, more than $332,000 was contributed to the Hesston Tornado Fund. A local committee dispersed the funds to those in need along the tornado's path.

Wrapped in the Arms of God

Even people whose homes were destroyed confirm that if the tornado had to come through Hesston, it came through the "best place in town" and at the right time. At night there would likely have been many more casualties. If it had clobbered the south edge of town, it would have hit the Schowalter Villa retirement community on the southwest, and the trailer park on the southeast. A couple blocks farther north, the tornado would have hit Hesston College and a residential area. Weather specialists debate whether a "microburst" just west of Hesston diverted the tornado slightly north and away from Hesston College. A couple more blocks north would have damaged downtown and the schools. North of the actual path are more residential areas, several churches, and Hesston Corporation. "Couldn't have gone through any better" is the typical refrain.

The churches of Hesston played a major role in the response. The Mennonite Brethren Church had a small part of its roof damaged; all other churches were spared and served various roles in the recovery days. The Hesston Ministerial Alliance met the morning of March 14, joined by mental health staff from Prairie View, who helped local churches respond to counseling needs.

Thus the churches became sanctuaries for people with both material and emotional needs. Donated clothes were sorted and distributed at Hesston Mennonite Church and donated food at Whitestone Mennonite. All churches provided counseling and coordinating services to meet varied needs of members and others. Special services, with time for sharing stories, provided meaningful healing during those first weeks.

Left: The amazing force of a tornado— a piece of straw and a spoon embedded in a tree!

Believe It or Not!

- Home delivery: Before the tornado, Milton Miller had taken a pair of his trousers to the cleaners, about a half-mile farther west. After the tornado, those trousers were found near his destroyed home (and fixed a certain way, so he knows they were his)!
- At Hesston College, dinner was put on hold so students could go to the shelters. Several hungry students decided they couldn't wait and headed for the Pizza Hut across town. So did the tornado. Along with others, they took shelter in the walk-in cooler. The Pizza Hut was destroyed; those in the cooler were unharmed.
- Marcella Diller remembers that one of the first things they did on emerging from their basement into a destroyed home was to pick up family pictures. In most cases frames and glass were broken, but one was found intact. Later they took it apart and saw insulation inside, even though the frame and glass had not been broken.

Reflections—One Year Later

The one-year anniversary was a day of quiet reminiscing for many in Hesston. Some shed tears as they remembered things lost or expressed gratitude for all the help they had received. One-year updates showed about 95 percent of the town rebuilt. Some businesses like Kropf Lumber expanded as other business moved to new locations. MDS Kansas built its state headquarters on the North Main Street site of a house destroyed by the tornado. Disaster coordinator Evelyn Rouner signed copies of her scrapbook-like director's report. In one day, all 200 copies were gone. For the remarkable recovery, she gives credit to the work of thousands of volunteers as well as excellent church, city, business, and county cooperation.

Hesston Mayor Waltner reflects, "It's been a very significant event in our community experience. I think what has come of it has been very positive." But he cautions considering Hesston a "model for disaster response," as some have suggested. "We cannot simply discount the significance of not having fatalities [in Hesston]. It would have been as easy as not to have 50 to 100 people dead. If we had been cleaning up our homes and streets and burying our dead, it would have been a much different experience. We can look back and be thankful we didn't experience the depth of human trauma that other communities do when something like this happens."

Right: Milton and Lorraine Miller helped start MSO/MDS in 1950. Milton remembers going on the first projects in Wichita and Udall, Kan. Now the Millers view scattered remains of their home at 108 Park Avenue, Hesston, and await arrival of MDS volunteers, bringing hope in a full circle.

Full Circle: MDS Returns to Its Roots

As the tornado traversed Hesston, several people felt the tornado's fury and the volunteer assistance in an unusual way.

Bob and Marcella Diller

At 404 North Weaver Street, the home of Bob and Marcella Diller took a direct hit. Bob was president of Kropf Lumber Company, located two blocks west of their home. Concerned employees reported the warning to Bob in his office. As the sirens sounded, most employees left. At the last minute, Bob and his son Mel decided they had better get out too. Mel dropped Bob off at home before heading to his place on Hesston's north edge. Marcella was anxiously waiting on the porch. Their view southwest was limited, but they could see the dirt swirling, so they headed for the basement. In what seemed just a minute, the tornado hit.

After the roar subsided into eerie silence, Marcella asked, "Is it over?"

Bob responded, "Yes," not knowing what waited above them. He reports, "We went up the stairs, opened the door—and there was no roof. Our house was gone! It was hard to believe. These things don't happen to you. I had lived in Kansas 70 years and had never seen a tornado in my life.

"Our car remained in the garage area but was totally smashed. In minutes the Wichita TV people following the storm were in our front lawn, interviewing Marcella. Relatives in Oregon saw her and immediately knew our plight."

Marcella vividly remembers the next day: "We got up, came back to our house, and couldn't believe how everyone was working. MDS and other groups were there. It was amazing how people were right there and helping. They'd say, 'What

Dave Williams, courtesy of the *Wichita Eagle*

do you want to do with this, or this?' Finally I said, 'Anything that's broken, get rid of it.' Cleanup went fast. Later we wondered if a few more things might have been worth saving. But it was okay. We were just getting that part of it over with and starting the next thing.

"On Thursday while Bob went back to work, I watched the backhoes raze the remains of our brick home. I knew this was it. It was gone. This was where we raised most of our family, so we had a lot of memories that were going down the drain. We did have a lot of good times here. But in the end, we had a feeling of thankfulness—thankfulness that Bob got home in time and we were alive."

Milton and Lorraine Miller

At 108 Park Road, on the northeast edge of Hesston, the tornado also destroyed the home of Milton and Lorraine Miller. Lorraine remembers coming upstairs when it was over. "At the top of the stairs was a bicycle that had come in through the front door or the windows. Across the floor lay our grandfather clock that our daughter Brenda and her husband and little boys made for us, and that hurt."

As Milton recalls, later in the evening it was determined that Lorraine was in shock, so she was sent to the hospital to rest. The next day college students helped them sort through and pack whatever could be sent to storage. "What impressed me the most," Milton recalls, "was standing there, looking across town as far as I could see—and everywhere were people in town to help clean up. They came from all these towns where MDS had been, plus others. They sent in food, clothing, equipment, trucks, men."

Giving Hope . . . Full Circle

In 1950 Milton, Lorraine, Marcella, and Bob were members of the two Sunday school classes that joined to start Mennonite Service Organization (MSO), the forerunner of MDS. The vision of those founding members was to establish an organization that would serve God and give hope to others. Now, 40 years later, thousands of MDS volunteers were carrying out that mission. Full circle . . . bread cast upon the waters, returning to the shores from which it was launched (Eccles. 11:1).

God, Come to Us as a Gentle Wind

Associate Pastor Phil Harrington offered this invocation at the Whitestone Mennonite Church on Sunday, March 18, five days after the tornado ravaged town:

Once again, O God, we gather in this place as your people. But we are not the same people we were last week. We have been visited and violated by a force of nature we did not invite. A force invoked by large and unusual air masses and currents that we do not even understand. Yet it came and in a way is still here because our lives have not recovered.

Our lives feel like a photograph of scattered debris. We are here and there and even lost. Part of us is still huddled in a basement, a corner, or a walk-in freezer, listening to frightening noises. Or waiting along the road outside of town, watching. Or racing in a car, trying to imagine.

Part of us is still worrying about friends and family across town. Or wandering through rubble or dirty streets, not quite believing yet that this has really happened to us. Wanting, even on our way to church today, to find things the way they were last week.

Part of us still feels the relief of being alive, reassuring others over the phone, telling our story over and over.

Part of us is wondering, Why our town? Why was our home destroyed? Or why was our home spared? Wondering at the miraculous way so many individuals survived when death was so close.

Part of us feels exposed. As a town, our roof has been lifted, our walls knocked down, our privacy taken. The hundreds of volunteers are here with desperately needed help and care. The National Guard was here. The news people showed our pictures and told our stories to the world around us. The onlookers came and left.

Part of us feels loss. Loss of homes, the places we always felt secure. Loss of possessions, things we were attached to, that we invested part of our lives in. Loss of memories. Loss of regular schedules and activities.

Part of us feels weariness. We are tired from cleaning up, from caring in many ways for victims and volunteers. We have felt the excitement, the adrenaline that keeps us going in times like this—but it is running out.

And so, in the midst of all our feelings of fear, anger, pain, and uncertainty, part of us is looking this morning. Looking for regularity. Looking for things that have not changed. Looking to see if you, God, are still the same.

Come and find us, God. Come to us as a gentle wind this morning. A wind that can gather together our scattered parts. That can soothe our bodies and spirits. A wind in which we can catch our breath. Amen.[2]

Courtesy of MDS Kansas

The Servant Song

Will you let me be your servant,

let me be as Christ to you?

Pray that I may have the grace to

let you be my servant too.

We are pilgrims on a journey,

we are trav lers on the road.

We are here to help each other

walk the mile and bear the load.

I will hold the Christ-light for you

in the night-time of your fear.

I will hold my hand out to you,

speak the peace you long to hear.

I will weep when you are weeping,

when you laugh I ll laugh with you.

I will share your joy and sorrow

till we ve seen this journey through.

Richard Gillard[1]

CHAPTER TWO

In the Beginning

Fifty-year-old memories are delightful to explore, even though they do not always agree on all details, such as the organizational beginnings of what has become MDS. Yet memories and records of the founders intent are clear: We should seek opportunities to be engaged in peaceful, helpful activity just where we find ourselves.

On the early beginnings of MDS, two persons have contributed significant writings that are used extensively in this chapter. In 1950 Fred Brenneman was a teacher of the Young Marrieds Class of the Pennsylvania (Pa.) Mennonite Church near Hesston, Kansas. The following excerpts from his diary are probably the earliest and most accurate records of the organizational beginnings of MDS. (The Pa. church moved into Hesston in 1964 and became Whitestone Mennonite Church.)

John Diller was chosen first coordinator of the emerging organization. Fortunately, he was an excellent writer and record keeper. Much of the material for this chapter comes from his writing.

Courtesy of MDS Kansas

In 1887 a Mennonite church was built near Zimmerdale, four miles southeast of Hesston. Since most of the members came from Pennsylvania, it was called Pennsylvania Mennonite Church. A Sunday school class from this church held the picnic in the park where the idea of a disaster service organization was born on July 28, 1950.

The Fred Brenneman Diary

Photo, page 18: Henry Loewen checking in MDSers at the MDS Kansas bus for the Dodge City, Kan., flood project in 1965.

Friday, July 28, 1950. Sunday school class picnic in Newton. Paul Shenk led discussion on "What can we as COs [conscientious objectors to war] do to help our country and people in need now and in war?"

On May 17, 1951, the Little Arkansas River in Wichita threatened to overflow its dikes. MSO responded promptly and in less than three hours had 35 men in Wichita. A new group came the next morning, and these efforts help save the town from flooding.

This is really when Mennonite Service Organization (MSO) began. Paul Shenk was active in developing the constitution and served as the first vice president. In all this, I had the pleasure of working with these young people, serving as chairman of the constitutional committee and then as first president.[2]

Tuesday, August 8, 1950. Pa.-Hesston S.S. classes joint picnic—ball game with Pa., winning 20-8—basket supper—enthusiastic plans for supporting Puerto Rican girl at Hesston—buying washing machine & refrigerator for Albert Buckwalter.

Friday, August 11, 1950. Meeting of committee—Daniel Kauffman, Allen Diller, Harold Dyck (Hesston S.S. class); Paul Shenk and myself (Pa. S.S. class); Allen Diller sec.; myself, chm.; to consider ways in which we may as COs serve our land.

Wednesday, Nov. 29, 1950. Committee meeting to draw up constitution for Hesston-Pa. group, tentatively named Mennonite Christian Service Organization.

Tuesday, Jan. 9, 1951. David Schrag [General Conference Mennonite (GC)] came to get materials to study for a service organization—gave what we of Hesston-Pa. have.

Monday, Jan. 22, 1951. Meeting and adoption of constitution for MSO; elected me as president.

Sunday, April 15, 1951. Executive committee of MSO met at Paul Brenneman's place to consider appeal by Nelson Kauffman to send a group to help at Hannibal if flood emergency develops.

Monday, April 16, 1951. General meeting of MSO, in student lounge of Hess Hall. Good representation present—wonderful spirit of cooperation; enough volunteers for 3 loads to go to Hannibal, Mo., if called; good reception by local Red Cross.

Thursday, May 17, 1951. Almost torrential rains over a wide area; Black Kettle Creek east side of our place overflowing, as all other creeks; children played in water over the road; MSO, by contacting KFBI [radio station], arranged to send volunteers to Wichita to help with the work sandbagging the dikes and rescue work; 33 went in the evening; Lyle Yost saw to on-the-spot arrangements.

Friday, May 18, 1951. By contacting Rev. Peter J. Dyck, pastor of Eden Mennonite Church, we were able to supply another 35 men today for flood control work in Wichita; of these, 2 carloads from Hesston College. Leaders in Wichita told me when I went down to see if there was need of a third shift of workers, "We have never had such workers." They were assured that we will be ready to help anytime they need us.

Thursday, July 12, 1951. Heavy rains continue—flood situation in eastern half of state very serious—at least five people have perished by drowning. In response to a call from Mayor Ramsey of Salina yesterday, informed him of MSO and that we are ready to help in Salina if help is needed; the mayor called this morning, asking for motor boats; they were sent. Toward evening Lyle Yost, chairman of Service Committee, and Howard Hershberger, vice president of MSO, went to Salina; about 8:15 p.m., Lyle called asking for 100 cots and bedding; by general telephoning at Hesston and Moundridge, the response was "like a flood," and soon the request was more than met. Praise the Lord!

Friday, July 13, 1951. J. M. Brenneman and Howard Beck went to Salina to look after cots and blankets sent there by MSO. Waters generally subsiding. Forty men to Wichita to help in flood control. Very serious floods and fires in Kansas City. General damage very great.

Sunday, Sept. 23, 1951. MSO gave the first program—at Canton, to a large, appreciative audience; the work of MSO is attracting wide attention.

MCC photo, Mennonite Church Archives

Before the Beginning

"Bear ye one another's burdens, and so fulfill the law of Christ" (Gal. 6:2, KJV). MDS volunteers have always claimed that the reason for their organization's existence and work is simply their attempt to follow Christ's teaching "to love one another, . . . to help the neighbor in need along the road." Jesus and his followers modeled a life of healing the sick and caring for those in distress. The Anabaptists of the sixteenth century understood this truth and lived it by caring for others in need. In one famous example, an Anabaptist even turned back to rescue a pursuing persecutor who had fallen through ice on a frozen lake.[3]

Mennonites, Amish, and like-minded Christians have a biblical understanding of faith that embraces a community of caring for each other and for neighbors. For generations we have had barn raisings and gathered for planting or harvesting bees when neighbors had accidents or sickness. Extending this model to helping those affected by natural disasters happened in communities before 1950. Manitoba Mennonites rallied to help neighbors flooded by the Red River in 1948. In 1947 there was a significant response to tornado activity in Woodward, Oklahoma, particularly by members of the Church of God in Christ (Mennonite), who count that date as the beginning of their disaster response program.

CPS Experiences in Disaster Response

Mennonite, Amish, and other young men (plus women volunteers) who chose Civilian Public Service (CPS) during World War II were required to perform work approved to be "in the national interest." In their camps, CPSers chiefly did agricultural work, dairy herd testing, soil conservation, and service in mental hospitals. Some tasks, such as forestry services and fire prevention—as with the popular smoke jumpers—were responses to emergencies. Sometimes CPSers, involved largely in nondisaster work, were called to respond when disasters struck nearby.

While stationed at a sanitation experiment camp in Florida, John Horst of Akron, Pennsylvania, spent several weeks in hurricane cleanup. Stanley Regier and 60 other CPSers from Camp 64 in Terry, Montana, helped repair several miles of railroad track washed out by the rampaging, ice-choked Yellowstone River.

Ralph and Elizabeth Hernley of Goshen, Indiana, were educational director and dietitian for Henry, Illinois, CPSers. They recall the CPS response to a late afternoon tornado that hit nearby Lacon. Seventy-five minutes later, 55 CPS men with tools and heavy equipment were in Lacon. They spent all night cleaning the streets; another

Bear ye one another's burdens, and so fulfill the law of Christ.
—(Gal. 6:2, KJV)

Courtesy of Elizabeth and Ralph Hernley

Courtesy of Elizabeth and Ralph Hernley

Far left: CPS men from Camp Henry (CPS Camp 22) working at tornado site at Lacon, Ill., in March 1942.

Near left: CPSers at Lacon in the midst of cleanup operations. The bulldozer operator is Loray D. Koerner.

crew from camp relieved them early in the morning. After many days and nights of such CPS service, the Hernleys remember a warming in the Henry and Lacon communities' critical view of "conchies" (COs).

Ervin Miller of Sullivan, Illinois, was at camp in Dennison, Iowa, in spring 1943 when the muddy Missouri River endangered the nearby towns of Council Bluffs, Iowa, and Omaha, Nebraska, on opposite banks. He remembers CPSers spending long days and nights with little sleep, bolstering the dike on the Iowa side, which held partly because the Nebraska-side dike burst, relieving the pressure. Grateful Council Bluffs town leaders sent city engineer Jack Boyne to thank the CPSers. He visited the men in the armory where they were bunked.

"You've done a swell piece of work, boys," Boyne said. "How'd you like to go to a show?"

"We never go to shows," they said.

"Well," Boyne countered, "can I send you some cigarettes?"

"We don't smoke," the conchies replied.

Boyne made a third attempt, "How about some beer then?"

"No!" they shouted, horrified.

"Isn't there anything I can do for you?" he asked.

"Yes," they said, "you can send us two new aprons for the cook and four dish towels." These were promptly provided.[4]

The purposes of MSO were clearly stated:

• To promote the Christian ideals of peace and service.

• To promote a corporate group for mutual inspiration and stimulation.

• To activate the principles of peace and service in a constant program when and where needed.

• To provide personnel, equipment, and provisions on short notice in any disaster, whether by force of nature or by war.

Now we have an opportunity or should seek opportunities to be engaged in peaceful, helpful activity just where we find ourselves.

The CPS Influence

Those who conceived the vision that led to MDS saw the World War II CPSers as instrumental in bringing this new venture into being. In writing the early MDS history, John Diller recalled the first 1950 Sunday school class discussions. "The conviction held by those in the group who had served in Civilian Public Service in WWII was aired, namely, that we as professed peacemakers find any type of participation in the prosecution of armed conflict impossible as we strive to follow the Prince of Peace and his message for us. All who served in CPS shared their experiences and exchanged ideas."[5]

Lois Hershberger remembers earlier class discussions: "Paul Shenk and Ray Spicher were the CPS guys who came back and felt they needed to do something in peacetime as well as war." Naomi Weaver reminisces, "I can just see Paul Shenk leaning up against the bench when he was our teacher, just see him standing there, talking about it. I think after that was when those picnics were held."

Lawrence Brenneman, son of the Fred Brenneman who taught the Pennsylvania class (whose diary is quoted above), describes that early picnic: "There are two ways to escape the midsummer heat in Kansas: air-conditioning and a watermelon feast. The latter was the method employed by the young married people's Sunday school class of the Pennsylvania Mennonite Church in Hesston. On July 28, 1950, they met in the Athletic Park at Newton to have an 'old-fashioned watermelon feed.' Paul Shenk and his wife and Ray Spicher and his wife had charge of the program.

"Paul Shenk led in the discussion: 'What can we as conscientious objectors do to help our country and people in need, now, and in war?' Through their discussions and convictions, they finally came to the conclusion 'that not only are we to be ready to respond in time of national crises when the circumstances almost compel us to do something constructively helpful; but now we have an opportunity or should seek opportunities to be engaged in peaceful, helpful activity just where we find ourselves.'"[6]

Where did they acquire these convictions and the inspiration for serving others? Paul Shenk, a chief promoter of this new venture, articulates his feelings: "In CPS we were more or less shuttled off in society. . . . We should have been out there where there was some human need. It seemed to me that one of the ways to witness would be to get out where danger was involved; because this is one of the things they always said, 'You're afraid of danger; you stay here where it is safe.' I wanted to go 1-A-0 and join a medical unit, but my church said if I did, I would be excommunicated.

"The thing that really challenged me was that in the war the British Quakers were given the opportunity of going into the battle and working, not under the army, but in their own ambulance corps. It seemed to me that this was much better than going out and sawing down trees for forest fire trails, etc. I feel we should be trained and we should be ready to give a Christian witness where needed, not by withdrawing, not in a monastery-type circle, but right where it is needed."

Mennonite Service Organization Begins

This contagious enthusiasm was shared with the corresponding class at Hesston Mennonite Church, where similar discussions were taking place, guided by teacher Daniel Kauffman. In early August 1950, the two classes met jointly and selected a committee of five "to look into the possibilities and practicalities of forming a more organized group."

They met on the nights of August 11 and 14 to organize and prepare a statement of convictions and suggestions to send to Mennonite Central Committee (MCC) and the Mennonite Relief Committee of the Mennonite Church. The statement was also read on August 18 to the South Central Mennonite Conference meeting near Harper, Kansas. There the classes were encouraged "to find ways of practical expression of their convictions."

By November the committee had drafted a constitution for the new organization to be called Mennonite Service Organization. On January 22, 1951, the two groups jointly met, approved the constitution, and elected its first executive committee: Fred Brenneman, president; Paul Shenk, vice president; Allen Diller, secretary-treasurer; Paul Brenneman, chair of the medical committee; and Lyle Yost, chair of the service committee.

Membership requirements were modest: "Any Christian who subscribes to the objects of this organization may attend the meetings and will be considered a member." Though other (GC) Mennonites made inquiries, the initial organization was mainly "Old Mennonite." Yet in the minds of leaders like John Diller and Peter Dyck, the early vision included the whole MCC constituency.

Called to Serve

One of the first persons called into early service by the emerging MSO was John Diller. The constitution did not call for a coordinator in its organizational outline but indicated that the Service Committee "shall effect its own organization." Before the first calls for help came in the spring of 1951, John clearly was in place as "coordinator"—the stay-at-home person phoning around to line up volunteers requested by the field director. An early paper details his involvement in the May 1951 floods and states several coordinator qualifications:

- Have a telephone number known by the highway patrol, city officials, and the Red Cross.
- Have a list of personnel and equipment.
- Be able to organize a group quickly to meet needs that arise, making decisions at a moment's notice.
- Be willing and able to stay at home and serve by sitting at a telephone.[7]

John, paralyzed by an accident, met these qualifications. Thanks to his writing gifts, there are excellent records of many early MDS actions and activities. We give a tribute to John Diller at the end of this chapter.

Called to Wichita

The year 1951 brought record floods to many parts of Kansas. On May 17 the first call for service came from Wichita, where the Little Arkansas River was threatening to overflow the dikes. John Diller, coordinator, conferred with Lyle Yost, chair of the service committee. Lyle headed for Wichita at about 6:00 p.m. After checking with the city engineer, he called back in about an hour and said he had promised 15 men equipped with flashlights, shovels, and boots, with one or two trucks.

According to John, "A couple of us were keeping the wires [phones] hot, and by 8:30 p.m. we had 35 men in Wichita, ready to go to work." More went as the night wore on. All night they hauled and filled sandbags. In the morning, another group of 35, including Hesston College students and volunteers from Eden Mennonite Church in Moundridge, relieved the night workers.

The Rains Came Down

The rains and floods in Kansas continued. One week later, Grand Bend called for help. Two carloads went out and lugged sandbags through nearly foot deep mud to dikes 200 feet away. That extra

Courtesy of MDS Kansas

Women from the Service Auxiliary, the MSO women's division, took sandwiches to the weary men. They had also made armbands with the MSO identification on them, which during the rainy night earned the workers the label "Mighty Soaked Outfit."

Left: As the first MDS Kansas coordinator, John Diller spent countless hours on the phone, often finding more volunteers than requested. He would give the switchboard operators his list of people to call, and when he completed one call, the next person was waiting to talk to him!

help was credited with saving the city from flooding. Again the MSO team was relieved the next day by two carloads from Eden Church (GC). Already the projects were inter-Mennonite.

The floods of summer 1951, the greatest then on record in Kansas, presented MSO with an opportunity to stretch its growing muscles. In July , MSO took boats, cots, and blankets to help evacuate Salina. MSOers returned to Wichita and Great

Courtesy of MDS Kansas

Response to a 1953 tornado in Hebron, Neb., spread the word and organizing of MDS units in neighboring states.

Bend for second rounds, and to Florence and Kansas City as floods continued.

In fall and winter 1951-52, MSO sent extra people to an MCC flood-response unit in Topeka, working at longer-term flood rehabilitation. The early concern about lack of enthusiasm and low attendance at meetings was supplanted by a "Here we go again!" spirit as MSO gained experience in responding to the many calls for help.

Going Inter-Mennonite

When a tornado hit Arkansas in early March 1952, Peter J. Dyck, pastor (1950-57) of the Eden Mennonite Church (GC), asked coordinator John Diller, "What are we going to do about Arkansas?" They agreed that John would invite all "MCC constituent churches in central Kansas" to a meeting that Peter would chair. The purpose was to meet the need in Arkansas and be prepared to address any future major disaster. Over 80 persons from four Mennonite conferences attended a March 31 meeting. After discussion, they took actions:

• That we select a Temporary Disaster Committee to represent and guide us in the work in Arkansas and to be prepared in the event of another disaster. That this committee be composed of two men from each branch of the MCC constituent churches who want to cooperate, each church choosing their representatives.

• That the Disaster Committee effect its own organization, consisting of chairman and secretary-treasurer.

• Not to replace our present relief committee, brotherhoods, and service organizations.

• In a major disaster, the Disaster Committee shall immediately investigate the need and avenues for service and report to each local organization.

• Without soliciting funds, the Disaster Committee shall provide personnel and projects through which funds already contributed can be disbursed.[8]

Peter J. Dyck was elected chair of this Temporary Disaster Committee and John Diller secretary-treasurer. This inter-Mennonite coordinating group did not immediately replace the congregational-based MSO organizations, particularly in Old Mennonite churches.

By 1952 John Diller had prepared information on MSO operations and had written a proposal called "MSO in a Churchwide Program of Service." He suggested that "we need a unit of MSO in every congregation." He proposed getting these units together to form a "Central Council of MSO" and—in light of similar activity in the General Conference and Church of God in Christ (Mennonite)—a "unification of all Mennonite Service Organizations." Peter Dyck had experience directing the MCC relief program in Europe after World War II and saw the emerging disaster service program as something "we need to do together."

The Good News of MSO Spreads

This activity captivated the attention of people across the country. On December 1, 1951, a presentation about MSO was given to a Christian businessmen's meeting in Goshen, Indiana. Oklahoma and Nebraska initiated similar discussions.

By 1953 there were organized MSO units in Indiana, where the Relief Committee of the Mennonite Church promoted their formation. The idea soon spread east to Pennsylvania and north into Canada. Robert Kreider, noted Mennonite historian, suggests that the rapid spread of this grassroots laypeople's organization was partly due to the "CPS network" through which the inter-Mennonite mix of younger persons excited about service found avenues for implementing their visions.

By 1954 "Mennonite Disaster Service" was used in Kansas to refer to the organization coordinated by the Temporary Disaster Committee (as compared to the MSO congregational activity). With the spread of disaster activity, there were more calls for Mennonite Central Committee to take a coordinating role. John Diller, in a 1952 proposal for a churchwide program of service, showed awareness of an MCC Executive Committee action of May 3, 1952, that set up permanent disaster relief readiness organizations.

By 1954 there was a call for broader discussion of the many service programs emerging around the church, including expanded voluntary service, disaster service, social service, and peace organizations. The General Conference of the (Old) Mennonite Church sponsored a "Study Conference on Local and Area Service Programs," at Wayland, Iowa, February 12-13, 1954. Persons from any church conference were urged to attend. Much discussion centered on MSO, with strong affirmation for its expansion and consideration of its name. Noting that the Kansas inter-Mennonite group had changed its name to Mennonite Disaster Service, conference participants recommended that all area groups carry that same name.

MCC Takes Leadership

The 1954 MCC Executive Committee minutes noted the growth of local MSO groups and the need for wider coordination and counsel. Leaders felt central coordination was needed for liaison with civil defense and Red Cross in Washington, D.C. On May 15, 1954, the MCC Executive Committee took action to appoint an "MCC Disaster Relief Coordinating Com-

mittee." The first committee was composed of William Snyder (MCC), Elmer Ediger (GC), Boyd Nelson (MC), and Edward Snyder (Ontario, Canada). They met on January 31, 1955, and took their report to the March MCC executive meeting. Included were these points:

• MCC should provide a coordinating committee composed of a member of the Akron staff and representatives to be designated by their respective constituent groups.

• MCC should make an insignia available to Mennonite Disaster Service based on the MCC symbol.

• Contacts with National Red Cross and with civil defense will be handled by Akron staff.

• When disasters occur where MDS is not organized, Akron is to be the clearinghouse for response.

• MCC recommends use of the name "Mennonite Disaster Service" to provincial, district, and state groups.

• MCC shall facilitate information sharing, including mailing lists, reports, and basic materials for new groups.

• MCC will help with the organization of disaster services in new areas.

MDS Is Officially Born

On December 29-30, 1955, the MCC Board at its annual meeting adopted the recommendation of the Disaster Coordinating Committee. Mennonite Disaster Service as a binational inter-Mennonite organization was officially born.

During the 1950s, Civil Defense organizations were responsible for government disaster responses. The emerging MDS

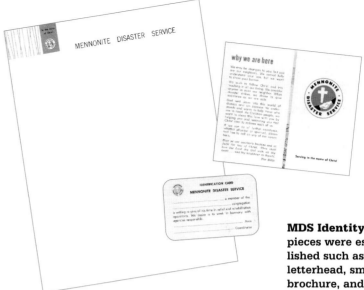

MDS Identity pieces were established such as the letterhead, small brochure, and identification card.

organizations were thrust into cooperative ventures with civil defense, whose major mandate was civil and military preparations for wartime activity. This uneasy partnership became the focus of many discussions, including study conferences cosponsored by the MCC Peace Section.

First Annual Meeting

The first annual meeting of this new Mennonite Disaster Service was held March 2, 1956, at the Hotel Atlantic in Chicago. Thirteen states and one province sent 28 representatives. They chose a Coordinating Council: Boyd Nelson (MC), Paul Martin Jr. (BIC), Elmer Ediger (GC), Dale Rufenacht (EMC), and Laban Swartzendruber (CM). Other groups were invited to send representatives. There were requests for a common insignia, letterhead, and identification cards.

Below: A letter of commendation from the governor of Indiana, addressed to Boyd Nelson.

Top right: In 1964 the MDS section (board) met in Lansdale, Pa. At the table, from left: Lewis Britsch, Region II director; Laban Swartzentruber, Conservative Conference; Raymond Hess, Brethren in Christ; C. Wilbert Loewen; Wayne Clemens, staff coordinator; Ivan Martin, Region I director and chair; Albert Ediger, Region III director; John Jantzi, Region IV director; Eddie Bearinger, Region V director; "visitor." Standing Fred Unruh, General Conference Mennonite (left); and Norman Shenk, Lancaster Conference.

Bottom right: The 1966 MDS executive seated around the table, from left: Laban Swartzentruber, Ernest Weaver, Eddie Bearinger, Ivan Martin, Delmar Stahley, Harry Martens, Norman Shenk, William T. Snyder.

Participants also suggested that a leaflet and handbook of operations be prepared. They highlighted project leadership as a key issue and asked about payment for extended services. The meeting concluded with recognition of the importance of such meetings and the call to get together "possibly a year hence."

In summer 1956, Harry Martens served the Coordinating Committee in a special volunteer assignment. He traveled extensively, helping new units to organize and MDS to establish its symbol, insignia, letterhead, and identification card. MDS prepared a descriptive folder containing much of the same written message as the one used now. The handbook was not completed that summer; in 1960 Vernon Wiebe developed one in Kansas.

Training schools for MDS project leaders were held as early as 1955 in Kansas. In October 1956, "Activity Summary No. 1" was distributed from Akron. By April of 1958, it had become the *Quarterly Bulletin*. At the 1959 annual meeting, there was considerable discussion regarding the role of women in MDS. Participants had "general agreement that there is a vital role to be filled by women in disaster areas." Some units bought radios, and a filmstrip was authorized. Volunteers like Harry Martens, Wilbert Loewen, and C. L. Graber performed special assignments for the Coordinating Committee.

A New Direction for the 1960s and Beyond

At its 1962 annual meeting, MDS representatives took several more steps that shaped the MDS organization. They approved a plan to reorganize the local units into six regions, four across the United States plus eastern and western Canada. The MDS Coordinating Committee would become a "section" of MCC. The new section (board) would be made up of the regional representatives along with the conference representatives already on the Coordinating Committee. Finally, an $8,000 budget was approved so that MCC could identify a half-time staff coordinator to give leadership to the growing organization. In the summer of 1962, R. Wayne Clemens began his assignment as the first staff person for the binational MDS.

A Grain of Mustard Seed

The 1950s MDS story is an amazing one, a lasting legacy of those early visionaries wanting to be faithful servants of Christ in their home communities. While their initial motivation was personal faithfulness, their vision soon included a larger organization. An active disaster year in 1951 compelled them to become an inter-Mennonite organization by 1952. Widespread interest and other disaster activity gave rise to new organizations in other locations. By 1956, MDS was a binational organization, with units in Canada and under general MCC coordination.

This rapid burst of activity during that first decade also brought to light some perennial problems that have faced MDS during its first 50 years. Early leaders tackled tough issues:

- The need for key longer-term trained leadership was noted in 1951, with discussions about how project foremen could be identified, trained, and kept on site for longer periods of time.
- Contact and cooperation with other agencies, especially Red Cross and civil defense organizations, raised questions of relationship to government.
- How do we manage the perils of bureaucracy in a way that fosters grassroots local autonomy, yet retains some semblance of coordination?

Larry Kehler, Mennonite Church Archives

Courtesy of Mennonite Weekly Review

"Wow," exclaims Ray Spicher, who helped lead that first picnic, "starting with a Sunday school group, look at what the organization has developed into now! It's overwhelming. This is a mustard seed story! We thought we were on the right path, but we had no idea it would develop into what it did."

Harold Dyck, chosen from the Hesston class to be on the first committee and still a resident of Hesston, reflects on "what a little seed planted in the right kind of soil can do." Of the MDS response to the 1990 Hesston tornado, he says, "It was a good feeling to see that what we started way back was bearing fruit. The organization amazes me; it got started so that there was some planned organization when something hit. What would the people [of Hesston] have done without such help and support? People are so grateful. Thank God for MDS!"

Fifty years later we thank God for the visionaries who in 1950 dreamed of MDS, indeed "an idea whose time had come." One key to implementing the dream was John Diller.

A Tribute to John Diller

Even though John Diller lost the use of his legs, he served with his head and his hands. On February 8, 1944, John helped his three-year-old son and one-year-old daughter build a doghouse. That evening he milked his cows and finished the evening chores except for feeding the cattle silage. It was already dark. His silo, built in Depression days, was a round hole dug 25 feet into the ground. He went to pull up silage with a winch arrangement. Apparently the cattle had bumped the winch, so when he stepped onto the platform, it gave way. He fell headfirst 16 feet to the silage below. While lying injured in the silo, he thought, *Maybe this is God's way of getting me into some other kind of work*.

Somehow John crawled out of that silo and walked to the house. There he collapsed. Over the next three years, he spent 12 months in various hospitals, seeking relief from paralysis. His brother Robert, stationed at a CPS camp in Montana, remembers receiving the telegram about John's accident, then obtaining release on a one-year agricultural deferment to take John's place on the farm. During that time, Robert recalls, John insisted on being placed on the tractor seat in the busy farm season and taking his six-hour turn as they ran the equipment around the clock. John's son, Don, credits the strong support they received from church and relatives as a model that led John to give himself to serving others.

Physical healing from paralysis never came, but the call that would lead him to another kind of work did arrive. John, Emily, and family left the farm and moved back to his hometown, Hesston. He made a living by repairing radios and filing saws. They ran the Book and Bible Room for 10 years, then John worked as an accountant for Kropf Lumber. Later, John had an income tax service.

When those early leaders of MSO were looking for that "stay-by-the-phone coordinator," John said yes and served nearly 20 years. He became legendary for working the phone for hours and often finding more volunteers than requested. God in his providence had called a person with just the right gifts. John's records and writings of those first years are invaluable insights into the beginning years of MSO/MDS.

John answered requests for information and counsel from many states and provinces wanting to set up similar organizations. In 1962 John presented a major paper on MDS to the Mennonite World Conference in Kitchener, Ontario, and said, "One is led to exclaim 'What hath God wrought?' when one views the development of MDS over the past 10 years." "What hath God wrought" is also a fitting tribute to the gift of John Diller to Mennonite Disaster Service and the church he loved.

John Diller died in Hesston, Kansas, on February 6, 1995. His wife, Emily, who helped John in many of his tasks, had died on July 7, 1994.

At the MDS 25th anniversary banquet in Hesston in 1975, Region III director Marvin Hostetler presented John Diller with a plaque recognizing his long years of service as MDS Kansas coordinator. His wife, Emily, is at the right.

Courtesy of Mennonite Weekly Review

CHAPTER THREE

Why Are You Here?

Carl Hiebert

Mennonites

We keep our quilts in closets, and do not dance.

We hoe thistles along fencerows

for fear we may not be perfect as our Heavenly Father.

We clean up his disasters.

No one has to call.

We just show up in the wake of tornadoes with hammers,

and after floods with buckets.

Like Jesus the servant, we wash each other s feet. . . .

Julia Kasdorf[1]

No question is asked MDSers more often than Why are you here? Why do we drive hundreds of miles at our own expense to help someone we don t know? Why do we just show up in the wake of tornadoes with hammers, and after floods with buckets?

Every MDSer has a personal response to this question, but it usually comes down to stating one s faith: I believe this is what Jesus would do if he were here. One may pull out the MDS brochure Why We Are Here, and say (abridged):

We may be strangers to you, but you are our neighbors, because we consider anyone in need our neighbor. We cannot fully understand your loss, but we want to share your burden. We wish to follow Christ and his teaching in all of our living. As Christians, we want to share God s love with you.

After that, people often ask, Tell us more about the Mennonites. Who are they? What do they believe?

MCC photo files

Two MDS volunteers salvage materials at the MDS work site in northern Alabama after the super outbreak of tornadoes in 1974.

Who Are the Mennonites?

A family stopped by the Mennonite booth at the Kansas State Fair in Hutchinson. Mennonites? Who are they? questioned the daughter.

Her father s reply was quick: Mennonites are an outfit who go around doing good after floods and tornadoes. [2]

Photo, page 28: A large group of weekly volunteers joins the MDS long-term staff led by Dean and Pam Denlinger (kneeling, center) at the Birmingham, Ala., project in early March 1999.

Longtime Mennonite pastor and church leader Peter Wiebe claims, "More is known about the Mennonites in the United States through MDS than by any other program. We have mission boards and MCC; they're mostly overseas. We have Mennonite schools, Mennonite relief sales, Mennonite restaurants, Mennonite music—but what people know about is Mennonite Disaster Service."

Jason Yoder, MDS board member representing the Conservative Mennonite Church, illustrates this typical perception: "I was flying home from our MDS meetings in Calgary in 1998," Jason reports, "when the gentleman beside me asked why I had been in Calgary. I told him about our MDS meetings.

"'Oh,' he said, 'I heard of MDS when I lived in Pennsylvania. I remember when a group of Amish people made a bunch of corn chowder soup, put it in milk cans, and hauled it to Harrisburg to distribute after Hurricane Agnes in 1972.'

"On the next leg of my flight, I sat beside a gentleman from Texas, and he remembered MDS from our work there."

MDS is also known as the inter-Mennonite organization with the broadest spectrum of Amish, Old Order Mennonite, Mennonite, and Brethren in Christ constituent support. When a woman rescued from a tree after a flood resists going to a hospital "until I've seen a Mennonite," which one does she want to see?

Images of Mennonites

On any Sunday you will find over one million Mennonites (including related groups) gathering for worship in more than 60 countries around the world. In existence since 1525, the Mennonite church includes a wide variety of people and their practices. Though they speak dozens of languages, the thousands of congregations count themselves as one family of faith—one of many faith families in the Christian church.[3]

In the United States, there are at least 46 varieties of Mennonites numbering more than 300,000 members.[4] This creates many Mennonite images, none complete in itself. John A. Lapp, Mennonite educator,

A Dream

From our beginnings in 1525 to the present, Mennonites have dreamed that it is—
- Reasonable to follow Jesus Christ daily, radically, and totally in life.
- Practical to obey the Sermon on the Mount and the whole New Testament, literally, honestly, and sacrificially.
- Thinkable to practice the way of reconciling love in human conflicts and warfare, nondefensively and nonresistantly.
- Possible to confess Jesus as Lord above all nationalism, racism, or materialism.
- Feasible to build a church that is voluntary, disciplined, and mutually committed to each other in Christ.
- Conceivable to live simply, following the Jesus-way in lifestyle, in possessions, and in service.
—*David Augsburger*[5]

Amish volunteers raising a barn at the Sam Beiler farm near Salisbury, Pa. The Beiler farm was hit by two separate tornadoes on the evening of June 2, 1998.

MCC photo by Pearl Sensenig

historian, and former executive director of MCC, states, "All of us have to own the great diversity in the Mennonite world. We come from all sorts of different backgrounds and varieties.

"I think the image of MDS is as good as any other Mennonite image I know," Lapp continues. "We've created the activist image of MCC and MDS. We've created the cultural and media images of plain people. We've created the theological and ethical images of the great minds among us. Now with more Mennonites in Africa, Asia, and South America than in North America, we have a new international image. We should be grateful for all the images."

What Mennonites Believe

At the center of Mennonite teachings is the belief in Jesus Christ as the one who died and rose from the dead so people can live in union with God. Mennonites believe the life and teachings of Jesus guide daily living. They believe the church should keep Christ's life and ministry alive in the world.

Mennonites believe the church is made up of people whose sins have been forgiven and who choose to follow Christ's teaching. Mennonites believe Christians should aim to relate to each other and the world in the same loving and forgiving way that Jesus did.[6]

For more about Mennonites and their beliefs, see publications[7] and web sites such as www.thirdway.com and www.mennolink.org.

Mennonite Beginnings

In the 16th-century Protestant Reformation in Europe, small groups of earnest young believers said Reformers Martin Luther and Huldrych Zwingli had not gone far enough. Conrad Grebel led one group in an attempt to recover New Testament Christianity. On January 21, 1525, in Zurich, Switzerland, members of this group baptized one another and verbalized their faith in Jesus Christ.

The movement also sprang up and spread all over South Germany and the Netherlands. Mennonites were nicknamed after an early Dutch leader, Menno Simons. But just as Menno Simons was a follower of Christ, so Mennonites today are followers of Christ, not Menno.

Fired by their new faith, the believers began to evangelize. The official churches immediately opposed the movement and scoffed at these "Anabaptists"—whose name literally means rebaptizers. The state would not tolerate this change to believers baptism because it defied the government-run church. Many Anabaptist leaders were martyred. Over the next two generations, thousands were tortured and killed.

Fifty years of persecution took a terrible toll. The small groups lived without the right to own property or to meet publicly for worship. They moved to many places, including Russia and North America, seeking freedom to live their faith according to conscience. From 1575 to 1850, the movement grew mainly by winning its own children to faith. In nearly every generation over the past 475 years, the church has experienced persecution somewhere in the world.[8]

As the movement spread, geographic distances and theological differences created divisions between groups of Anabaptists. The nonhierarchical nature of the new church coupled with the need for strong individual leadership during times of persecution led to growing differences in interpreting Scripture on how to live out faith in daily life. One of the most noted divisions was the separation of the Amish from other Mennonites in 1693. By the early 20th century, there were many denominations or conferences of Anabaptist-Mennonites, a trend that regretfully has continued.

Into the World

North American Mennonites organized home and foreign missions beginning in the late 1800s. During World War I, Mennonite young men who were conscientious objectors were often imprisoned for refusing to join the military. A few were able to join the Quakers or others in alternative service, including some international ventures.

In 1920 Mennonites living in Russia faced increased hardships from new political changes and extreme drought. They sent a delegation to North America to appeal for help. North American Mennonites and related groups joined to form Mennonite Central Committee (MCC). Following a significant relief response, MCC also helped in a major migration as Mennonites fled Russia to North America in the 1920s.

As World War II approached, MCC as an inter-Mennonite (including Amish and Brethren in Christ) agency joined the Quaker and Brethren peace church denominations in seeking more favorable options for alternate service by conscientious

Jan Luyken

Menno Simons

This movement of young men (and volunteer women) from a wide variety of Mennonite groups into service camps has probably had a more profound effect on North American Mennonites than any other single experience.

The MDS Melting Pot

Mennonites discovered each other during WW II and CPS. MDS has been a persistent continuation of that story.
—John A. Lapp

MDS has been a melting pot for us in the various expressions of the Anabaptist family. We are drawn together here and discover we don't have to practice everything precisely the same to work together.
—Norman Shenk

objectors. Through these efforts, the Civilian Public Service (CPS) program was launched. Thousands of Mennonite young men found "service in the national interests" in CPS camps around the country.

This movement of young men (and volunteer women) from a wide variety of Mennonite groups into service camps has probably had a more profound effect on North American Mennonites than any other single experience. Once the "quiet in the land," Mennonites began to look outward for service ministries. MCC expanded its service programs both in North America and around the world. Other inter-Mennonite organizations were born—including Mennonite Disaster Service. The CPS, MCC, and MDS movements, with various Mennonites serving, living, and working together (and often marrying each other), were crucial factors moving the two largest Mennonite bodies to an integration effort at the close of the 20th century.

MDS Fits the Mennonite Mold

The story of MDS beginnings was told in chapter 2. Is there some connection between the basic tenets of Anabaptist-Mennonite teaching and this amazing organization of almost all the Mennonite and related groups who came together to serve neighbors facing crisis? In February 1993, John A. Lapp gave the keynote address at the MDS all-unit meeting held in Seward, Nebraska, and stressed the importance of MDS in the Mennonite mix. He edited that speech for use here:

Why MDS? God's People Doing God's Work

The most persistent question MDS workers are asked is "Why?" What has motivated thousands of Mennonite, Amish, Brethren in Christ, and a considerable number of other friends to leave homes and regular employment to give themselves to disaster cleanup and reconstruction?

The question is important; the answer cannot be glib. Volunteers would likely use a variety of explanations. Yet there are common themes. There is that spontaneous concern for one's neighbor who suddenly experiences catastrophe. The good Samaritan of Jesus' story illustrates this kind of response. One theologian dares to call the merciful Samaritan the "ideal human being."[9] Fortunately, there are many good Samaritans.

A Tradition

Mennonites like to think of themselves as biblical people. They like to begin with the Scriptures, citing the living response of Jesus to the hungry and the hurting and his teachings to love the neighbor, care for the needy, and be compassionate in all situations. Mennonites remember the prophet Isaiah's definition of authentic faith: "Is it not to share your bread with the hungry, to bring the homeless poor into your house, . . . and satisfy the needs of the afflicted?" (Isa. 58:7, 10, NRSV).

This Christian tradition emphasizes the practice of faith. One recurring theme of sixteenth-century Dutch reformer Menno Simons was that true faith should "bear fruit." In his classic words, "True evangelical faith . . . cannot lie dormant, but manifests itself in all righteousness and works of love: . . . it clothes the naked; it feeds the hungry; it comforts the sorrowful; it shelters the destitute; it aids and comforts the sad."[10]

When MDS was formed in 1950, the founders were drawing on deeply held convictions that motivated a tradition for hundreds of years. They were not only responding to victims of floods and tornadoes. MDS represents the passionate belief that authentic faith is expressed in every dimension of life. It was no accident, however, that this organization was formed in the years following World War II. During that war, more than 7,000 Mennonites, Amish, and Brethren in Christ were placed in government-sponsored alternative service in the U.S. and Canada instead of doing military service.

After the war Mennonites decided that public service, such as responding to disasters, could also be a good way to connect their faith practice to public need. MDS is intimately linked to the Mennonite desire not to participate in war and to find a positive way of being good neighbors. During the American Revolution, Pennsylvania Mennonites and Dunkers (Church of the

Brethren) told the State Assembly, "It being our principle to feed the hungry and give the thirsty drink, we have dedicated ourselves to serve all men in everything that can be helpful to the preservation of men's lives."[11] Since 1950, MDS has been a continuing practice of that kind of alternate service.

This tradition came alive for me in January 1993, when I [Lapp] visited MDS at work in Homestead, Florida, following Hurricane Andrew. I was moved by the extent of the destruction and was struck by the spiritual and social chaos. The people felt numb, depressed, and victimized. I was deeply inspired by the dedication of the MDSers and the heroic presence of the Homestead Mennonite Church. A remarkable MDS video, *A Church Without Walls*, has captured the witness of that congregation and the MDS workers. The following themes from that video illustrate the unity of a tradition dedicated to helping and serving in the life of a congregation as well as through disaster response workers.

MDS photo

For Mennonites, when Jesus invites people to come and follow him, it is not only a fad for the moment. It is an invitation to a way of life, not only for the present but also for eternity.

A Church at Work

Ann Salazar was then a Homestead resident. On the video she says, "A miracle came into my life. God's people are doing God's work." After the hurricane, the MDS office in August 1992 was inundated with offers of help and inquiries as to how soon they could be on location. God's people wanted to do God's work. Recall the concluding words of Jesus' story of the good Samaritan: "'Which of these three, do you think, was a neighbor?' The lawyer responded, 'Well, the one who showed mercy.' And Jesus said, 'Go and do likewise'" (Luke 10:36-37, NRSV, adapted).

Ann Salazar went on to describe those first days. She said the MDSers "were so caring, so compassionate, not expecting even a thank-you." Jesus taught his disciples, "As you go, proclaim the good news, 'The kingdom of heaven has come near.'" Then after telling them to heal the sick and cleanse the lepers, he added, "You received without payment; give without payment" (Matt. 10:7-8, NRSV).

As the video says, MDS moved in unnoticed and expected to be around for a long time. God's work is not something that can be done in a flash. God's work is done by people committed to the long haul. To be sure, God's work is not only done amid natural disasters; but for many people in many places, life is close to being a disaster. Think of the wars, diseases, homelessness, and helplessness that permeate the

lives of nearly half the people of our world. God's work is best recognized when people are needy and responsive.

This is a time to show that at the heart of the universe there is not destruction and violence but love and compassion. God's work is to overcome the alienation, to restore health and wholeness, to create the holy community, and to heal creation. Jesus "went about doing good" (Acts 10:38). In this way he announced that God's new order is at hand. He said, "As the Father sent me, so I send you. As I have demonstrated God's love, so you should demonstrate God's love" (John 20:21; 13:34, NRSV paraphrased).

Ann Salazar spoke well. Miracles happen when God's people do God's work.

A second theme in the video is equally striking. Vic Miller was one of the persons who stayed put in Homestead. He observed, "The only thing left standing was the church." Then he added, "The Lord wanted it that way."

One immediately thinks of Matthew 16:18. After Peter makes his great confession of faith, similar to Vic's, Jesus says, "On this rock I will build my church, and the gates of hell [the winds of Andrew] shall not prevail against it" (KJV). Today there are not many established landmarks. Change rather than stability characterizes our culture. Buildings (even church buildings) come and go, and so do roads, politics, ideas, farmland, theologies, friendships,

Left: MDS leaders in Puerto Rico were active in recovery operations after Hurricane Georges struck the island in September 1998. Isaias Martinez (left), Ramon Bermudez (second from right), and Angel Rivas (right) join family members in front of their home being rebuilt by MDS.

MDS strives to be a statement about the shape of Christian community. Visitors to an MDS project discover experienced senior carpenters and craftsmen, and also volunteers who are not even apprentices. MDSers come from many places: Virginia, Saskatchewan, Oregon, Nebraska, and New Brunswick. Some are clean shaven, some have beards. Some are women, some are men. Some are Old Order; some no longer use the name "Mennonite" for their congregations. But MDSers eat at the same table, are constrained by the same God of love, and throb with the same Spirit. This sense of community comes alive, not simply in words, but as the walk proves the talk.
—John Lapp

and corporations. Jesus insists that some things in life ought to be more than seasonal. Something basic and timeless should shape our lives. For Mennonites, when Jesus invites people to come and follow him, it is not only a fad for the moment. It is an invitation to a way of life, not only for the present but also for eternity.

The set of relationships called "church" involves life on earth and in heaven. This community is a rock that stays put amid the changes of life and the struggles of society. The Homestead Mennonite Church stands as a wonderful parable of the community of faith built on the rock of Jesus Christ. Amid massive destruction, the roof stayed on, as Kathy Hartzler noted, "so we could be a blessing to the community." Others in the video observed that the church was a hub; the people never felt alone. "We knew," they said, that "we'd be taken care of."

Pastor Walter Sawatzky articulated a third significant video theme: "Building networks of community is what church is all about." The video ends with the Homestead congregation singing movingly, "We are only one body, that is why we sing, bind us together with love."

The apostle Paul uses the image of the body to describe the Christian community. "Just as the body is one and has many members, and all the members of the body, though many, are one body, so it is with Christ. For in the one Spirit we are all baptized into one body—Jews or Greeks,

slaves or free—and we are all made to drink of one Spirit." Later he adds, "If one member suffers, all suffer together with [that one]. If one member is honored, all rejoice together with [that one]" (1 Cor. 12:12-13, 26, NRSV).

MDS is a statement that the church is never complete in one congregation or in one locality. Every local church is a part of a community of churches and indeed part of the seamless body of Christ that ties together churches and congregations around the world. MDS is a network of communities, as the Homestead congregation aspires to be. Walter Sawatzky spoke, not only for Homestead, but also for MDS: "Building networks of community is what the church is about."

A Parable

Mennonite Disaster Service can be understood as a living parable embodied by a committed group of people, an organization that seizes the opportunity to demonstrate Christ through story and action. In our age, when there is too much talk, the best word of the church is to act out the never-ending love of God. The parable made flesh by MDS in hundreds of American and Canadian communities represents a deeply held tradition of biblical Christianity: "Faith without deeds is dead" (James 2:26).

The meaning of the MDS parable is "God's people doing God's work." This parable is rooted in the only thing left standing—the church, "for the Lord wants

Carl Hiebert

Jamie Alderfer from Pennsylvania, Pam Denlinger from Ohio, and Lois Schrock from Maryland enjoy getting to know each other during a meal at the Birmingham, Ala., project.

it that way." The parable witnesses to the church's purpose: building networks of community. Why Mennonite Disaster Service? Because that's the way God's people do God's work, by mending a torn land. —*John A. Lapp*[12]

God's People Aiming to Be Faithful

"MDS captures gospel motivation in its simplest form," states Robert Kreider, former president of Bluffton College and noted Mennonite historian. "The cup of cold water, feeding the hungry, giving shelter to the homeless; . . . this we do in MDS. It is so beautifully simple in dramatizing the gospel message—good news."

Kreider acknowledges another motivation we may be reluctant to admit: "MDS is fun. It's exhilarating. You drive through the night. You enjoy meeting people. It's great to tell stories when you come back. We think of this as a lower level of motivation, but I have a notion that most of the good work of the kingdom has a fun dimension to it."

One unique aspect of MDS in the context of the church is that it is a laypeople's movement, bringing members of all constituent groups together as they work and fellowship in a focused service ministry. MDS receives support and encouragement from church leaders of all the constituent churches. A dozen Mennonite and related groups have representation on the MDS board.

The Church Needs MDS

MCC administrator Reg Toews says, "The church needs inter-Mennonite, inter-church activity. I go to a lot of meetings, and MDS is the one that has by far the broadest range of participation from the inter-Mennonite constituency. It is difficult for us to maintain our prejudices about other Mennonite groups when we have rubbed shoulders, working with them."

Dan Houck, representing the Brethren in Christ on the MDS board, explains, "The Brethren in Christ still practice foot washing in our churches. To me, responding to a disaster, cleaning up someone's mess from a hurricane or a tornado, is the ultimate act of foot washing."

"We believe in helping the needy, especially in disaster or sudden crisis," adds Emmanuel Fisher, Old Order Amish representative. "MDS has brought a constructive unity among many church affiliations and congregations throughout all of the United States and Canada. We need to give the honor and glory to our almighty God."

MDS volunteers come from all walks of life: young and old, women and men,

MDS photo

> **The Word in Action**
>
> I have heard the Word preached, I have heard the Word taught, I have memorized the Word, I have quoted the Word, but I saw the Word in action as the Mennonites came in the doors of our church month after month. What a revelation! —Jeanie Tyson, member, First Assembly Church, Albany, Ga., which hosted MDS workers for over a year
>
> **Left:** Student groups from many schools add to the MDS mix. In January 1999 some students and faculty from Central Christian High School, Kidron, Ohio, worked on the Hurricane Georges project in Puerto Rico.

Sermons We See

I'd rather see a sermon than hear one any day;
I'd rather someone walk with me than merely tell the way.
The eye's a better pupil and more willing than the ear,
Fine counsel is confusing, but example's always clear;
And the best of all the preachers are the [ones] who live their creeds,
For to see good put in action is what everybody needs.
I soon can learn to do it if you let me see it done;
I can watch your hands in action, but your tongue too fast may run.
And the lecture you deliver, may be very nice and true,
But I'd rather get my lessons by observing what you do;
For I might misunderstand you and the high advice you give,
But there's no misunderstanding how you act and how you live.

—*Edgar Albert Guest*[13]

tradespeople and novices, farmers and professionals. Anyone possessed by a flexible attitude and a servant's heart can find meaningful involvement in MDS.

A story shared by Ron Mathies from his Kitchener (Ontario) Mennonite Brethren church illustrates this point. At a testimony meeting, a man back from a week of service with MDS shared, through tears, his experience. He had always supported the church and those going into MCC or mission work, but as a machinist and handyman, he never felt qualified to be involved in missions. Through his week with MDS, he was able to enter the lives of other people, walk with them, and share his faith in a wholesome and unforced way. He returned with a powerful testimony: "I can contribute. I can be part of the mission of the church."

Word or Deed?

On their return home, MDSers are often asked, "But did you share the gospel?" The MDS image is often the one suggested by the title of an early MDS filmstrip: Sermons in Overalls. Some are inclined to recite the poem "Sermons We See." Like the members of the churches from which we come, some of us are better at verbalizing faith than others.

Evangelism in MDS?

In 1968 Fred Unruh led a workshop on "Evangelism in MDS." Thirty years later his points remain well-stated principles for us all:

• Service is not self explanatory; actions do not intrinsically carry Christian truth.
• Christian truth is communicated when

there is integrity among the act, the explanation, and the character of a person.

• Words and actions are both symbols, things we use to share a truth. Both are needed.

• We can confuse issues of therapy ministries and crisis evangelism. Love suggests that we move gently in, pushing for decisions amid crisis, when emotions and search for security are at a high level.

• The key word in witnessing is not action, but interaction.

• Christian service points away from self and points to Christ.[14]

Is MDS Only for Mennonites?

Does MDS serve only Mennonites? No. Only a few of the following stories are about Mennonites helping Mennonites. Our neighbors are found anywhere between St. Croix in the U.S. Virgin Islands and the shores of Mennonite Creek in Alaska.

Can non-Mennonites serve with MDS? Yes. Many persons from many faiths join us in serving those affected by disasters. In recent years more church denominations

Sam Resendez

MCC photo, Mennonite Church Archives.

Ronnie Giel

Mudout

You didn't have to.

The mud was in my house, not yours.

But you came.

You sloshed in foot-deep mud,

cleaned out my house.

Did you know that you also cleaned

some long-caked mud from my heart,

And I saw God?

—Norman Wingert

Right: "You sloshed in foot-deep mud!" Mudding out, a typical MDS activity, at the Rapid City, S.D., flood project in 1972.

have their own disaster response programs; others join MDS in partnership programs or individually. The MDS "badge" has been worn by some unusual partners.

Urie A. Bender and Katie Funk Wiebe share an eloquent story and commentary in *Day of Disaster*, from a 1974 flood response program in Cambridge, Ontario:

Claudette Millar, the mayor of

Cambridge, was a good administrator and served her community well. Her sensitive spirit was almost overwhelmed by the human need and frustration she felt from those who looked to her for leadership during the flood crisis.

Mayor Millar told Urie Bender, "I met Eddie Bearinger—Eddie. He was the head of MDS [Ontario]. He said in his strong gentle voice—he's over six feet—with a quiet smile on his face, 'Don't worry.'

"You know, when he looked at me and spoke, I had the distinct impression that I was not to worry. It looked like chaos: pumps, buckets, ropes, shovels, Mennonites everywhere. But amid all this chaos was Eddie, and a superb organization.

"I knew of the Mennonites and MDS—Mennonites going to Ohio and New York. I thought they helped only Mennonites. Yet here they were, hundreds of them, to help us.

"The condition of the town was unbelievable. I was ready to accept assistance from anyone. I thought that just moving the furniture out on the street would be a big help. I didn't realize the Mennonites would go right into the basements and shovel out the crud.

"The owner of the New Albion Hotel is a Jew. He told me, 'You wouldn't believe the way the Mennonites cleaned up our synagogue! Then they came to my hotel—a group of Old Order Mennonites—and asked if they could help. I said they could lift out the carpet. They did. Then they asked, 'What about your basement?' I told them they shouldn't go there. I couldn't stand the smell myself, the muck and sewage.'

The mayor asked, "Do you know what he said? 'They started there.' Those Old Order Mennonites mucked out the whole messy basement. I had offered 10 dollars an hour to get it cleaned up. No takers. They went in, cleaned it from end to end, because, they said, they wanted to help me.'"

Mayor Millar noted, "I used to think those Mennonites just helped each other, to an extreme degree. That it was a kind of ethnic thing. Then we found the Mennonites helping us just as much. I knew it was more than ethnicity. It had to have something to do with your faith.

"You know, that faith was almost a silent thing. And it wasn't so much what your people did—it was the way you did it."

"The way you did it" started a long time ago, when Jesus responded to the needs of people around him. The Anabaptists of the 16th century understood the same truth and lived that way, caring for others.

Their children, the Mennonites, have never been able to escape this heritage. In Europe, in Russia, in North America, and around the world, Mennonites have committed themselves again and again to service in Jesus' name.

This is the heart of Mennonite Disaster Service. Cleaning out a basement in Jesus' name is one way of loving. One gratifying result is having other Christians say to the MDSer, "Next time, we want to be part of what you are doing."[15]

Join us! Join us in our churches, in our ministry of service via Mennonite Disaster Service, in our sincere but incomplete attempts to be faithful servants of our Lord Jesus in today's hurting world.

Top left: Men from the Hispanic Caucus of the Mennonite Churches of California load packages of food distributed to families in need because of the winter freeze in 1999.

Bottom left: Only for Mennonites? Many kindred servants join in MDS response efforts, including this group of Hutterite-Bruderhof young adults from Pennsylvania assisting in cleanup at the Albany, Ga., flood project in 1994.

CHAPTER FOUR

After Seedtime Comes the Harvest

Large photo: MCC photo, Mennonite Church Archives. Inset: Courtesy of Harold Miller

Just to watch them work is enough to make an agnostic stop and think.

—*Observer of MDSers at the Stroudsburg, Pa., flood site in 1955*

This chapter touches on a few highlights of MDS projects during its first 25 years. More early activity is recorded in *Day of Disaster.*[1] A few stories here are from that book. Most of these scenes illustrate the seedtime-harvest theme. Many seeds planted by MDSers in the early years are still being watered, nurtured, and harvested. People's lives keep reflecting the hope brought by MDSers; churches planted have borne fruit.

Litany

It helps now and then to step back and take the long view.
The Kingdom is not only beyond our efforts, it is even beyond our vision.

We accomplish in our lifetime only a fraction of the magnificent enterprise that is God's work.
Nothing we do is complete, which is another way of saying that the Kingdom always lies beyond us.

No statement says all that could be said.
No prayer fully expresses our faith.
No confession brings perfection. . . .
No program accomplishes the church's mission.
No set of goals and objectives includes everything.

This is what we are about:
We plant seeds that one day will grow.
We water seeds already planted, knowing that they hold future promise.

We lay foundations that will need further development.
We provide yeast that produces effects beyond our capabilities.

We cannot do everything, and there is a sense of liberation in realizing that.
This enables us to do something, and do it very well.
It may be incomplete, but it is a beginning, a step along the way,
An opportunity for God's grace to enter and do the rest.

We may never see the end results, but that is the difference between the master builder and the worker.
We are workers, not master builders; ministers, not messiahs.
We are prophets of a future that is not our own.
Amen.

—*Archbishop Oscar Romero*[2]

Early Disasters Plant Seeds for Spread of MDS

Large photo, page 38: Flooding from Hurricane Diane in 1955 in the Stroudsburg, Pa., area led to the first MDS response in the eastern states.

Inset, page 38: MDS work in the Corning, N.Y., area following Hurricane Agnes in 1972 led to formation of the Community Mennonite Church of Corning. Emily Berkey is being baptized by Pastor Harold Miller (left) and her father, George, in the Chemung River, that flooded the area.

North of the Border

Mennonites in Canada gave mutual assistance long before the organized beginnings of MDS. Early immigrations of Mennonite refugees into Canada brought an outpouring of support from churches and relatives as thousands of Mennonites carved homesteads out of the prairies in the 1870s and again in the 1920s. By the 1940s, MCC and other relief organizations were active in Canada when another wave of Mennonite immigrants arrived.

When the Red River flooded southern Manitoba in 1948, there was instant "help your neighbor" grassroots activity. Long-time MDSers C. N. Friesen and Fred Kathler were then living in the area. C. N. remembers the call spreading through churches and many volunteers gathering to sandbag. Others evacuated people and cattle.

On the same land, the 1950 floods were even worse. Meanwhile, the churches had organized Mennonite Disaster Relief; C. N. served as coordinator for the southern Manitoba churches. MDR had solicited lists of volunteers with their skills and equipment. Merchants provided tools. People lived with family and friends on higher ground, even for extended periods. Syd Reimer, longtime MDS leader in Canada, had moved to Rosenort in 1949. He remembers that Henry Loewen from Meade, Kansas, brought several men to help.

All this took place before MDS was organized, but it was clearly part of Anabaptist practice. By 1956, these local organized efforts blended into the MDS network.

In the Great Lakes Area

In September 1949, CPS alumni in northern Indiana formed a committee called "Crusaders for Peace." Like those initiating Sunday school classes in Kansas, their records give the group's purpose: to "stimulate and challenge our thoughts along the nonresistant life of a Christian today." They sponsored CPS reunions in Indiana, Ohio, and Illinois. A 1951 CPS reunion in Indiana supported establishing "disaster units." On March 24, 1953, an Emergency Relief Unit was organized at Goshen, Indiana, with temporary officers instructed to obtain information from Lyle Yost in Hesston, Kansas, about their Mennonite Service Organization.

On June 8, 1953, a deadly tornado struck around Flint, Michigan, and killed 127 people, the state's worst disaster (up to 1999). The Indiana group expressed immediate interest in relief work and soon sent two men to Flint to investigate possibilities. In 10 days they agreed to start a three-week response, later extended. Mennonites and Amish from Ohio and Michigan joined them. That effort was the seed to establish MDS units in those states.

In the Midwest

On May 25, 1955, devastating F-5 tornadoes hit Udall, Kansas, and Blackwell, Oklahoma. With unit coordinator John Diller working the phones overnight, there was an amazing response, recalls Albert Ediger, early unit leader in Kansas. By the next morning, 100 men were ready to start searching the rubble for victims and valuables. By the second morning, the count was over 300; by Memorial Day over 1,000.

In Blackwell, 40 miles south, the damage was major, though casualties were fewer than in Udall. Marvin Dester, long-time MDS leader, says the churches of Oklahoma helped clean up, then used the opportunity to organize an MDS unit in the state.

In the East

On August 18-19, 1955, Hurricane Diane sputtered up the Delaware Valley on nearly the same path as Hurricane Connie a week earlier. The weather service proclaimed Diane a "well-behaved hurricane." Yet the upper Delaware landscape, soaked by Connie, could hold no more water. Diane dumped billions of gallons on the Pocono Mountains, causing dozens of mountain streams and rivers to go berserk.

During the night, the Broadhead Creek flowing through Stroudsburg rose 30 terrifying feet in 15 minutes. Caught unaware, campers and homeowners were swept from their beds. Cabins and homes were demolished and bridges torn out as the crest roared down the valleys at 60 miles an hour. An estimated 200 lives were lost. Diane, with "too pretty a name for a demon," according to the Easton Express, became the first hurricane in U.S. history to cause over a billion dollars of damage.

On Saturday, August 20, as floodwaters started to recede, a small private plane circled and pilot Andrew Rosenberger banked low over the stricken area so Norman Good and David F. Derstine could see the devastation. That night, back at Blooming Glen (Pa.) Mennonite Church, where Derstine was a minister, the scouts reported to an emergency meeting of representatives from 50 Mennonite churches. They agreed to call for 100 workers to enter the disaster area on Monday morning. The meeting concluded with a simple prayer: "Help us, Lord, to lift high the banner of Christ by bending low into the mud."

On Sunday at each church, men signed up to indicate what day they would be available. That afternoon, reports were phoned to the temporary Mennonite Disaster Service committee. More than 300 men had volunteered to work on Monday!

Early Monday morning, 7 buses and 21 trucks loaded with volunteers, shovels, brooms, pumps, and wheelbarrows were on their way to Stroudsburg, under police escort. Each morning for the next two weeks, never less than 275 workers left to "bend low into the mud." The banner of Christ was clearly raised. One flood victim said, "Just to watch them work is enough to make an agnostic stop and think."

In nearby Lancaster County, churches also heard the call for help; many volunteers joined those from farther east. After they worked throughout the summer, a meeting was called on September 19,

Our 50 Years in MDS Service

MDS photo

After nearly 50 years of marriage and MDS service involvement, Sue and Fred Kathler really know how to work as a team! They've led MDS projects in many locations, including this assignment in St. Thomas after Hurricane Marilyn.

In 1948 I was living with my parents on a dairy farm in southern Manitoba. When the Red River flooded that year, we waited too late to move our cattle, but finally got them out at the last minute through mud and rain. In late April 1950, as the flood was on the way north from Fargo, my dad listened carefully to the radio weather forecasts. He said, "If we have to evacuate, we're not going to do it like we did in 1948." When he heard the crest would reach Emerson (18 miles from us on the N.D.-Man. border), in two days, he said, "Today we're moving our cattle."

My dad phoned different people to get help, including my soon-to-be brother-in-law John, who had a truck. It was a warm day, with no sign of water or snow; we could have been out sunbathing.

When John arrived, he asked, "Mr. Kathler, what are you doing?"

My dad responded, "We're going to move our cattle. The radio says that in two days the crest will reach Emerson, so we're moving our cattle today."

John shook his head but used his truck to haul the cattle to a neighbor's place on higher ground. We moved the chickens into the second floor of the dairy barn. Dad moved Mom and the rest of us out too.

The next day my brother and I went back to feed the chickens. We couldn't get in our yard. Overnight the water had risen about eight feet and backed up into the creek running by our house. We couldn't get to the barn except by boat, which we had tied to a handy post. Later, when I told John, he couldn't believe it. Then we went out to help other people.

I was getting edgy. May 6 was the wedding date set for Sue and me. Sue's folks lived along another river, but as a rule it doesn't flood. Yet the water kept rising. A day and a half before our wedding, we decided to postpone it. On May 6 we moved Sue's family out; two of her brothers and I stayed to guard the place. The second floor didn't get water, and the electric box was above water, so we had electricity—and a boat.

After we moved them out, there was nothing else for us to do, so we decided to get married anyway, on May 14, eight days later.

Where could we go for our honeymoon? We couldn't get to Winnipeg. Sue's folks' house was now an island, with water in the first floor. So we had an "island honeymoon" on the second floor. We used a hot plate to make food—very primitive! We went around helping other people who needed help.

Now we're planning our 50th anniversary honeymoon for June 2-4, 2000, in Hesston, Kansas. Our 50 years in MDS! (Fred and Sue have served on many MDS projects. In 1999 Fred was chairman of the MDS unit in British Columbia.)
—*Fred Kathler*

1955, at Mellinger's Mennonite Church. With the encouragement of Orie O. Miller, Raymond Charles, and Paul Kraybill, a temporary emergency organization was established for the greater Lancaster area. Ivan Martin was selected as field coordinator and Landis Hershey as home coordinator. Both men gave many years of leadership to MDS.

The work at Stroudsburg became the seed that grew into strong and permanent MDS units in eastern Pennsylvania and the Lancaster area. Throughout the years, these units have provided thousands of volunteers when the call has come to "send forth laborers into the harvest."

And in the West

In late 1955, heavy rains pounded northern California mountains for several days. A levee protecting Yuba City from the swollen Feather River broke on Christmas Eve. Family after family found Christmas trees and toys destroyed by mud and water. The next morning, August A. Schroeter, Otto Reimer, and Arthur Jost headed to Red Cross headquarters in San Francisco. They left home early to complete the five-hour drive by the time the office opened, but they received a cool reception. ARC staff said the situation was so serious that "inexperienced persons" could not be allowed in the area.

What followed was a scene countless MDS investigators were to face in years to come. During the disappointing meeting, a Red Cross official walked in; he had just flown from the East. When the Mennonites were introduced, his face lit up. He had just been working with

Mennonites in the East and heartily recommended them to the West Coast officers. After a short briefing, the Mennonites were on their way to Yuba City. There the National Guard had already received word of their coming and waved them through to Red Cross headquarters.

After another investigating day, they returned to the Reedley-Dinuba area and on December 29 called a meeting of 38 men, representing six Mennonite groups, to organize the California MDS unit. By January 2, MDS leaders were back in Yuba City to arrange accommodations and work assignments for volunteers. Reporting for work on January 4 were 45 men. In a few days, the count was 74 men and 10 women. Before the month's end, volunteers had also arrived from Oregon and Idaho. MDS on the West Coast was off to an exciting start.

Palm Sunday 1965

Tragedy on Palm Sunday

On Palm Sunday, April 11, 1965, a staggering total of at least 37 tornadoes slammed through six states in the Midwest. The twisters started in eastern Iowa, swung through Wisconsin and Illinois, then stunned Indiana, Michigan, and Ohio with their mightiest blows.

In one afternoon and evening, the storms killed at least 279 persons and injured thousands more. The toll in Indiana alone, the state hardest hit, was 140 dead and 1,250 injured, with damage estimated in hundreds of millions of dollars.

Two of the hardest-hit parts of Indiana were the Sunnyside area near Elkhart and

Right: Where shall he begin? This lone person faces the stark reality of a town in ruins, no longer existing: Udall, Kan., in 1955. On the Memorial Day weekend following the tornado, over 1,000 MDSers descended on Udall to assist in the cleanup.

Courtesy of Mennonite Weekly Review

the Shore community near Shipshewana. In each community, a Mennonite church was completely demolished. One young girl from Sunnyside Mennonite Church and nine Shore Mennonite Church members were killed.

The Sunnyside Story

Leonard Garber, pastor at Sunnyside Mennonite Church, remembers when those tornadoes struck: "We had company that day and were out walking the streets in the afternoon. There was a lot of turbulence in the skies; the clouds were very agitated. Evening services were to begin at 7:00. When I went to the church, three or four families were there. Some brought word that a tornado had hit the Midway Trailer Court. Thinking about the way the skies looked and not having any outside com-

Life Follows Death in Indiana Storms

On Palm Sunday in 1965, a series of vicious tornadoes ripped through northern Indiana and part of the adjoining states of Michigan and Illinois. The following week I was one of a group of congressmen who flew out with the late President Johnson to inspect the damage and provide what moral support we could to the unfortunate victims.

I'll never forget that scene as we surveyed the damage. The destruction was awesome. Those tornadoes had struck a cruel blow to the lives and hopes of many Hoosiers and other residents of the Midwest.

Although that tragedy was something I'll never forget, there was something else I'll always remember about that day. That was the sight of the many volunteers of Mennonite Disaster Service from Indiana and other states who were on the scene helping the dazed victims rebuild their shattered lives. In this hour of need, the Mennonites truly appeared to be heaven-sent. —*Birch Bayh*[3]

President Johnson leads a delegation of Washington officials, including Indiana Senator Birch Bayh, through the devastated Sunnyside community in northern Indiana after the Palm Sunday tornadoes.

Courtesy of Leonard Garber

munication at the church, we decided it would be wise to go home. No more than 5 or 10 minutes later, the next tornado wiped out the church. I stood outside our back door, several blocks away, and watched the debris fall on our yard.

"I spent the night trying to help people get out from under the debris. Several families who lived near the church were wiped out. A few other families were home, some

Paul Huffman

Left: This unique photo from the Palm Sunday storms shows twin twisters roaring through the Dunlap-Sunnyside area near Elkhart, Ind., on April 11, 1965.

MDS Works in Other States

Much of the response to the Palm Sunday tornadoes took place in northern Indiana. MDS units also worked in other states, particularly Ohio and Michigan (see story on page 171).

were in their basements, and most got away without injuries. One four-year-old girl from our church was killed and found under a car a couple of days later. We faced a lot of trauma. Twenty-seven lives were lost in the Sunnyside community."

In a week the elders stood on the bare floor of the former church and made three decisions: they wanted to build again, immediately, and on the corner lot nearby. In a month they were ready for the groundbreaking. MDS was spread thin, given all the surrounding areas in need of cleanup and rebuilding, but there was

43

Courtesy of Leonard Garber

tremendous interest in supporting these efforts. Masons came from as far away as Pennsylvania. Most of the church was built with volunteer labor.

By November the Sunnyside congregation was worshiping in its new building. Clare Schumm, pastor at Sunnyside following Garber, says that following rebuilding of the church, the congregation experienced renewed vision for outreach and growth. Steady membership growth brought a building expansion program a decade later.

The Shipshewana Story

In the mid-1800s, Mennonites and Amish from Pennsylvania rode covered wagons to new settlements in Lagrange County, Indiana. Many settled near the village of Shore, beside Hood Lake, about two miles south of Shipshewana. In 1865 the first Mennonite church was built by the lake and named Shore. A hundred years later, the congregation had just completed an addition for the growing membership. The late evening tornado devastated the Shore community, demolished the Shore Mennonite Church, and left 17 dead within a quarter mile of the church.

Paul Haarer, longtime MDS leader in the Indiana unit, remembers the day vividly. He lived six miles away, but his parents lived next to the church, and his uncle and aunt right across the road. Paul and family were headed for the evening service at the Marian Mennonite Church, but someone reported a bad storm in the Shore area. "I knew my folks were there, so a couple of us went over. I couldn't believe what I was seeing. It was the worst disaster I have

ever witnessed. My parents' property was totally destroyed. My mother's life was spared, even though she was outside trying to enter the house at the back porch when the house went down around her."

Across the road at his uncle Frank Haarer's residence, Paul's cousin Noble and family were visiting Noble's elderly parents. The children playing outside brought in hailstones. Those inside had not realized a storm was coming. Steven, 16, saw the tornado crossing Road 5, a half a mile away, and shouted, "It's a real tornado."

Noble looked out the west window and yelled, "There goes somebody's roof! Quick, everybody to the basement."

The children and Noble's wife darted for the basement door. Noble helped his parents, who could not move as fast, but they never made it. Those in the basement survived, but Noble and his parents were taken with the house and carried several hundred feet. Their bodies were not found till the next morning, stripped of clothing and covered with mud and rubble.[4]

A Loving Response

Still a fledgling organization in 1965, MDS had little experience in responding to so massive a disaster. The stories of overwhelming devastation quickly spread through the Mennonite and Amish communities from Kansas to Pennsylvania. Over the next months, thousands of volunteers came to northern Indiana. The Shipshewana Amish-Mennonite community had strong connections with the Amish of Pennsylvania, who brought support. Their story is a sample of hundreds of oth-

Courtesy of Leonard Garber

Courtesy of Leonard Garber

Top: The Sunnyside Mennonite Church Elkhart, Ind., was destroyed by the Palm Sunday tornadoes. Within a month they held groundbreaking services, led by Pastor Leonard Garber (left foreground).

Middle: Masons from the Lancaster, Pa., area laid most of the blocks for the new church.

Bottom: In just over six months, services were held in the new building. MDS and other volunteers provided most of the labor. This 1999 photo shows a recent addition.

ers that could be told.

Carpenters Stephen Esh, Jacob Flaud, and Jacob Esh organized the Amish response from the East. In a week they were on their way to investigate the need. A local business provided a driver and transportation. After riding overnight, they arrived early in the morning.

Jacob Flaud reports, "We were pretty tired from traveling, but right after breakfast Dan Hochstetler took us on a tour of the storm area. We soon forgot how tired we were. Each place we went, we thought, Now we've seen everything, but the next place would be different and worse. We saw right away there would be no problem finding work for our men.

"Wednesday morning we started home again, but our thoughts remained in Indiana. We arrived home Wednesday evening, and many interested friends came to find out what we had learned. We dis-

covered that our local Red Cross had agreed to provide a school bus and driver for our groups to travel, charging only for the bus. It was decided I would start out with the first load of 42 men the following Monday. By Thursday evening we had 42 signed up, the exact number we needed. In addition to the bus, we ended up taking two pickup trucks to carry our tools."

The bus didn't start till Monday noon. They expected to arrive Tuesday morning but were there by 3:00 a.m. The Brick House Restaurant opened and served them breakfast. Then they went to work. Tuesday evening they commented, "We forgot to be tired after seeing how it looked."[5]

There are no accurate records of how many volunteers helped in the recovery efforts after the Palm Sunday tornadoes, but it surely stands as one of the largest MDS operations ever. MDS leaders set up

one office at the fire station in Dunlap, another at a mobile home in the Shore area, and organized efforts in several other communities. Hundreds of people just showed up and tackled the tasks. One newspaper reports that MDS provided 6,342 volunteer days during the first nine days following the storm. According to an MDS Akron headquarters news release, the Indiana-Michigan unit estimated that 5,000 persons were operating under their organization on Saturday, April 17.

In the Amish communities, records were kept of noon meals served. The largest number served at the Bishop Bontrager home on one day was 250. At the Reuben Miller home, 3,700 people were served during the first six weeks. Jacob Flaud estimates that around a thousand Amish from the Lancaster area volunteered. The MDS offices were not closed until the week of September 6.

A Big World

Some of the men had never been out of Lancaster County before. To them the journey seemed a tremendous undertaking. At a rest stop, one man remarked, "If the world is as big the other way as it is this way, it must be awful big."[6]

Courtesy of Paul Haarer

Courtesy of Paul Haarer

Far left: The Palm Sunday tornadoes that tore through the Shipshewana, Ind., area leveled the Shore Mennonite Church. The storm hit a half hour before the evening service was to begin.

Near left: From all around volunteers flocked to Indiana to assist in cleanup and rebuilding. Here, volunteers from Pennsylvania register at a local headquarters. About 1,000 Amish volunteers from the Lancaster area helped.

Camille, She Was No Lady!

Right: During the first 50 years of MDS history, the most intense hurricane to strike the United States was Hurricane Camille. The August 17, 1969, monster storm had winds over 200 miles per hour and a tidal wave that carried huge ocean ships onto shore.

On Sunday, August 17, 1969, a terrible storm struck the Mississippi Gulf Coast. Hurricane Camille, the second most intense one (as of 1999) ever to strike the U.S. mainland, swept ashore just before midnight, with devastating waves of 20 to 30 feet and winds over 200 mph. Three ocean freighters and scores of smaller boats in the Gulfport harbor were beached. Mennonite communities nearby, at Camp Landon (a former CPS camp) and around the Gulfhaven Mennonite Church north of town, were far enough inland to escape the tidal surge but not the ferocious winds.

Three days later Camille paused over Virginia's Blue Ridge Mountains, dumping 27 inches of rain in Nelson County and causing terrible flash flooding. In Virginia 106 people died. Many MDSers were among emergency crews who searched and dug for bodies buried under mud and rubble. Virginia MDSers organized an immediate cleanup and long-term rebuilding project.

In Mississippi, the death toll reached 135. The total dead from Camille reached 256 in the affected states. Chris Graber, MDS Region II director, wrote, "I saw more destruction than anyone could imagine possible."

Most Intense Hurricanes in U. S. History

1935 hurricane in Florida Keys: 892 millibars of atmospheric pressure (worst)

1969 Hurricane Camille: 909 millibars of pressure

1992 Hurricane Andrew: 922 millibars of pressure

Saffir-Simpson Hurricane Scale

Category	Wind Speed	Damage	Storm Sea Surge
1	74-95 mph	Limited to trees, mobile homes	4-5 ft. above normal
2	96-110	Roofing and window damage, much damage to mobile homes and trees	6-8 ft. above normal
3	111-130	Some structural damage, trees and signs down, mobile homes destroyed, flooding likely	9-12 ft. above normal
4	131-155	Extensive structural damage, roofs gone, major damage along shores, evacuations required	13-18 ft. above normal
5	Above 155	Complete roof failure on most buildings, many whole buildings destroyed, landscape obliterated	Greater than 18 ft. above normal

MCC photo by Burton Buller

MCC photo by Burton Buller

Courtesy of Gene Ramsey

Far left: The effects of Hurricane Camille were felt all the way to Nelson County, Va., where 27 inches of rain caused terrible flash flooding and killed 106 people. MDSers worked for many months in cleanup efforts.

Near left: A casualty of Hurricane Camille, this house in Woods Mill, Va., was almost buried in mud from flooding streams.

Riding Out Camille

MDS photo

George Reno, born and raised in Louisiana, was one of the first converts at an emerging Mennonite mission church at Akers and later became its pastor.

George and his wife still live in southern Louisiana. As a shrimp fisherman, his livelihood depended on his boat. He often rode out storms and hurricanes in his boat, to keep it safe. George remembers Hurricane Betsy in 1965, then Camille in 1969, as the worst storms to hit the Gulf:

I come from an interesting family. Mother's people are deathly afraid of weather. If a black cloud passes over, they're running. On my dad's side, they defied the weather; nothing scared them. I guess I inherited my genes from my dad's side.

My brother and I rode out Camille, the storm of the century, near Venice, Louisiana. We took a lot of rope and spider-webbed our boats into the trees just outside the levy. We tied them into willow trees. They are leathery and bend but don't break. These winds would lay the trees on the ground, just bend them, stripping off bark and limbs.

As the wind and water rose, we adjusted the ropes. The peak of the storm hit at midnight with winds up to 200 miles per hour. We had huge tidal waves; at one time we were in the tops of the trees. When the wind changed and the water began to recede, we had to back our boats out to get them over the waterway so we wouldn't be left up on land.

By five in the morning, it was dead calm, from 200 mph plus to zero, in six hours. Our boats took some damage, but we survived. The Lord was with us.

Outside the levee was a big ballroom restaurant. They had an air-cooled generator built about 10 feet high and a roof over it. When the storm was over, everything was gone—nothing but four pilings sticking up and a naked green generator setting on top. It was still running; it never stopped. Nothing there to furnish electric to, but it was still running.

People inside the levees were supposed to have evacuated, but not all of them left. My brother took a small boat and went inside the levee, up over the highway. I took my shrimp boat in the river and followed along. I saw a man standing out on a big pile of debris; he was stripped to his shorts, all scratched and bloody. He had about 100 feet of water between him and the levee but couldn't swim. I told him to relax, my brother was coming in a smaller boat and would pick him up.

While I waited, I heard a kid screaming at the top of his voice. I walked along the top of the levee, through the debris and snakes. A gable of a house was sticking out of the water, washed up against the levee. A child and his parents were in there. I picked them up and took them back to Venice.

We live in a precarious place. Age has taken its toll, and I no longer ride storms out. My wife has finally persuaded me that it's more fun to leave with her than stay and enjoy the storm. But for many years I wouldn't leave my boat. Out on the boat, I didn't have a feeling of fear, but a feeling of uncertainty, not knowing what would happen. It was exhilarating.

MDS Deploys in a Unique Mobilization Effort

MDS Region II leaders made immediate contact with Mississippi unit leaders on August 18. Meanwhile, Region III MDS leaders had special connections with Harold Regier, a Kansan in a continuing ministry at Camp Landon. Region III director Marvin Hostetler arranged for an air force plane to take 100 MDS men and women to Gulfport that week. They worked out of Camp Landon and the neighboring Crossroads Mennonite Church, providing cleanup services, clearing trees, helping the Red Cross serve meals, sorting clothes, and providing emergency relief.

Ronnie Geil, MDS leader in southern Mississippi and living in the Gulfport community when Camille hit, says, "It was a real lift to our spirits when I passed the airport several blocks from our home and saw those C-130 cargo planes with all those MDS volunteers who came to help. After that I knew how it felt to receive help and why victims of other disasters had been so happy to see anyone who came to work. It brought home to me how important it is to give of our time when people are in need."

Within a week Region II director Chris Graber and MDS binational coordinator Delmar Stahly were on site for long-term planning. The two-pronged response by two regional bodies created confusion and tension that led MDS to develop further guidelines for responding to major disasters.

In the first month, MDS sent in over 650 people. Over the next six months, almost 1,800 volunteers traveled to southern Mississippi to help in the recovery effort. Harold Regier, pastor at the Crossroads Mennonite Church where 20 people huddled as the storm beat down, remembers the outpouring of help: "The MDS response was an affirmation that those of us there long term were represented by a much larger constituency, people who had service and mission as a motivating part of our faith commitment. People were surprised at the enormity of the response and how MDS got people into places so easily and quickly."

Warren Miller, member of the Gulfhaven Mennonite Church, recently reflected, "One thing that impresses me is that, even though Camille was 30 years ago, hardly a month goes by that I don't meet somebody who learns that I am a Mennonite and says, 'Oh, yes, I remember them in Camille.' Thirty years later those stories are still here."

Below: Communities say thanks to MDS in many ways, such as a bridge dedicated to MDS, on the Tye River, Nelson County, Va.

THIS BRIDGE IS DEDICATED TO
THE MENNONITE CHURCH
IN THANKS FOR ALL THAT ITS MEMBERS HAVE DONE
TO HELP THE CITIZENS OF NELSON COUNTY
FOLLOWING HURRICANE CAMILLE,
AUGUST 20, 1969

Courtesy of Gene Ramsey

Right: Many Mennonite women who traveled to Mississippi to work after Hurricane Camille volunteered to help the Red Cross serve hundreds of meals.

Burton Buller

Courtesy of MDS Kansas

Below: MDSers from Kansas entering a U.S. Air Force transport plane for the noisy ride to Gulfport, Miss., to work on the Hurricane Camille project. Two planeloads went in late August 1969.

Some Fruit Ripens Slowly

David Kniss shared this story as part of his devotional for the MDS all-unit meeting at Columbus, Mississippi, in February 1997:

I am pastor at the Gulfhaven Mennonite Church near Gulfport, Mississippi, an area that experienced a lot of MDS work in 1969 when Hurricane Camille went through. Regularly, as I talk with people and they find out I'm Mennonite, they say, "Oh yes, the Mennonites came down and helped us in Hurricane Camille." We have good rapport with people because of the witness you have left. I'd like to share a beautiful experience I had in 1992.

I got a call one day from a woman whose father was in the hospital and very ill. She said her father wasn't a churchgoing person but a very rough character, a shrimp fisherman and construction man who had never darkened the door of a church.

She had asked her father if he would like to see a minister, and he said, "Yes, I think I would."

He had never accepted Christ in his life. She asked, "Who should I call, my Church of God pastor or a Baptist pastor? What kind of pastor would you like for me to call?"

"No, I want you to call a Mennonite pastor."

She didn't even know what that was but looked it up in the yellow pages and gave me a call. I went to see him.

As I visited Tallis in the hospital, I asked about his relationship with the Lord. He explained why he asked for me to come. He said that 23 years before, "when my house was leveled in Hurricane Camille, I heard about these Mennonites who were helping people. I looked them up at their office and talked to someone there. I took a set of plans along of what I'd like to do to reconstruct my house.

"They said they'd send someone out to see my place that evening. So they did. This man came out, and I showed him the plans and said I'd like to have some help laying the foundation. I went to work the next morning. That evening, the foundation was laid.

"I went down to the office and asked, 'Who do I thank for this? This is wonderful. Who did this?'

"The person in the office said, 'Well, I can't really tell you who did it. I'm not sure.'"

Tallis said they didn't even act like they were too interested in his thanks. He said it was just so wonderful to see that kind of a spirit.

He went to work the next day. When he came home, all the debris was cleared. He said, "I had a nice clear lot. Again, I went to see

them, and again the same response: 'We're not sure who did it, but someone did.' I have never, never forgotten that act of kindness."

I talked to Tallis about the Lord, and he accepted the Lord. I had the joy of baptizing him and seeing him brought to the Lord. I asked him if he simply wanted to be baptized into the family of God or as a Mennonite. He wanted to be a Mennonite.

We grew a lot in our friendship together, Tallis and I. His wife loved it when I came to visit because that was the only time he'd shave. Once she called me: "Please come and visit Tallis; he needs a shave bad." When I visited him, he was clean-shaven.

Tallis really grew in the Lord during those months we knew him. Then he went on to be with the Lord. We were in the north somewhere when he passed away and not able to be there for the funeral. That was a terrible heartache for me.

Twenty-three years after you were there, someone reaped what you sowed. This is repeated more often than you might realize. People are touched by your witness. Some time later, in a time of crisis, they turn to the Lord. So I just share with you the beauty of what you're doing and the results that may come years later.[7]

1972: Year of the Floods

Top right: The Community Mennonite Church of Corning, N.Y., was built on land donated because MDSers helped that community after Hurricane Hazel.

Middle right: The Bible Fellowship Church in Rapid City, S.D., grew out of the witness by MDS volunteers after the floods of 1972. With about 300 attending, it even has a Christian school for 150 students.

Bottom right: By the shores of Mennonite Creek, so named because MDS helped to rebuild after USA's most intense earthquake, in 1964 in Alaska.

Near right: In 1971, C. Nelson Hostetter became the first full-time MDS coordinator. Outgoing coordinator Delmar Stahley (right) and Nelson are flying from Memphis to an MDS project in Inverness, Miss.

Among the busiest years in MDS history was 1972. Three major floods in three parts of the country all required long-term response programs. On February 26 a 30-foot wall of water from a ruptured slag dam cascaded through Buffalo Creek, West Virginia. It killed 125, destroyed 450 homes, and damaged 1,600 more. By the end of the summer, MDSers had logged more than 4,000 volunteer days.

On June 10, a vicious cloudburst dumped up to 14 inches of rain in the Black Hills of South Dakota. In the dark of night, torrents of water crashed down the slopes, bursting dams and sending a devastating wall of water through Rapid City, South Dakota. In the town of 43,000 people, 230 were killed.[8]

During June 19-24, Hurricane Agnes dropped as much as 19 inches of rain as she roared out of the Gulf of Mexico and across every state from Florida to New York. More than 210,000 people were forced from their homes, and 122 were killed. Long-standing flood records were shattered in six states. Damages totaled over $3 billion, making it the most costly disaster in the United States at that time.

The MDS response was as widespread as the disaster; in the first two months about 37,000 volunteer days were logged from Florida to New York. The total response to Hurricane Agnes may be the largest volunteer response to any disaster in the first 50 years of MDS. In Wilkes Barre, Pennsylvania, and Corning/Elmira, New York, work continued for up to two years. The Community Mennonite Church in Corning, New York, was planted as a result of the MDS response.[9]

Corning Update: Planted Seeds Save Money

As the Community Mennonite Church grew, the group in Corning started looking for property on which to build. In 1981 trustee Clayton Tuttle approached prominent businessman John Eberenz, who owned the biggest piece of undeveloped land in the city. The spot looked just right for a church.

Eberenz was negotiating to sell it for $200,000 but said he had dreamed that the land should go to a nondenominational church. "If you have a nondenominational church, I'll sell it to you for $60,000."

Clayton replied that the group was Mennonite, not nondenominational. Remembering the Mennonites working after the flood, Eberenz responded, "Well, if it can't be nondenominational, it can be

Courtesy of Harold Miller

Courtesy of Dick Nickel

MCC photo, Mennonite Church Archives

Courtesy of Abe Froese

Mennonite." The next day he dropped the price to $30,000. Clayton said they didn't have that much money, but he would ask the church.

Before the church could decide, John Eberenz and his wife left on a trip. On the way Eberenz called back and said he and his wife had concluded that if he gave the land to the church, it might help when they came to the pearly gates. Clayton didn't counter his theology; the property went to the church!

Rapid City Update: From Broken Dam to Haven for Broken People

The tremendous witness of the MDSers who responded to the Rapid City floods also left a lasting impression on the whole community. As MDS was closing down in 1973, city officials said they would welcome having a Mennonite church started in town.

In 1978, the Mennonite Brethren Church sent Dale Wiebe to Rapid City as a church planter. In November, they started meeting in a school, and the church grew rapidly. In December 1979 they started building a church that was completed in July 1980.

Today this Bible Fellowship Church is a haven for over 200 members, with attendance averaging 275-300. Current pastor Dick Nickel says the church "cares for broken people and people looking for answers in their lives. We have seen the Lord turn many lives around."

MDS Goes International

In earlier years, MCC and MDS had no clear understanding about which organization would respond to international disasters. On several occasions in the 1960s and 1970s, MDS sent rebuilding teams to other countries. Later, as MCC sent personnel into more countries, they usually took the lead in responding to disasters occurring overseas, sometimes requesting MDS assistance. By the late 1970s, that division of responsibilities became official policy: MCC is responsible for organizing disaster response efforts internationally. MDS directs efforts in Canada and the United States, including U.S. territories like Puerto Rico and the U.S. Virgin Islands. MCC has continued to request MDS teams for some international programs during the 1980s and 1990s.

Below: During racial unrest of the 1960s, many southern churches were bombed and burned. MDSers helped rebuild five churches for African-Americans and two for Choctaw Indians. MDS volunteers and local workers pause for prayer before lunch at a project.

MCC photo, Mennonite Church Archives

MCC photo

Courtesy of Albert Ediger

MDS International Involvement

1956	Hurricane Betsy, Puerto Rico
1961	Hurricane Hattie, British Honduras
1963	earthquake, Yugoslavia
1963	Hurricane Flora, Haiti
1966	earthquake, Turkey
1972	earthquake, Nicaragua
1974	Hurricane Fifi, Honduras
1977	earthquake, Guatemala
1988	Hurricane Joan, Nicaragua
1989	earthquake, Armenia
1991	earthquake, Costa Rica
1995	earthquake, Japan

A Challenge to Traveling MDSers One source of mutual blessing is ongoing contact and visits to sites of MDS projects. If you have worked in a location and know individuals, you'll be welcomed with open arms. Hugs are standard, even for shy MDSers!

Everyone should plan a stop at a church MDS has helped start or build, such as Rapid City (S.D.), Corning (N.Y.), Gulfport (Miss.), and Crestview and Homestead (Fla.).

Tell them you're an MDSer, and enjoy the warm welcome!

Far left: MDS volunteers join local workers rebuilding in Honduras after Hurricane Fifi in 1974.

Near left: An MDSer gathers an appreciative crew as he rebuilds in Haiti after Hurricane Flora in 1963.

51

CHAPTER FIVE

Mending the Torn Land

MDS photo

You shall hear of wars and rumors of wars: see that you be not troubled: for all these things must come to pass, but the end is not yet. For nation shall rise against nation, and kingdom against kingdom; and there shall be famines, and pestilences, and earthquakes, in various places. All these are the beginning of sorrows.

—Jesus, in Matthew 24:6-8, KJV

Eight months after Hurricane Camille flooded Nelson County, Virginia, the local Episcopal rector preached. He referred to the Mennonite work and witness he saw through the MDS response: "Sacrifice. We talk about it, but they live it. Try to imagine what it would have been like without them. Who is still out there working to rebuild the country, the county? So far as I can see, nobody but Mennonite Disaster Service."

He added that in his congregation after the flood, many people had patterned their lives on a biblical example. "We read in Genesis 9:21 that after the great Flood, Noah got drunk. Many of my people did the same. But not the Mennonites. Cheerfully sober, they toiled to mend the torn land."

The Torn Land

Of disasters there has been no end. Records of recent years list more disasters and more people affected by those disasters than ever before. It is difficult to select only a few disasters of MDS's second 25 years (1976-2000) to illustrate its ongoing work. Text and photographs highlight disasters with sample projects where MDS has had a major impact, where MDSers have helped heal the torn land. Several major disasters of these years appear in following chapters.[1]

Chaos in the Canyon

On Saturday evening, July 31, 1976, the beautiful Big Thompson River was flowing peacefully down its Colorado mountain canyon. In a few hours that night, it was

Photo, page 52: A house in Coalinga, Calif. shows the effects of earthquake damage, although it didn't stop the paperboy.

Below: It is hard to imagine this tranquil river as a raging killer. On July 31, 1976, heavy rains and breaking dams sent a 19-foot wall of water racing down the Big Thompson River canyon in Colorado, killing 139 people. MDS launched a major response and made many friends.

transformed into a killing torrent. A severe thunderstorm had stalled over the upper valleys around Estes Park and Glen Haven and dumped up to 12 inches of rain in four hours. In the dark these waters thundered downstream at unbelievable speeds, catching and surprising residents and campers in the beautiful canyon. Dams collapsed, bridges were washed out, and trees, homes, automobiles, and boulders as big as cars were swept down the narrow canyon.

Six persons were never found, and 139 were confirmed dead. One family survived by scrambling through the second-floor ceiling, chopping a hole in the roof, and spending the cold night in the falling rain. Many survived by climbing canyon walls to escape the wall of water reaching 19 feet high; they clung to trees till rescued by helicopter the following day. Many tell of the horror of seeing others in trouble or listening to the screams of those being swept downstream. They remember the smell and sound of gas hissing from propane tanks,

busted from their moorings.

That weekend Mennonites from the nearby church at Greeley had a retreat at the YMCA campground in Estes Park. They were concerned about the heavy rains but had no clue of the terrible disaster taking place in the canyon below. The next morning they heard that the canyon road was out, so they would need to take other routes home. Most knew little about the disaster till they reached home later that day.

Delmar Schroeder, MDS Colorado coordinator, and Paul Martin, pastor of the Mennonite Church of Greeley, immediately initiated a response. Regional and other network teams soon joined them. Cleanup crews joined local residents and other volunteers to shovel through many feet of mud and tackle massive boulders. MDS set up a longer-term response unit, based at the Sylvan Dale Ranch at the bottom of the

canyon, where volunteers were housed and fed.

After MDSers completed rebuilding one home, the family erected a sign: "Built by the Mennonites, the Best Friends We Ever Had." Over 1,000 volunteers provided over 10,000 workdays of canyon service.

In 1996, the 20th anniversary of the event, the community helped compile *Reflections of the Heart*, a book of memories of the Big Thompson flood.[2] Survivors recall the horrors of the night and the long, hard road to recovery. Many remember the wonderful assistance of "the Mennonites." Florence Kratzer writes, "There were so many people who helped us. The Mennonites were wonderful. No job was too hard or too dirty for them to do, and they would accept nothing in return. My husband asked them why they did this, and the answer was because they 'love the Lord.'"

MDS photo

Follow the Flood

In March 1999, while researching this book, I traveled up and down the Big Thompson Canyon. I encourage you to do the same. Some call it "the most beautiful drive in Colorado." The natural wonders of the canyon also make it easy to visualize the devastating disaster in 1976.

In advance, you might read *Reflections of the Heart*s.[2] The map and stories in the book will come alive as you travel east from Estes Park, down the canyon on Highway 34. Along the way local folks will share their memories of that night; signs and memorials dot the route.

Halfway down the canyon, stop at the Indian Village Arts and Crafts store run by Lena and Howard Carman. Howard recalls, "If it weren't for the Mennonites, we wouldn't be here anymore. We could never have cleaned up and gotten back on our feet without your help."

As you leave the canyon, look for the Sylvan Dale Guest Ranch, where MDSers were housed and fed. Spend the night and enjoy the same hospitality from the Jessup family that MDSers did in 1976. Susan Jessup, current manager, responded to my thanks for their hospitality with heartfelt gratitude of their own: "The healing became so much more important than the flood. We thank you for helping bring healing to our community."

MDS photo

MDS photo

MDS photo

And Hugo Was His Name

It started innocuously as Tropical Depression 11, over the Atlantic between Africa and South America. By the time it had spun itself out over West Virginia two weeks later, Hurricane Hugo had left a path of destruction stretching across the Caribbean and up the southeastern seaboard of the United States.

Hugo increased in strength as it headed for the U.S. Virgin Islands and struck St. Croix dead center. There are no Mennonite churches on the island. Audrey B. Shank, one of four women living together and serving in a literature mission, was MDS representative there. Audrey and her colleagues survived the night huddled with neighbors who fled from room to room as the roof was torn off above them. In the morning they found their own house withstood the storm better than the neighbor's, though it too suffered significant damage.

Eventually Audrey was able to contact MDS and hosted the initial MDS and mission board investigators. She led MDS to the Sunny Isle Baptist Church, which became MDS local headquarters.

Taking Aim on the Carolinas

After devastating the Caribbean, the sprawling Hugo roared into South Carolina on September 21, 1989. Winds over 140 miles per hour wreaked havoc in a swath 100 miles wide northward from Charleston, South Carolina. Losing intensity slowly, Hugo created tremendous devastation as far as Charlotte, North Carolina, 200 miles inland.

Historic Charleston was hard hit, but in rural areas and small towns north along the coast and further inland, almost nothing remained. A storm surge over 15 feet high sent boats sailing into people's yards far from water and moved houses into the middle of the road.

Forty miles inland, the 7,000 residents in the Moncks Corner (S.C.) community were not particularly concerned about Hugo. Severe storms seldom reached that far, but Hugo did. Frank McCoy, pastor of the Pinopolis United Methodist Church, remembers: "Hugo pounded us for eight terrifying hours. It had been predicted this could be a monster, but Hugo turned out to be the Goliath of all hurricanes. Huddled in our home breaking apart around us, we felt sure we were entering the valley of the shadow of death, never to return.

"Finally the storm roared off to the west. As the September dawn began lighting the countryside, my wife, our teenage son, and I picked our way out of our nearly collapsed parsonage. Trees not already broken leaned at crazy angles, as did the telephone poles and almost everything else. To seek help, we stepped gingerly over downed power lines and scrambled over trees piled three to four feet high. Everyone wondered how and where to begin clearing out the chaos."

Paul Brubacher, East Coast regional director, and other MDS leaders were immediately on-site to investigate and set up a long-term response. Even before volunteers were allowed into the more devastated areas along the South Carolina coast, MDSers were cutting trees and clearing debris around Charlotte. Then God led

Top: MDS carries responsibility for disaster response in the U.S. Virgin Islands. When Hurricane Hugo devastated St. Croix in 1989, MDS sent teams to assist in reconstruction. Project director Wes Heinrichs (left) and his crew catch their breath after another roof repair. Other MDSers include Willard Heatwole (center) and Keith Allen (right), a Mennonite pastor from Jamaica.

Middle: Hurricane Hugo tossed a yacht onto the road in S.C.

Bottom: MDS women restore a house in S.C. after Hurricane Hugo.

BENTON MENNONITE CHURCH LIBRARY 15350 CR 44 GOSHEN, IN

MDS project leader Ed Eby and pastor Frank McCoy together; the Pinopolis United Methodist Church become MDS headquarters for two months till larger facilities were found.

The Long Road to Recovery

The damage from Hurricane Hugo was massive; in 1989 it ranked as the most destructive hurricane ever to hit the U.S. mainland. Because the havoc was spread over hundreds of square miles, MDS placed volunteers in over a dozen locations. They used churches, fire stations, and warehouses in (S.C.) places like Charleston, James Island, Mount Pleasant, McClellanville, Cordesville, Cross, Isle of Palms, Johns Island, Awendaw, Sumter, Macedonia, Eutawville, and Moncks Corner.

The widespread need and the overwhelming constituency response pushed the MDS network as never before. Where would MDS find leaders to oversee all these locations and keep hundreds of volunteers busy? Where would MDS find vehicles, tools, and other needed equipment? The half-million dollars designated

by the compassionate constituency helped immensely; vehicles and equipment were donated or bought. By December 1989, MDS had outgrown the Pinopolis church facilities. An unused Pepsi Cola bottling warehouse became headquarters. An office, a large kitchen, and a dining room were installed, and lodging quarters arranged. Soon the large warehouse was filled with tools, vehicles, and building materials.

Back in the Caribbean

In St. Croix, the MDS team was also working at rebuilding. Winds on St. Croix were estimated to be over 200 miles per hour. Based at the Sunny Isle Baptist Church, an average of 25 to 30 volunteers at a time worked mainly at replacing roofs. Beryl Forrester, MDS volunteer and writer from Oregon, reported:

"The reasons we should be on the island of St. Croix in the name and Spirit of Jesus Christ are everywhere present. Anywhere one looks, homes are roofless, open to the elements. Some have plastic tarps for temporary protection.

"While MDSers minister with hammers

and manpower, they are also offering witness to the good news of God in indirect ways. It is not lost on our Crucian brothers and sisters that here are Christians who have taken time away from jobs and families to help. This stands in striking contrast to hundreds of locals and expatriates using the emergency for gain. Price gouging and profiteering are rampant. Even families of average means cannot put roofs back on because of overcharges.

"One easily understands why people say to the MDSers, 'God sent you here.' God really did. God is in the business of helping those who are victimized and helpless. This witness has been particularly needed in the St. Croix situation."

Despite bouts of dengue fever and tropical heat, MDSers replaced about 140 roofs along with doing other jobs before they left St. Croix in May 1990.

Lessons from Hugo

MDS learned many lessons dealing with a disaster the size of Hugo, lessons useful for addressing the even larger disasters to come in the 1990s. We relearned the importance of having many trained leaders available and began leadership training workshops. Hugo taught us that no one organization can do it alone. We continued our partnership with American Red Cross and added important new alliances with the Salvation Army and other groups.

We learned to depend more effectively on our own network and asked individual MDS units to organize and run satellite locations. The Eastern Pennsylvania MDS unit provided leaders and a vanload of volunteers each week for the Mt. Pleasant

Below: A used car lot? No, MDS vehicles supporting the Hugo response at its Moncks Corner, S.C., base. This was one of the largest projects in MDS history.

Below right: Amish young men from Lancaster County, Pa., tackling the massive tree damage caused by Hurricane Hugo in S.C. in September 1989.

MDS photo

Courtesy of Grace Burkholder

(S.C.) satellite location. The Virginia Shenandoah unit did the same for Cordesville (S.C.). We initiated a revised summer youth program that is ongoing and important.

When the Hugo project closed in summer 1991, over 7,000 volunteers had given over 40,000 workdays to help with recovery efforts in South Carolina. Another 100 had given a month of service in St. Croix. This is still one of the largest MDS projects ever. Yet its value is not measured in numbers so much as in work offered and witness given. Here are two testimonies from dear friends we learned to know and love.

Southern Hospitality and Humor

David and Ann Matthews, members of Pinopolis United Methodist Church, opened their home and hearts to many MDSers. The long-term workers spent many an evening or weekend with the Matthews,

who remember "our Mennonites."

"I went up to the church one day," Ann says. "These two ladies were in our kitchen, and they were just busy cooking, some of the best-smelling cooking I ever sniffed. Later we met some of the young people in Wal-Mart. They were so delightful and personable that we followed them home. We went to church with them, ate with them, brought them home with us, and introduced them to South Carolina iced tea. They just became part of the family. There in our church it was like regular Mennonite city. It took the edge off our hurt to know there are still people willing to give up so much so we could have shelter. If it took a hurricane to bring that into my life, I'm glad for it."

David mentioned to one MDS leader that he needed to hire someone to get the roof back on his garage. The MDSer said, "That's not a problem; we'll take care of it." That Wednesday evening, after they had worked all day, this Mennonite van drove

Below: Marlin (left) and Nancy (right) Gingerich from Iowa enjoy the hospitality of Helen White (center) and her family in the new home MDS built for the White family near Moncks Corner, S.C.

up. Six men and one young girl got out.

"So here they came with hammers and nails. They got up on the roof, put up the rest of the trusses, 35 sheets of plywood, and the girl was nailing on hurricane straps. I said, 'Now listen, we don't pay workers comp; don't fall off that roof.'

"The man turned, looked down at me, and said, 'We don't have time to worry

Below left: Mom and Dad Matthews (Ann and David, center) enjoy showing off Ev's 10-pound catfish! Beth (Noll) Lehman (left) and Evelyn Ediger (right) were two of many long-term MDS young adult volunteers who enjoyed the special hospitality of the Matthews.

The Sunny Isle Baptist Church became the MDS headquarters and church home for the many volunteers who traveled to St. Croix to assist recovery efforts. In May 1990, MDS left many friends behind, who said thank you via a bulletin announcement: "We say Good Bye and Fare Well to The Mennonites with a FELLOWSHIP LUNCHEON in the kitchen area immediately following today's Worship Service. To them we say a very Big THANK YOU! on behalf of us here at Sunny Isle and on behalf of the people of St. Croix."

A Peculiar People

Frank McCoy, Pastor, Pinopolis United Methodist Church, shares this story:

One evening a small slim Amish man with long gray beard, black felt hat, homemade clothes, and suspenders came up to me. He said, "People around here think we are peculiar."

I looked him up and down and blurted, "You are."

He was startled, so I quickly added, "You've left your homes, families, friends, and all that's familiar. You've never met

us before and probably never will again. Yet here you've come hundreds of miles from home to work on other people's houses in Moncks Corner. You work from sunup to sundown without pay. You bring your own tools. If we can't supply the material you need, you furnish it yourself.

"You ask nothing in return. It seems to us that all of you are working in the way Jesus would if he was here in this mess. Now that seems awfully strange to us. Yes, we do think you MDS workers are peculiar."

Courtesy of Beth Noll Lehman

about falling. Hand me the plywood.'"

Despite Ann's dislike of travel, the urge to visit their Mennonite friends was so strong that some years later they made the trip to Pennsylvania. Ann reflects with pleasure on the visit. "Wilbur Lentz arranged a place for us, and we visited all our friends. It was the most beautiful country, cows and horses out in the fields; I love country people. Beth [Noll] took us to her fiancé's home on a farm. When I got out of the car, this smell took the breath out of me. I said, 'Perfume, somebody has a perfume factory around here.' They had a pig parlor in the barn, and we parked right near the barn. I thought I would die, and they all laughed at me."

Now Ann is trying to get the courage to visit the Plessingers in Ohio and the Gingerichs in Iowa. Meanwhile, MDSers keep going back to Moncks Corner, where they're always welcome at the Matthews: "You-all come anytime."

Map: A sixth Great Lake? No, just the area over nine states affected by the great Midwest floods of 1993. The "500-year flood" sent six times the normal flow past the Gateway Arch in St. Louis, with enough topsoil every 24 hours to cover five 1,000-acre farms a foot deep.

Providence, R.I., *Journal-Bulletin*

UNFORTUNATELY, IT'S NOT A RAINBOW... IT'S ST. LOUIS!

Right: Boats and large vehicles were the only way to get around in many towns during the 1993 floods. In places like Keithsburg, Ill., on the Mississippi River, many people were forced from their homes for several months.

Ol' Man River . . . He Just Keeps Rolling Along

In 1993 thousands of Midwest residents learned what Mark Twain knew 100 years earlier. About his favorite subject, Twain wrote, "The Mississippi River cannot be tamed, curbed, or confined; . . . you cannot bar its path with an obstruction which it will not tear down, dance over, and laugh at."[3]

Excessive continuous rains during spring and summer in the Mississippi and Missouri river basins brought record flooding across nine Midwestern states. In Iowa, already-saturated land could not absorb the 38 inches of rain from June to August, more than the annual average.

Threatened dams were opened wide. Hundreds of levees failed, affecting 150 major rivers and their tributaries in the most widespread and largest U.S. flood to that date. By July 12, the early rains in the upper Mississippi basin pushed the crest at St. Louis to a record-tying 43 feet. Iowa waters pushed the new record to 47 feet by July 20. Then the record-breaking crest on the Missouri River reached St. Louis. By August 1 the record was pushed to 49.5 feet.

Tens of thousands of people were evacuated, some never to return. Fifty people died in the flood and dozens more from its effects. Total damage exceeded $15 billion, with 10,000 homes destroyed. At least 15 million acres of farmland were inundated, many lost to productive farming for several years.

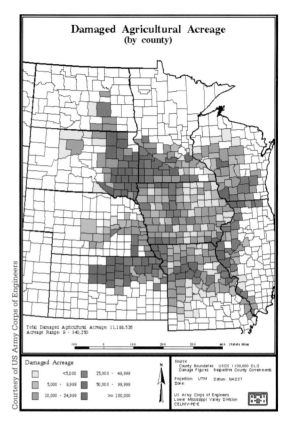

Damaged Agricultural Acreage
(by county)

Total Damaged Agricultural Acreage: 11,188,525
Acreage Range: 9 - 340,250

Courtesy of US Army Corps of Engineers

Damaged Acreage

<5,000	25,000 - 49,999
5,000 - 9,999	50,000 - 99,999
10,000 - 24,999	>= 100,000

Source
County Boundaries: USGS 1:100,000 DLG
Damage Figures: Respective County Governments
Projection: UTM   Datum: NAD27
Zone:

US Army Corps of Engineers
Lower Mississippi Valley Division
CELMV-PE-E

Willis Kuhns

IA 8528AC

We're in the Middle of It All

Mennonites, Amish, or both live in all the nine states affected (North and South Dakota, Minnesota, Wisconsin, Illinois, Iowa, Nebraska, Kansas, and Missouri). Mennonite farms of southeastern Iowa looked like swamps, with acres of stunted, yellow corn and beans.

Newsweek, AP photographer Cliff Schiappa, and Wide World Photos

Courtesy of Irvin Oberholtzer

Images of Amish and Mennonites joining in the massive sandbagging efforts flooded the media. Jacob Hochstetler, Amish farmer from near Canton, Missouri, spent 15 hours one day sandbagging. "Can't do much farming anyhow; too much rain. Might as well help," *USA Today* reported him saying. Help we did. This one was happening to us, in our neighborhoods.

The tensions and feelings of that stressful time are shown in a story from Irvin Oberholtzer, MDS Missouri unit chair then. He lives in northeast Missouri and had helped gather volunteers to sandbag at Canton, on the west bank of the Mississippi.

"Under direction of the Corp of Engineers, we were making a three-foot fence on top of the levee. We would put a stake every four feet, brace it, fill in with solid boards, and line this with plastic and sandbags to seal it against the rising waters. With water already up a foot on the boards, it was beginning to cut through the north end of the levee, under our sandbags and fence. The director said, 'We need 25 guys with shovels in the water inside the fence.' I remember so well: there were Amish boys in the water. There was no choice; we were desperate to get the job done. About 4:00 p.m. we thought we heard a waterfall, a rushing sound. Then it came over the communications system: the levee had broken on the Illinois side. It flooded 36,000 acres. The water went down, and we were able to repair our side. When the water came back up, our town was saved.

"Later, on the street, a man I didn't know came to me and said, 'You're a Christian; would you agree with me that God saw it better to save my house and let the land flood over there, where there aren't nearly as many farmhouses as we have houses in town?' I thought for a minute before replying, 'Sir, those are the things the Lord decides.' But I wonder. The people on the other side had a great loss."

Where Do We Start?

In good MDS style, we begin at home, at the grass roots, neighbors helping neighbors. In each of the affected states, local MDS units began such work. By July it was clear that this would be an immense disaster, so regional and binational leaders joined in the investigation.

Experience in large disasters like Hurricanes Hugo and Andrew again provided valuable lessons for MDS response. The flood affected nine local units and two regions; it would require the support of the whole network. We had a coordinating meeting in early September in Hannibal, Missouri. Each state was invited to send representatives to join regional and binational leaders in planning for a long and massive response. Each affected state selected an area on which to focus, each region took responsibility for another area, and MDS Akron set up a coordinating office in Hannibal. Over nearly two years, almost 6,000 volunteers gave about 23,000 workdays in flood recovery efforts. Only a few special stories can be shared to illustrate one of the largest MDS response projects in our 50-year history.

Pontius' Puddle

I'M SORRY. THAT COVENANT OF YOURS EXPRESSLY FORBIDS DESTROYING THE WHOLE EARTH WITH FLOOD, BUT I DID FIND A LOOPHOLE THAT ALLOWS YOU TO SOAK THE BEJEEBERS OUT OF IOWA!

Top left: Amish volunteer Solomon Schwartz, Anabel, Mo., struggles against the rising floodwaters during a sandbagging operation on July 9, 1993, along the Mississippi River, as shown on this July 26, 1993 "Newsweek" cover.

Bottom left: Note the waterline two-thirds of the way up the house. Homeowners and MDSers faced a mess after finally reaching these homes weeks after the first floodwaters.

Behind the Scenes in Disaster Recovery

The Silent Disaster

Beyond the photos of endless water and record flooding are people—sisters, brothers, and neighbors facing frustrations, discouragement, and tremendous economic loss. They ponder hard issues: When can they return home? Farmers wonder when the next crop will come—maybe not even next year. Many factories are closed; people are unemployed. Stress pounds finances, marriages, frayed nerves, and ulcers. During the year after the flood, in many communities more people died from causes related to flood stress than directly from the flood. Could MDS help in this arena?

Pastors and healthcare professionals in Iowa called for a seminar to give local pastors more training and resources to work at stress-related issues in their own congregations. MDS project leaders attended a similar workshop at Hannibal.

I Want to Go Back Home

After a flood there is always debate and often people feel pressure to move to higher ground. Moving makes sense to FEMA (the federal agency often paying for repeated repair of homes in floodplains) and to MDSers (who sometimes repair the same home flood after flood). Yet a house may have been in the family for generations. Residents want to return there to die. MDS leaders often get caught in the debate: Do we help these people rebuild or do we encourage them to move by building new houses elsewhere? Depending on

circumstances, MDS does either.

Alexandria, Missouri, is a small town on the west bank of the Mississippi, just south of the Iowa line. When the levee broke, the entire town was flooded; it took months for the water to go down. People were encouraged to rebuild elsewhere. Some did, helped in their rebuilding by the Christian Reformed Disaster Response volunteers. Yet many of Alexandria's elderly residents wanted to return home, even to houses in terrible condition. Project leaders were Irvin Oberholtzer and Marlin Gingerich. Marlin and his wife, Nancy, have served on many MDS projects from coast to coast, yet Marlin said, "This town is by far the worst I have seen; it looks like a war zone."

Irvin remembers that by the end of December 1993, there were five funerals in Alexandria for those who could not handle the stress. MDS repaired many homes and built several new ones, three for widows. Often they needed help to work through rebuilding decisions and the maze of paperwork required to get assistance. One time Marlin asked Irvin, "What do you do if Geraldine starts crying when you want to talk about the plans for her house?" Irvin responded, "Cry with her." Five years later, after a visit to see Geraldine and others in Alexandria, Irvin said, "We made a lot of friends here. Those bonds will stay as long as we live."

Moving to Higher Ground

Upriver 75 miles on the Illinois side lies Keithsburg, population about 750. In minutes after the levee broke in August, its highest flood on record swamped over 100 of the 150 homes. About 60 percent of the

Response Projects
In addition to local activities, MDS long-term flood response projects were located in Elwood, Kan.; Alexandria, Boonville, Jefferson City, and Hannibal, Mo.; Des Moines and Wever, Iowa; and St. Genevieve, Prairie de Rocher, Nauvoo, Hull, and Keithsburg, Ill.

Sabotage
There were confirmed reports of people going across the river to sabotage the levees on the other side so the water would go down and save their side.

MDS photo

Marlin Gingerich

Left: Probably no task is required more often in MDS recovery efforts than "doing drywall." "We can at least make it fun" appears to be the motto of this youth team in Keithsburg, Ill., in January 1995.

Below: Laverne Shetler (upper right) directs a crew preparing to pour the walls of the first basement in the flood relocation project in Keithsburg, Ill. Nine homes were built on higher ground, away from the Mississippi River floodplain.

MDS photo

Martin Gingerich

Left and above: Adopt a flood family? A great idea that worked well in Alexandria, Mo. Churches from nearby Iowa Mennonite and Amish communities picked families and rebuilt their homes. Pastor Scott Swartzendruber of the Kalona Mennonite Church helps rebuild the home of Helen Tucker.

people were displaced, many for months, some forever. From the city hall, on the higher side of town, the National Guard and others launched boats to patrol the town for the next 30 days.

Pastor Chuck Reynolds, First Christian Church, took a boat to check damage. Never before had floodwaters reached the upstairs sanctuary level; now his 12-foot boat floated in the doors and down the aisle. According to Chuck, even God moved to higher ground as the church was rebuilt on the hill outside town!

Willis Kuhns, MDS Illinois coordinator, led the investigation into Keithsburg and other Illinois towns. Ted Shattuck, first MDS on-site project leader, spent most of his time directing the town's volunteer response, using many who just showed up. Later, MDS did repair work for those who chose to rebuild. Yet our most significant work in Keithsburg involved longer-term buyout and relocation.

After waiting months for funding, MDS returned to Keithsburg and through February 1995 built nine new homes in a relocated subdivision. "If it hadn't been for MDS, the homes probably wouldn't be there," stated Sharon Reason, current mayor of Keithsburg. "There are now good things happening in Keithsburg. It's not a dying town."

Willis Kuhns reflects, "Seeing where it was and where it's at today is exciting, rewarding for all the phone calls and headaches that go along with trying to help people rebuild their lives. I'm glad I was a part of it." Pastor Reynolds concludes, "Your faith in action touched many lives. Several people who had never

been to church started coming. The Mennonites definitely touched lives for Christ that no other minister had been able to reach before."

Grandpa Smurf and Christmas for the Children

Downriver on the Illinois side, seven miles across the rich river-bottom farmland from Hannibal, lies the rural town of Hull, population 500. For 30 days as the Mississippi made it relentless rise, the farmers and townsfolk, joined by hundreds of volunteers, fought to shore up the levee. On July 25 the battle was lost and the levee breached. The second largest levee district in the United States (69 square miles) went under water. It took 24 hours for the waters to spread over the farmland to Hull. Then six feet of water arrived, flooding the town for the first time. Given ample warning time, people moved out with many possessions. It was almost two months before they could return to homes and businesses.

The town meeting place was the small restaurant and motel owned by Oliver and Helen Friedlein. It served coffee and food to keep the sandbaggers going before the water came and was the gathering point for families returning to work on their homes after the water receded. Willis Kuhns discovered this staging point and became acquainted with Paul and Jan Kenady, local farmers on the emerging flood-recovery committee. These folks were key contacts as MDS entered the community for a long-term recovery program.

MDS offered to clean and repair the restaurant and the motel if we could use it to house volunteers as we worked in Hull

Richer People

After the Ohio River floods in 1995, Paul Kenady and two other men from Hull traveled to Shepherdsville, Ohio, where Dan Bontrager was leading the MDS flood recovery program. They spent a week as MDSers helping other flood victims and concluded, "We're richer people in a lot of ways because of the loss we sustained. Without a doubt, we're richer because we've met these people."

61

Right: Tearing apart—before putting back together. Gutting a house after a flood is a messy job. An MDS crew in Albany, Ga., had to reduce this one to bare cement walls and floor joists.

and surrounding farm communities. The MDS Indiana unit led this project. Project director Dan Bontrager and coordinator Willis Hochstetler became close friends of people in that community. Hundreds of volunteers, mostly from Indiana, pitched in over the next nine months.

When Willis Kuhns offered help, the Kenadys remember wondering, *What are we going to do with the Mennonites?* But a little later we thought, *What are we going to do without the Mennonites?* Our perceptions altogether changed, because we didn't know anything about them, and we met so many super friends along the way."

By Christmas 1993, few families had been able to dry out and repair their homes. The Friedleins and other community leaders felt it important to find a way to bring the community together again, so a Christmas party was planned. A key goal was to reunite children going to school in other communities who missed friends and home.

MDSers heard about the activity and joined in raising support. One church in Indiana took up a freewill offering of $4,000. Another gave a new Bible for each child. Costumes for different Christmas figures, including a Smurf, appeared. An Indiana Amish MDSer had been to Hull several times, and Helen Friedlein joked with him that he would make a great Grandpa Smurf. Later he quietly asked Helen, "Now just what does a Grandpa Smurf have to do?" She replied, "Anyone with 56 grandchildren just does whatever they want to do." He had checked with his church and received permission to don the costume, to the delight of the whole assembly.

That evening 105 children, their families, and guests were fed. Santa Claus came on a boat behind the fire truck with three gifts for each child. Oliver reflects, "It was one of the warmest experiences I ever had in my life. Yes, we've had some tough times, but a lot of smiles, too."

Forever Friends

On July 3, 1994, Tropical Storm Alberto limped ashore on the Florida panhandle and, with winds of only 60 miles per hour, didn't even qualify as a hurricane. But as it moved north over Georgia on July 4, it hit a cold front heading south and stalled over western Georgia. The collision of warm moist air and the cold front produced an unstable weather pattern that resulted in days of heavy thunderstorms and drenching rain.

In Americus, Georgia, headquarters of

Courtesy of Lee and Mary Lois Martin

Mennonite Pilot's Association (MPA)

On various occasions over many years, pilots with access to small planes have provided valuable service to MDS. Chapter 4 tells of a pilot in eastern Pennsylvania who flew MDS leaders over the 1955 Stroudsburg flood area for an investigative trip. A view from the air is a quick way to gather perspective on the size of a disaster and identify the hardest hit areas. On short notice, MPA has also flown MDS leaders to meetings or to hard-to-reach locations.

In 1976 Mennonite pilots joined in an informal organization known as Mennonite Pilots Association. The purpose of MPA is to encourage Christian fellowship among pilots and to promote the safe and efficient use of general aviation in the mission of the church. Along with organizational officers, MPA has named "wing leaders" for each MDS region. These contact persons help MDS leaders find a qualified pilot when they need the service of a small plane for investigation or travel.

In 1989 Rocky Miller, chairman of MPA from Sarasota, Florida, was invited to become a member of the MDS board. MDS has supported MPA by sending out periodic newsletters and inviting reports of cooperative activity at all-unit meetings. Pilots interested in involvement in MDS are encouraged to make connections with MPA via the MDS Akron office.

Courtesy of Lee and Mary Lois Martin

Habitat for Humanity International, 21 inches of rain fell in 24 hours. Over 27 inches fell on July 3-7. Nearby Montezuma, a community with several Amish-Mennonite congregations, received over 15 inches. The flash flooding was instant and devastating. In Sumter County (around Americus), 15 persons died, swept away by rapidly rising waters. In Montezuma, the entire downtown business area and dozens of residences were submerged.

All the waters gathered into the Flint River drainage basin and headed south toward Albany. When the dam on 20-mile-long Lake Blackshear broke under relentless pressure, floodwaters in Albany rose 23 feet above flood stage, more than five feet higher than any previous record. The flooding from Alberto killed 31 people, caused about $1 billion damage, and became Georgia's greatest disaster on record.

The MDS Network: The Key Is Flexibility!

On Wednesday, July 6, the MDS office in Akron received a call from Millard Fuller, founder and president of Habitat for Humanity. While the Habitat facilities were not flooded, Americus was surrounded by water, and Fuller appealed for MDS help. At the same time, Lloyd Swartzendruber, Georgia MDS chair living in Montezuma, was alerting MDS to the desperate situation unfolding in south Georgia. In a conference phone call, MDS leaders developed an action plan. Habitat offered to provide housing for volunteers. Field consultant Tom Smucker made plans to head to Georgia with area investigators to organize the response.

Meanwhile, in Lancaster County, Pennsylvania, the Pequea Brethren in Christ youth were making final plans for their annual MDS work week. As part of the continuing 1993 Midwest flood response, they were preparing to leave for Iowa on Saturday, July 9. On Thursday, Dan Houck, their pastor and organizer, received an urgent phone call from MDS Akron: "Could you head south to Georgia?" The response was immediate: "Wherever you need us most."

They spent Friday gathering different tools and supplies, and Saturday headed south. Both they and Tom Smucker arrived in Americus on Sunday, ready to begin cleanup on Monday. Veterans of several years of MDS summer service projects, many of that youth group still consider this experience of being the first people on site one of their most meaningful work experiences—regardless of the mud and smell.

Below left: Wouldn't it be easier to move the ladder? But Dennis Martin is in good hands. His daughter Sonya (right) and Charlotte Witmer are holding the ladder so he can reach that far corner.

MennoNet, an Arm of MDS

Communication is a crucial link in disaster response services. Mennonites interested in amateur radio felt they could provide an important service to MDS. Various MDS supporters viewed television and even radio with mixed feelings. Yet as early as the 1950s, Mennonite ham radio operators established a network and offered their services to MDS.

Several Mennonites were involved in local emergency communication organizations helping to cope with disasters. Jake Swartzendruber was a radio pioneer who assisted with communications in northern Indiana after the 1965 Palm Sunday tornado. He joined Dick Weaver in keeping the issue on the MDS agenda. Finally by 1983, Jake represented the MennoNet group on the MDS section. In 1991 his son, Sandy, became the board representative.

With the counsel of our radio operators, several MDS units have purchased radio equipment for use on project activity. Today MDSers use many forms of communication in disaster response, such as radio, cellular phones, and the computer Internet. For more information about MennoNet, look for their link on the MDS website at www.menno-disaster-service.org.

New Volunteers
Of the 1,175 volunteers who spent time at Albany, 485 (41%) were on their first MDS project, and 458 (39%) were age 25 or younger. MDS is alive and well!

Top: A symbol of precious friendships: Lee Martin celebrates his birthday while serving for nearly two years as project director at Albany, Ga.

Bottom: Wow! Mary Lois and Lee Martin get to have their pictures taken with President and Rosalynn Carter. Many MDSers who worked in Georgia traveled to Plains to sit in former President Jimmy Carter's Sunday school class, and have a chance for a photo.

In Georgia for the Long Haul

In Montezuma, Lloyd Swartzendruber added "flood-response coordinator" to his hats labeled "fire chief" and "MDS Georgia chair." Lloyd and others from the Beachy Amish churches managed the cleanup for the downtown business district as well as surrounding areas where homes and farms were hard hit. They also coordinated food services for hundreds of volunteers, mostly non-Mennonites, who flocked in from Atlanta and elsewhere. Later, volunteers spent months in the area, leaving behind people extremely grateful to have Mennonite "neighbors."

By September, Lee and Mary Lois Martin arrived in needy Albany for a two-year volunteer MDS assignment and spent most of their time there. They established headquarters at the First Assembly of God Church, which graciously hosted hundreds of MDSers over the next 20 months. During early months, their women eagerly cooked for MDS volunteers, then kept helping as MDS cooks took over their kitchen. This close working relationship forged friendships that will never be broken.

In November 1994, a second flood recovery unit was located around the Lake Blackshear area, 40 miles north of Albany. During the winter of 1995, the famous MDS snowbirds flocked to Albany and Lake Blackshear to help with rebuilding efforts. The Lake Blackshear location closed in September 1995, but the work in Albany continued through March 1996. In Albany alone, over 1,175 volunteers provided over 8,000 workdays. By conservative estimates, this saved over half a million dollars for victims of Alberto.

Stepping Over into Abundant Life

Many close friendships were formed during the 20-month MDS project in Georgia, especially between the Martins, other long-term volunteers, and our brothers and sisters of the First Assembly of God and Albany Christian churches. Addise Capuzzi and Jeanie Tyson spent months working alongside MDSers in the kitchen, serving hundreds of meals to volunteers working in Albany. Here are testimonies from these special friends:

Addise (writing after MDSers left Albany): "Things are so different here in Albany. You can't begin to realize how lonely we are, the emptiness and void you left behind. I thank God for the chance to work at the church so I could get to know our dear friends, a chance of a lifetime. It was just a little slice of heaven to be with you all, a blessing from above. I would be there at

6:30 a.m. and leave late in the evening but was never tired. I ask God every morning to bless each of you wherever you are."

Jeanie (in a letter to Pastor Robertson and the deacon board of First Assembly Church, February 20, 1995): "Thank you for opening up the doors of church to the Mennonite Disaster Service. My spiritual life will never be the same because you did. Somewhere in the midst of working these last months in cooking, mopping, and scrubbing lots of pots and pans, I stepped over into abundant life. For the first time in my life, I saw real Christian love in action. Now I have seen what Jesus meant when he said, 'If you have done it unto one of the least of these, you have done it unto me.'"

Living on the Edge in California

MDSers in Arizona like to kid their California counterparts that they will own "oceanfront property"—when California slides into the ocean. No scientific evidence says this is about to happen, but records suggest that no other state has the range or numbers of disasters that occur there. Earthquakes, floods, fires, mudslides, riots, blizzards, and even the occasional tornado and hurricane visit this rapidly growing state. During the past 15 years, and likely earlier, no state could rival California for the "active MDS project" record.

Left: Eva Zuniga (front) and her son (left) proudly welcome Ann and Wes Heinrichs into their home in April 1999. Eva's home in Watsonville had been destroyed by the Loma Prieta earthquake, and MDSers rebuilt it for her. MDSers are always welcomed back by former clients.

MDS photo

Courtesy of Lee and Mary Lois Martin

Above: Ladies of the First Assembly Church in Albany, Ga., where MDS had its headquarters for nearly two years, spent countless days providing food for hundreds of volunteers. Deb Short, MDSer from Archbold, Ohio, is joined (from left) by Shirley Goff, Jeanie Tyson, Lois Cox, and Joyce Tye. Thanks, friends!

Learnings Old and New

In five years MDS coped with Hurricanes Hugo and Andrew, the California earthquake, and the major Midwest floods. What we learned from those experiences helped us later.

1. *Communication is crucial.* Conference calls with representatives from all levels of the MDS network begin immediately and continue as needed. The Akron 800 number, fax and e-mail updates, and the Internet website make information available widely.

2. *Begin involvement immediately.* Investigate right away. Be prepared to stay. MDSers like to be involved in the emergency and cleanup phase, even though dozens of other groups may also appear. That way they make contacts for longer-term opportunities.

3. *Be creative in setting up headquarters.* In addition to using churches, par-sonages, schools, armories, fairgrounds, mobile units, and RVs, MDS has learned to "Make Do Somehow" to obtain needed housing. In Albany we bought a flood-damaged home. Volunteers helped fix it up to house long-term volunteers. At the end of the project, we sold it for a profit, which helped cover project costs.

4. *Continuity of leadership is crucial.* Leading MDS projects is hard work, so leaders often rotate every two or three months. In Albany, Lee and Mary Lois Martin were project leaders almost the entire 21-months of the project. They had made a two-year service commitment to MDS and spent the first 20 months in Albany. This provided continuity seldom found in MDS projects. That was a key to building excellent relationships with other agencies and friends in the local church communities.

Major Projects in California Since 1985

1986 • Marysville/Yuba City/Sacramento floods
1987 • Whittier earthquake
1989 • Loma Prieta earthquake
1991 • Oakland/East Bay fires
1992 • Northern California earthquake
1992 • Landers/Big Bear earthquake
1992 • Los Angeles civil disorder
1994 • Northridge earthquake
1995 • Russian River floods
1997 • Marysville/Yuba City floods
1998 • Winter freeze

Photos on these pages illustrate some of this wide variety of California activity.

Right: Shaded by an elevated home, Wes Heinrichs pours a cup of coffee for C. N. Friesen, from British Columbia. Maybe the coffee breaks helped C. N. do such a good job of recruiting volunteers from B.C. for West Coast projects.

Courtesy of Wes and Ann Heinrichs

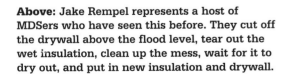

Eddie Neufeld

Above: Jake Rempel represents a host of MDSers who have seen this before. They cut off the drywall above the flood level, tear out the wet insulation, clean up the mess, wait for it to dry out, and put in new insulation and drywall.

Courtesy of Wes and Ann Heinrichs

Above: This photo from the 1992 northern California earthquake shows a common MDS job, putting a new foundation under an earthquake-damaged home. House movers with major jacks and blocking equipment elevate even large homes. After a new foundation is built, the house is lowered onto it.

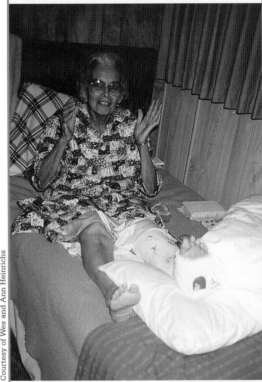

Maria Sousa

Courtesy of Wes and Ann Heinrichs

Maria Sousa's home near Watsonville, Calif., was badly damaged by the Loma Prieta earthquake in 1989. She lived alone. While she stood watching, a damaged porch roof being removed by MDSers fell on her, breaking her hip and leg. After a few days in the hospital, she was invited to live at the MDS center and stayed there many months. She became part of the MDS unit, playing games and going to church with MDSers. Even when her home was finished, she wanted to keep living at the MDS center.

Courtesy of Wes and Ann Heinrichs

Left: Aren't you glad your house isn't straddling this fault line? The Big Bear earthquake struck in 1992 and centered east of San Bernadino, Calif. MDS spent several months working in surrounding areas.

Eddie Neufeld

Below left: Not hard to tell how high the water was on this house! MDSers found plenty of mud to clean up after the Russian River floods at Guerneville, Calif., in 1995.

Below: How did that car get under there? During the 1997 Yuba City floods, high water lifted this California home, floated it over the car, and dropped it on top.

Conrad Yoder

Courtesy of Wes and Ann Heinrichs

MDS photo

Above: MDS always seemed to have a project going in California, so unit leaders have a long history of MDS work. In April 1999 a group of leaders gathered to share their stories. Seated around the table, from left: Roger and Barbara Friesen, Lowell Detweiler, Egon and Naomi Hofer, Wilma and John Miller, Ed Ratzlaff, and Carl and Mildred Pankratz.

Left: Some earthquake-damaged structures needed to be rebuilt from the ground up.

From Sea to Shining Sea . . . and Beyond

Courtesy of Roger and Barbara Friesen

A group of rotating volunteers, mostly from British Columbia, join MDS unit leaders on the front steps of the First Presbyterian Church, our headquarters for the fire rebuilding project near Wasilla, Alaska, in summer 1996.

MDS photo

In December 1997, wildfires burned hundreds of acres in southwest Alberta, many ranch buildings, and miles of fences. Mark Daley (second from right) was one of the ranchers assisted by MDS. From left: Herman Neufeld, MDS Alberta, chair; Tom Smucker; and Kevin Thiessen, MDS Alberta, treasurer.

MDS photo

In 1994 Kazuo Akamatsu came to the U.S. as part of the MCC International Visitor Exchange program. Because of his interest in helping churches in Japan plan for possible disaster response, he asked to spend some of his time serving with MDS. After working on the California earthquake project for several months, he was in the Akron MDS office when the Kobe earthquake hit Japan. He returned to Japan to help organize a volunteer response. Kazuo is explaining to Lowell Detweiler, who traveled there as a consultant, how they kept track of their client base.

MDS photo

The largest project on the West Coast was likely the response to the Loma Prieta (San Francisco) earthquake in 1989. A major headquarters was established in Watsonville, Calif.

Courtesy of Wes and Ann Heinrichs

In 1992, on the 500-year anniversary of Columbus reaching America, MDS worked on several projects with Native American people. One special project was building the new Black Mountain Church near Chinle, Ariz.

Courtesy of Orlan W. Martin

MDS photo

On March 14, 1992, arson fires destroyed six Amish barns in the Big Valley of central Pennsylvania. There was an overwhelming response. MDS coordinators needed to slow down the tide of volunteers. Within a month, all six barns had been rebuilt, livestock replaced, and machinery provided for spring planting.

The "ice storm of the century" hit eastern Canada and the northeastern U.S. in January 1998. MDS responded on both sides of the border.

Wilbur Litwiller

Mary Litwiller encourages Mattie Chandler as they prepare for the dedication services for Mattie's new home, rebuilt by MDSers in Birmingham, Ala., in 1998.

MDS photo

Leadership teams are one of the most crucial needs in MDS. Ottis Mast, Region II director (seated center), is surrounded by his long-term leadership team at Crestview, Fla., in 1995. Project directors Virgil and Leola Kauffman are on the right.

MDS photo

MDSers from the Puerto Rico unit were the first work team to arrive on the island of St. Thomas after it was smashed by Hurricane Marilyn in 1995. Hundreds of roofs were missing. MDSers spent months on this once-beautiful island in reconstruction.

CHAPTER SIX

Hurricane Andrew:
A Shaking and Shaping

MCC photo by Mike Hostetler

The wind blows wherever it pleases. You hear its sound, but you cannot tell where it comes from or where it is going. So it is with everyone born of the Spirit.

—Jesus, in John 3:8

Heed the Wind

omewhere on the way to Homestead, Florida, the MDS "book" that tells how to do things "got lost." Hurricane Andrew ranks number one in U.S. disaster history (as of 1999) in terms of property damage caused by any natural disaster. It also ranks first in shaking and shaping MDS and other disaster response agencies into organizational changes. MDS had to learn to do things in new ways. We sometimes wanted to use old wineskins when new partnerships and new programs were needed.

By God's grace, and however imperfectly, MDS changed. The stories of God at work in Homestead and the bayous of Louisiana are exciting.

In the Eye of a Hurricane

In 1988 fire destroyed the Homestead Mennonite Church (HMC). After years of fighting red tape and with MDS volunteer help, a larger church was built and dedicated in November 1990. In August 1991, Walter and Joy Sawatsky were called to be copastors. The couple was excited about the call to HMC because the people "felt they were at the edge of something new" and were seeking pastors who could help them enter a new stage of ministry. They expected the new building to help them grow into a community-oriented church. None dreamed it would take a hurricane.

Courtesy of Abe Froese

Above: The Homestead (Fla.) Mennonite church was destroyed by fire in 1988. MDSers helped demolish what remained and rebuild by November 1990, in time to face Hurricane Andrew and remain standing!

Photo, page 70:
Luann and Philip Martin with daughter Joelle return to survey the scattered remains of their home near Homestead, Fla., after fleeing Hurricane Andrew.

Top right: The Southmost Mennonite Church in Florida City was completely destroyed. Christian Aid Ministries helped to rebuild it and centered their disaster response in that community.

Middle right: Frame houses stood no chance against Andrew's fury. The walls are gone, but magnets remained on the refrigerator!

The following is a composite of first-person accounts from Walter and Joy Sawatsky in 1992; Kathleen Hartzler's story at the MDS All-Unit Meeting in 1993; later interviews with the Sawatskys, Hartzlers, and other HMC members in 1999; and excerpts from other interviews, news reports, and audiovisuals. On the night of August 23, 1992, the Sawatskys and several other church families took refuge in the church. David and Kathleen Hartzler welcomed five others to ride out the storm in their home, two blocks west of HMC. This is the Homestead story:

Hurricane Andrew Takes Dead Aim on South Florida

By Saturday afternoon, August 22, 1992, we were on hurricane watch and beginning to wonder, *Should we go through all the work of preparing for the storm?* By Sunday morning it was clear we would be hit. Some decided to evacuate to Sarasota.

Andrew Facts and Figures

Date: August 24, 1992, in south Florida; August 26 in south-central Louisiana

Casualties: 52 (39 in Florida, 9 in Louisiana, 4 in the Bahamas)

Damage estimate: $28 billion

Families affected: 137,000 in Florida; right after storm, 250,000 homeless, 1.4 million without electric

Homes destroyed/damaged: 63,000 in Florida; 8,000 in Louisiana

Other info: 22,000 federal troops deployed, largest U.S. military rescue operation ever. 700,000 evacuated

MDS response: 4,250 volunteers and 27,825 workdays in Florida; 2,350 volunteers and 14,200 workdays in Louisiana

A few of us met for church to pray, sing, and plan for the storm.

That afternoon we feverishly put up storm shutters, trimmed trees, and took loose objects inside. While we were trying to pull it all together, the telephone kept ringing: "Are you going to evacuate? Where do we go?" We were thinking, *If this phone wouldn't ring, we could finish getting ready!* But there was one very welcome call—from MDS: "We'll be there when the storm is over."

We finished boarding up the church on Sunday evening. We watched the TV news, seeing the eye coming right at us, never wavering. The intensity of the storm kept building. We had weathered 125-mile-per-hour winds, but we began to hear reports of 145, 165. Scary!

Yet at Homestead, the evening was still calm. I had a feeling of butterflies and excitement. I've always loved severe weather, but I had no idea what this hurricane would be like. Even up to midnight, we were watching the news on TV and cooking food so it wouldn't spoil. At one point we gathered to pray. We put the church and ourselves in God's hands. Then we slept an hour or so.

Andrew Comes Knocking

About 3:30 a.m. we heard the wind and lost electricity. The noise rose. Some of us went outside. It was fascinating to watch huge blue arcs from transformers exploding in the sky, and better than fireworks. Piece by piece, Homestead went dark.

At times we felt Andrew would suck the doors right off. We could hear shingles peeling back and then huge objects hitting

MDS photo

MDS photo

MDS photo by Mike Hostetler

the building. In the first half of the storm, some of the church roof went. Through openings, we could see the sky. So we frantically moved furniture and the piano into the fellowship hall.

The eye, moving over the church, was an unusual experience. We stepped outside. When we looked up, we could see it, like a crescent against the sky. The stars were crystal clear. This was something I wanted to experience and be able to tell about.

All of us raced out and moved cars to the other side of the church because after the eye passed, the wind would come from the opposite direction. In the backyard of the church, the storm had deposited a boat and broken pine trees. We knew it was going to be bad. Then the wall arrived, sounding like a freight train.

Suddenly it hit from the other side; the house began to shake. My husband came in and said, "The sliding glass doors are about to cave in. We've lost the Florida [sun] room." All seven of us were in the bathroom, praying and singing. I didn't really have a sense that we would lose our lives, but I did feel that the house would be coming apart around us. We prayed for the Lord to put his arms around us, around our house, and around the church, so it could be there as a place of refuge in our community.

After the wall hit, it stripped some shingles off the back half of the church. The rain poured in through the light fixtures. When I went into the kitchen and found rain pouring through the vents, I began to get frightened. But in there, a real sense of peace came over me: I knew it was going to

be a real mess, but we were going to be okay. People started getting under the tables and singing and praying.

On the night of the storm, the church was a real lifesaver. It was nice to be there with other people. We felt safe. Amazingly enough, it was the only thing left really standing around here. I think the Lord wanted it that way.

About 7:00 a.m. the winds began to subside. Neighbors started pouring in. We could tell by their faces how bad the hurricane was. They were in shock. We gave them blankets and towels. Vic had a little butane burner and made hot coffee, a real comfort. We started bringing people in— and have been bringing them in ever since.

As we went out after the storm and looked around, I thought maybe a tornado had hit our section. We walked around the streets, not having the slightest idea where to pick up the pieces. We began to hear reports that this wasn't the only place; it was like this for 20 miles. Someone said there was a pay phone working. I called my parents to say, "We're safe. Call MDS and tell them to come."

MDS Is on the Way

While Homestead and other south Florida residents were anxiously awaiting Hurricane Andrew, the MDS network was also watching, praying, and preparing. On Sunday afternoon, Lowell Detweiler, executive coordinator, set up a conference call with Atlee Schlabach, Sarasota, Florida, unit director; and Region I director Paul Brubacher, Morgantown, Pennsylvania. We agreed on a plan and cleared our schedules to go south.

Monday, August 24, brought reports of extensive damage, especially south of Miami. By early morning, MCCers in Miami and Belle Glade had reported they were okay and facing limited damage. None of us at MDS could make phone

Paul Brubacher

contacts with Homestead. By noon, Kathleen Hartzler's message reached MDS Akron via her dad, Wellington Moyer, in North Carolina: "Send all the help you can; Homestead is devastated." By late afternoon we had a direct call from Walter Sawatsky in Homestead: "We're all right but had a rough night. Homestead buildings 100 percent damaged, not complete destruction. Need help. Power out. Bring generators, water, own lodging, money, food, extra gas. Will need immediate help on roofing."

With this information in hand, MDS leaders again consulted by phone. Atlee had already lined up Martin Sommers and others in Sarasota to head south early Tuesday with a generator, water, food, and

Above: Damage to cement-walled homes was often limited to roofs. MDS teams immediately began covering roofs to protect from daily rains. By the end of the first week, MDS had "dried in" over 30 homes.

Bottom left: Hurricane Andrew's devastation totaled $28 billion, the most damaging storm in U.S. history (through 1999). It uncovered roofs and revealed some poor construction methods.

plastic. Paul Brubacher would get one or two others and leave as soon as possible with the MDS van and equipment trailer. Lowell would fly south Tuesday. We'd meet in Homestead.

As Atlee Schlabach led the first MDSers into Homestead on Tuesday morning, he thought he was in a war zone. Dodging debris and power lines, he worried about getting flats, like many others who were changing tires.

By Wednesday, Lowell and MCCer Phil Davis had reached Homestead. Lowell reported to Akron, "What you've seen and read and more is true. Andrew has devastated south Dade County. One is numbed as one drives south from Miami to Homestead and views the unending damage. By the time we were halfway to Homestead, the devastation was complete, with only a few persons cautiously moving about. At only an occasional place had any attempt been made to start cleanup or covering roofs, and the debris is unending."

Paul Brubacher

By Wednesday evening, Sarasota MDSers had the church dry. By Thursday teams had begun to cover house roofs with asphalt paper or plastic to prevent further damage from daily rains. Paul Brubacher and the Lancaster MDSers arrived with vehicles and more supplies. The VS unit from Americus, Georgia, went down to help. By Saturday over 50 volunteers were on-site, coming with self-contained living units plus water and food for themselves and local residents. By the weekend, MDS had dried in (covered) about 30 houses, many for HMC members, so they could return to their homes.

The Church That Stood Up to a Hurricane and Found Itself Without Walls

In November 1992, Cathleen Hockman, associate editor of Gospel Herald, *visited Homestead. This title and story are from her December 29 article (abridged):*

When Hurricane Andrew smashed into

southern Florida early on August 24, the walls of HMC were miraculously left standing. Today it's one of the resulting paradoxes to find that HMC is becoming a "church without walls." Walter and Joy Sawatsky, who pastor the church, explain: "Among leadership [in HMC] there is a keen sense that we are going to have to do church in a different way. In terms of relationships, we want to function as though there were no walls."

From that first Monday, Walter says, people were pouring in to use the church as a temporary shelter. Three months after the disaster, a steady stream of survivors, needing help of various kinds, has continued to flow in and out of the church doors.

Paul Brubacher

Above: The Homestead Mennonite Church suffered only minor roof damage, quickly repaired. It became the headquarters for MDS response in south Fla.

Near right: The Homestead Mennonite Church became a haven for all, a church "without walls." Everyone was welcomed, for meals, to share their journeys, and to connect with MDS and church leaders for help.

Far right: On Sundays, beds and food were stacked in the corners as Homestead Mennonite Church gathered for worship. Many area churches lost membership because of Andrew, but attendance grew at Homestead, even without counting MDSers. The mural, there before Andrew, was fulfilled as the church reached out to a community in need.

MDS photo

MDS photo

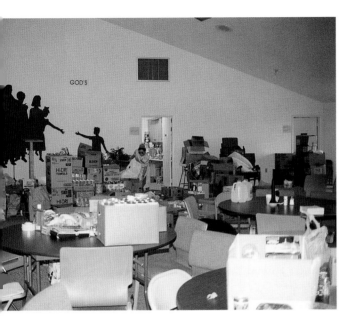

Hurricane relief has virtually taken over the HMC building.

Wooden shelves have been built in classrooms, and now the church is better stocked than the average convenience store—canned goods and paper products fill room after room. One long narrow classroom has been converted into a community pantry and clothes closet, filled with towels, blankets, shoes, toys, and toiletries.

Sixteen recreational vehicles are parked behind the church; some of these have been donated to MDS to house volunteers. Alongside them are rolls of tar paper, fiberglass insulation, stacks of plywood, and lumber. Two tents store more building supplies. MDS is constructing a building on the back lot to house and feed volunteers.

Three months after the hurricane, some neighborhoods were cleaning up, removing trash, and making repairs. Blocks of other houses, however, resembled deserted battlefields. Rubble mixed with broken furniture, crushed cars stripped of usable parts, and stuffed toys. Some places looked like

the owner evacuated before the storm and never returned. In one house, the walls were gone, but one could still see clothes hanging neatly in the closet.

To speed insurance reimbursements, homeowners spray-painted their addresses and insurance companies on the walls of their damaged property. Many left other messages—grim, hopeful, humorous, or simply sad: "You loot, I shoot." "We survived Andrew." "Mildew Manor." "This used to be home."

The material needs of Dade County people were obvious. Less apparent were their emotional and spiritual needs. Walter Sawatsky describes the emotional roller coaster his family experienced after the hurricane. First came a state of shock, when adrenaline fueled them to respond to immediate needs. Then came a sense of optimism in October, when cleanup was underway. By November, though, the Sawatskys were feeling some discouragement: rats in the house, mold growing on the walls, and insurance settlement still not

Top: During the week, the church was a resource center for the whole community, offering foodstuffs, cleaning supplies, counseling services, and sign-up lists for roof repair by MDS.

Below left and right: Two examples of messages from threatening to hopeful painted on houses.

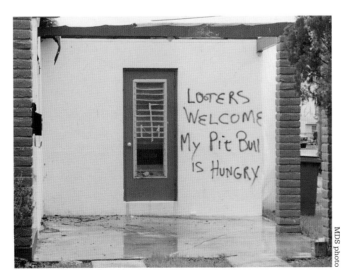

Strangers are becoming friends. Homestead Mennonite Church is a paradoxical place. Out of Andrew's indescribable destruction comes growth and renewal.

complete. "Most of all, we were tired of having to make so many decisions when we felt vulnerable, scattered, and unfocused," Walter says.

"Just to see the MDS volunteers come, and in such large numbers," Walter continues, "reminded us that we are cared about. When we doubt that God does care, these are concrete reminders that we are not alone."

In contrast to many other congregations in Dade County, Joy adds, the HMC members are still returning to church. Many congregations have shrunk to two-thirds or half their pre-Andrew size, but HMC attendance has increased—even without counting all the MDS volunteers who worship with the congregation. People in the community whose roofs have been repaired by MDS or who have received shelter or food at the church come to learn more about this church that served them—even though they were strangers to each other.

Strangers are becoming friends. Homestead Mennonite Church is a paradoxical place. Out of Andrew's indescribable destruction comes growth and renewal. People who have lost everything, whose homes are reduced to piles of twisted metal and concrete, suddenly have so much to give. Amid overwhelming stress, weariness, and feelings of vulnerability, church members are finding their own healing and an ability to give a powerful ministry and witness to others in a broken community.

As Paul writes in 2 Corinthians 12:10, the weak have become strong. Out of loss comes fulfillment. Death brings life. All these are taking place in a church that stood up to a hurricane—just to become a church without walls.

Creating Shelter

MDS leaders at Homestead faced many stresses, such as the lack of facilities to house and feed the volunteers flocking south. MDS wanted to give the Homestead Church building back to the congregation and could find no other available facility. On the back of the church grounds, MDS built a temporary headquarters, with bathrooms and an office-kitchen-dining hall. Volunteers slept in the church, in neighboring homes, and in RVs on the grounds. Even building this temporary facility involved delay and bureaucratic hassles. MDS leaders threatened to build anyway and bring in the media if authorities closed down the project.

Abe Froese

Gloria's Story

Gloria Hernandez grew up as a migrant worker in Texas, moved to Homestead, and bought a house not far from HMC. After a 1989 divorce, she spent time in Texas but returned to Homestead in 1992. The family renting her house had defaulted on payments, the bank had foreclosed, and the insurance had lapsed. Gloria and her children "migrated" that summer to earn money to reclaim their home. After time in Georgia and Missouri, they were in Illinois in August when Andrew hit. Gloria says:

I was picking bell peppers as a migrant farm worker. When I heard about Andrew, we didn't have TV. I went to use my neighbor's phone. He had the news on. They interviewed my neighbor Bonita in Homestead! She said her house had been destroyed. They showed her house and mine too. I couldn't get in touch with any friends. I tried morning, night, every hour. I started getting anxious. I wanted to go back and see the house, but my boss said I needed to finish the contract. I didn't get back till the first week of October.

We arrived at night, and the police escorted me to the house. They checked it and told me I couldn't get in. I'd have to park the car and stay outside. It was terrible to sleep with the car doors open, mosquitoes, and so much noise from generators. My kids, a little girl and three boys, were with me. At dawn, we went inside. The house was completely destroyed. No one had done anything to the house because it was empty.

We went to live in a tent city, but they wanted proof we lived [in Homestead]. I had my driver's license, but they wanted a light or rent bill, and I had nothing. I went to the bank to get copies of my papers. They told me it was foreclosed, and I owed them $28,000. I went outside and cried and cried, not knowing what to do. I was asking God, "Why did you bring me here to Homestead when there is nothing left for me?" I didn't want my kids to see me like that, so I spent the day outside the bank, crying.

The Spanish [Mennonite] pastor who lives in Kendall was visiting the neighborhood and inviting everyone to come to the Homestead Mennonite Church. I was ask-

ing God to tell me to leave this area, but it seemed God was telling me to stay. We went to the church; we were meeting there every night. I started helping distribute the food and clothes that came to the church. We helped those in the migrant camps. I know that was why God didn't let me go, so I could continue my mission work. In 1993 I started working with the outreach program here in the church.

I was a Catholic and searching for a church I could feel happy with. When I was invited here, I found the family I was looking for. In April 1994 I was baptized here and my children too. I'm still working for the church; I continue to do my outreach work to help people.

Since my house wasn't really mine, I couldn't ask for help to get it fixed up. I got a trailer to live in and worked as a volunteer with the farm workers. We kept dealing with the red tape so I could get my house back. Neighbors and church people wrote letters on my behalf. Finally, in early 1994, the bank called. They said they had payment (from another agency) and I could get help to fix my house. It was the last month MDS was to be here. MDS leaders said, "Okay, let's start working." MDS asked me to get money for the materials. They started on the roof, then worked in my house. It was pretty well done when they left.

I feel I am part of the Mennonite Church and proud of it. At Thanksgiving we had a lunch and served 390 people. Pastors cut the turkey, and members served. We had lines and lines and distributed 150 food baskets. We invited neighbors and people from four camps of farm workers. We fed

everybody and had food left. If I belong to a church, I want the doors open to everybody. I always tell people of the church we need to be here when they need us.

Nehemiah: Builder of Walls and Lives

Like Nehemiah of old, Walter Sawatsky looked at destruction and had a vision for making things better. Owners had deserted many homes around the church and were determined never to return. Yet hundreds of people were desperate for housing. Surely something could be done. Drawing on his experience in Miami, helping to establish a nonprofit housing corporation, Walter proposed a similar concept for Homestead. He talked about buying and repairing homes and making them available to families who could not otherwise afford them. The congregation was infected by his enthusiasm but too exhausted to carry the load.

Undaunted, Walter turned to Mennonite Central Committee. Providentially, MCC was looking for an assignment for Ernie and Mary Pries of St. Catharines, Ontario. A perfect match for the assignment, Ernie and Mary arrived in Homestead in November 1992. Guided by a board of directors from the church and community, the Prieses helped give birth to the Nehemiah Project of Homestead. Over the years this effort has provided good housing for many families and led many to the Homestead church.

The partnership between the Nehemiah Project and MDS brought mutual blessings. Seven houses near the church were purchased first, and MDS provided an

Top: Gloria Hernandez (left) and Kathleen Hartzler preparing a Thanksgiving meal. The whole community was invited, and 390 came!

Bottom: The Nehemiah team passes another house on to an excited family. Dora and Eliezar Cruz (center and right front) sign papers to take possession of their new home. The Cruzes have three children. Nehemiah staff include (back, from left) Ernie and Mary Pries, Marilyn McCready, and (front left) Rick Beutsch, lawyer.

Courtesy of Kathleen Hartzler

Courtesy of Ernie and Mary Pries

interest-free loan and volunteers to fix the houses. In return, MDS lodged volunteers in two or three houses within walking distance of the temporary building back of the church. The arrangement served both organizations well during the MDS stay in south Florida. Then the houses were sold to interested families.

Soliciting funding, buying houses, obtaining building permits, and selecting families were daunting tasks that challenged but did not intimidate the Prieses. By July 1993, the first families were moving into new homes. Hector and Louisa Vazquez were the second family to receive a Nehemiah home. Hector recalls, "It was hard to find housing; we went through a lot of obstacles. We are thankful to the Lord and Nehemiah. It really put my faith back, because my faith was low then."

Hector's connections to Mennonites began in Aibonito, Puerto Rico. When they moved to Homestead in 1989, he saw the Mennonite church and told his wife, "One of these days we'll have to visit that church."

It took Hurricane Andrew to make that happen. A friend invited Louisa to a service at HMC, and she began taking English lessons there. Hector attended a worship service with her. He reflects, "As soon as I walked in, I could feel God. I felt so much love and sharing. We had been searching for a church to call our own. I said, 'This is our church.' "

The housing needs of lower-income families in south Dade County remained long after MDS left in spring 1994. The Nehemiah Project still responds to that need. As of 1999, says current director

Louis Azan, it had rebuilt or renovated 37 houses sheltering 150 people. No family had lost its home: all 37 original owners still occupy their homes and have a new perspective on life.

In fall 1992, Fernando Sandoval was an MCC volunteer in Lancaster, Pennsylvania. He agreed to transfer to Homestead, where his Spanish and construction skills were needed. Seven years later, he is still there, one of three paid Nehemiah staff. As construction foreman, he faces daily the bureaucratic red tape that frustrated so many MDS leaders. Fernando says that if anyone wanted to build a house from the ground up, the Dade County regulations would require 32 inspections! "Sometimes we want to throw in the towel. It's hard. But in the end, we experience the joy of helping someone get a house. Once you give them the key, it's a real reward to see the smile. I guess that's what keeps us going. The bottom line is helping somebody else."

Forging a New Partnership

As Homestead Mennonite Church and MDS embarked together on the long journey toward recovery, additional resources were needed. According to a Miami *Herald Tribune* study, 55 percent of Homestead households reported that at least one family member experienced severe stress or other mental health problems as they faced gruesome sights and daunting tasks amid the clutter and stench. While HMC pastors and leaders had counseling and outreach gifts, they also were Andrew's victims. They struggled to find energy to achieve personal recovery and to

help others. They gave unselfishly of time and energy, but with MDS they welcomed new partnership discussions with Mennonite Health Services (MHS).

MDS photo

Courtesy of the Vazquez family

Top: Fernando Sandoval, long-term MDS-Nehemiah worker in Homestead, checks the next job with MDS project director Marlin Gingerich.

Bottom: The Nehemiah housing program, founded by Homestead Mennonite Church and supported by MDS, provided rebuilt homes for many hurricane-affected families. The Vazquezes were the second family to receive a Nehemiah home and later became members of that church. From left: Kim, Luisa, Kenneth, and Hector with David in front.

MHS leaders negotiated for and received the services of Sandy Kauffman from the staff of the Oaklawn Psychiatric Center in Elkhart, Indiana. For the first year, Sandy spent a week a month in Homestead, working with the church and mental health volunteers they recruited to provide additional counseling and support

Below: Art and Oma Smucker of Goshen, Ind., represent dozens of MDS leaders who spent many months on the Homestead project. Art and Oma were office managers and left many friends as they headed home.

Jean Hampton

MDS photo

to church and community. As either MDS workers or church members became aware of persons with special needs, MHS volunteers became their listeners/advocates. In cooperation with new HMC-sponsored outreach ministries, a CareNet counseling program was begun, including local Spanish speakers to serve in surrounding Hispanic communities.

MHS volunteers supported MDS leaders by leading devotionals and midweek services or taking on general support tasks. Finding the way in this new partnership was not without tensions. Evolving job descriptions were not always clear. Persons had different perspectives on who to help and how much to help. The test run did give MDS an ongoing relationship with MHS, which now appoints a representative to the MDS board.

The Homestead Project Winds Down

In February 1994, MDS held its annual all-unit meeting in Homestead, Florida. Over 400 supporters from all over the United States and Canada made the long journey south that thousands of MDS volunteers had taken over the previous 18 months.

In April 1994 MDS packed up and left Homestead after 20 months, among the most challenging in MDS history. Over 4,250 volunteers gave 27,825 workdays in Homestead alone, not the largest but one of the most concentrated projects. Except for the projects in Louisiana, MDS was unable to spread out efforts as with Hurricane Hugo or later Midwest floods.

Bottom left: As MDS prepared to leave Homestead in 1994, one of the delightful tasks was to assist the Homestead Mennonite Church in completing an addition required because of church growth—an unusual blessing from Hurricane Andrew. The MDS building and complex (background) had to be torn down before the church could get an occupancy permit for the new building.

Haven Old and New

In 1989 Haven of Hope opened its doors. A notorious crack house had become a home for pregnant teens. Supported by community churches, including Homestead Mennonite Church, it was destroyed by Hurricane Andrew; MDSers tore down the remnants.

It was rebuilt after a long struggle over permits and construction difficulties, with support by many, including MDS. It reopened in 1997 and is again serving the community.

Before and after. Karen Holmes, daytime housemother (left), and Mary Mayes, executive director, stand in front of the new building.

Courtesy of Paul Brubacher

Courtesy of Kathleen Hartzler

Forced to do things differently, MDS (and other disaster agencies; chapter 11) developed new partnerships and modes of operation. Like persons handling uninvited changes in midlife, MDS also matured for the turbulent years to follow.

If you question whether the struggles were worthwhile, travel south next winter. Spend a Sunday morning with the Homestead congregation. Go early and attend the Spanish language service. The warmth and presence of God's Spirit will transcend your language limitations. Join the coffee fellowship between the Spanish and English services, and you'll surely find someone eager to talk about how Hurricane Andrew reshaped the church into a growing multicultural congregation. You'll meet many members who have joined HMC "because of the work and witness of the church and MDS" after the hurricane. Stay for the English service. If you're as blessed as I was, you'll share a fellowship meal, like the many meals MDSers ate together in that crowded church in the time of storm.

The vision for being a "church without walls" remains. Pastor Chuck Goertz reflects (in 1999), "We need to continue reflecting the diversity we find around us. Reflecting that diversity in the community of faith is one of the strongest evangelistic tools we have. We look at the world and see that racism and ethnic groups and social status separate us. But Ephesians tells us God has broken down the dividing walls. If that can't be exemplified in the church, the church really isn't good news. If we aren't good news, we can't share good news."

Right: The low-lying La. bayou country was hard hit by Hurricane Andrew. Leroy Miller crosses a typical bayou canal to check progress of work for an MDS client.

Don't Forget Louisiana: We Got Hit by Andrew, Too!

Though given less attention in media coverage and even in MDS discussions, Hurricane Andrew did not disappear after devastating Dade County. After crossing the Everglades and the west coast of Florida, Andrew regained strength over the Gulf of Mexico and smashed into rural south-central Louisiana on Wednesday, August 26. Thousands of homes were damaged. The state suffered $2.4 billion dollars in losses—a large disaster compared to anything but the $25 billion damage in south Florida.

MDS Region II leaders Amos Miller, Ottis Mast, and Levi Miller were in Louisiana by Thursday and by the weekend had found housing for volunteers in Franklin. On Monday volunteers began cleanup. Repair and rebuilding efforts continued through August 1993. With damage widespread in south-central Louisiana, MDS later set up satellite locations in Houma and at the Live Oak Baptist Church of Pointe au Chiene, on the end of the bayou. The rural locations and cooperative welcome from local authorities stood in stark contrast to hassles met in south Florida. This was a favorite project for over 2000 volunteers who traveled down to Cajun country.

MDS photo

A Warm Southern Welcome

Mayor Sam Jones describes the people of Franklin as "a curious culture. I think if the Martians ever came, this would be a good place for them to land. We would certainly talk before we shoot. We genuinely like people. We enjoyed having you, being hospitable."

"I found out [Mennonite volunteers] didn't know what crawfish were," reported a smiling Kate Malloy, a local leader who provided many valuable contacts for MDSers. "I boiled crawfish for forty-seven people one night. When we dumped those crawfish out on the table, they didn't quite know what to do. But they learned!"

The learning included an immediate offer from the Episcopal church to use the parsonage for housing volunteers. When we needed more space and asked to use the local armory, David H. Stiel Jr. of the Marine Corp League remembers, "We couldn't say yes fast enough."

Others paid utility bills and gas. The local Texaco station fixed all the flats on MDS vehicles for free. A local businesswoman supplied all the ice the project needed, loaned furniture, and took long-term volunteers on boat rides on the bayous. The mayor helped arrange for after-hours inspections and electrical hookups. As we closed the project, the local community gave thanks by arranging a Cajun dinner for over fifty people. Both the effectiveness of our work and the enjoyment of MDSers were truly enhanced by this special partnership with local community and church partners.

Down on the Bayou

One road south of Houma, Louisiana, through the bayous of Terrebonne Parish (county), ends just beyond the Live Oak Baptist Church of Pointe au Chiene. Andrew smothered this flat heartland of Cajun country with winds up to 155 miles per hour and storm surges flooding every home for miles around. Many residents are fisherfolk of the Houma Nation, making their living plying shrimp boats beyond Land's End, where fresh water meets the salty Gulf. MDS was invited to use the Live Oak Baptist Church to feed its volunteers working in the area.

The Isle de Jean Charles, west of Pointe du Chiene, can be reached only by a narrow one-mile causeway that often floods at high tide. It is home to about 200 people. Their homes had several feet of water and mud in them, but they were most concerned about their church, which had been blown off its foundation.

Steve Cheramie, tribal councilman of the United Houma Nation, was a key contact for MDS work in Terrebonne Parish. Steve, a Mennonite pastor who grew up there, suggested MDSers might help. He recalls, "One week here comes this group of Anabaptist, Mennonite, Amish MDS volunteers. In no time they jack it up and put it back on its foundation. Even today when I speak at that

MDS photo

7-1

Courtesy of Virgil Kauffman

Near left: Rebuilding by required codes in La. lowlands often meant elevating homes many feet above ground level. This home is being built by MDSers near Houma, La., in 1993.

Far left: The MDS memorial wall! MDS was offered the use of the armory for the Franklin, La., headquarters. A temporary wall was erected to provide sleeping quarters, and MDSers were encouraged to autograph it. In 1999, six years later, Ottis Mast finds the wall in place, autographs and all—an ongoing tribute to hundreds of MDSers who worked in Franklin.

church, that's always brought up."

Steve adds, a twinkle in his eye, "They were puzzled by our diversity. They had been introduced to Mennonites when MCC had volunteers in these areas. But MDS was a more diverse group. Just when they thought they understood what a Mennonite was, the next week a different flavor came in. They'd just shake their heads and say, 'We haven't figured out what a Mennonite is yet. Are you still a Mennonite?' When I said yes, they responded, 'Well, we might join you when we figure out what you are.'"

On several occasions, Steve joined MDSers at Live Oak Baptist Church and shared his personal story and the area's history. As pastor, Steve attempts to blend Native American customs with Christian worship. For many volunteers, sitting on the floor of the community room, Indian-style, and praying and talking with Steve was a memorable part of their Louisiana stay.

Are You Real?

Ottis Mast, MDS regional leader who coordinated the Andrew response in Louisiana remembers with appreciation the excellent support from the local community. He recalls trying to explain what MDS does to a local resident who asked with amazement, "Can I touch you? Are you real?"

Turning Over the Shoebox

After Hurricane Andrew, the lists of those referred to MDS for assistance were long; it often took weeks to assess all the cases referred to us and offer aid.

In Franklin, Chris Eash, MDS construction foreman, went to the home of an elderly man. He was glad we had finally come. In the bedroom, he dug into a full closet and pulled out a shoebox with $11,000.

He had received a FEMA check for the damage to his home. Trusting neither FEMA nor the bank, he had cashed the check immediately and put his money in the shoebox.

With great relief, he handed the $11,000 to Chris, saying he had found someone he could trust and now could sleep at night.

Three Flavors of "Ma-Mas" [Cajun for grandma]

In October 1992, 15 people from Keystone Publishing, Shipshewana, Indiana, spent a week working for MDS at Pointe au Chiene. Owner Julie Barth and business partner Art Oswald led the group. Julie wrote of her experiences, abridged here:

After our 20-hour van ride, we arrived at Live Oak Baptist Church and were greeted by LeRoy and Ruth Miller, local MDS coordinators. I had offered to plan, organize, and prepare meals for our group. I entered the kitchen that Monday, anxious, not knowing if my plans for using the donated food we brought along would work or if there was a grocery store nearby. My Mennonite friends told me I need not fear and should have more faith. I wasted time worrying because I didn't know I was about to meet my guardian angel. She was a petite grandmother from Oklahoma named Ruth Miller, a model of flexibility, efficiency, and old-fashioned Mennonite make-do skills.

Ruth broke the ice: "Boy, am I relieved to find that you are here. I had no idea what was ahead, or how I was going to provide meals for all these people. I'm so glad to see you have some menus planned. Let's eat lunch; then we can sit together, see what else we need, and go up to the grocery store a few miles north." Ruth's candidness, humility, good cheer, and creativity in the kitchen sustained me all week.

During that time, Ruth and I talked of our children and children's children. We gave each other kitchen hints, and she became a living example of the *More-with-Less Cookbook*. We worked, prayed, and laughed a lot together. On the day we left, I was overwhelmed with emotion as I said good-bye to this tiny, fragile-looking, but mightily strong woman. In Cajun country, God blessed me with the presence of Ruth Miller.

Jane and Wilfred Chaisson lived just up the road from Live Oak Baptist. A crew from our group was assigned to repair their roof. On Thursday morning Art reminded me I was to record the events of our journey and encouraged me to visit Jane.

Since I had never conversed with a Cajun lady, I was uneasy about the interview. I started up the path to the porch where Jane was relaxing with her grandchildren before continuing lunch preparations. I reached out my hand and introduced myself. I was greeted by the warmest, friendliest smile I had seen in a long time.

In minutes Jane was telling me about her family. She is proud that her grandfather, a Houma Indian, gave her the land the family lives on. He also donated land for the Live Oak Baptist Church, a few doors down the road. "It used to be all farmland," she says sadly. "Now the land is eroding, just disappearing into the water." She looks out across the yard, across the narrow blacktop road, toward the bayou where the family's shrimp boats are docked. This is their life, their ancestral home.

From the first moments of our meeting, Jane and I begin to realize that our bond that makes us feel so comfortable together has nothing to do with hair color, accent, geography, or even the hurricane. The bond is that we're Christians.

As we move from porch to living room, Jane smiles and shows me her family gallery, pictures mounted high on the wall, as I have seen in other homes. I know why. You can still see the floodwater mark on the wall paneling in the living room.

She invites me to lunch, and I say, "Only if I can help." Our conversation moves from how to know when the shrimp cakes are just right for turning to discussions of our children and how God has been beside us as we raised them.

Finally the feast is ready. Hungry crews come down from the roof. We say grace together and serve ourselves shrimp cakes, with vegetables and rice. Mike shows us how they pour the hot sauce on their rice, "just to improve the flavor a little."

That evening Mike and Will take several of us riding in Mike's shrimp boat. On Friday the crew returns to the Chaisson home to finish fixing as much of the roof as possible before we leave that afternoon. I too return, and Jane tells me more about her grandfather and how he taught her faith in God, a faith we share. Just before we leave, Jane and I exchange addresses and hug each other, promising to pray for each other and our families. She and her husband and sons thank us again and again.

Love flowed through the room that sunny afternoon just as water had flooded it only eight weeks before. I was reminded of the remark of another Cajun woman, Theresa Verdin, whose church MDS had put back on its foundation. "I thank God for Hurricane Andrew," Theresa said, her eyes gleaming with tears, "because I have met so many of God's people."

On the Giving Side

The Houma Indian grandmother was apprehensive when a party of four MDS volunteers, two of them Cheyenne Indians, came to repair her damaged home. She stayed out of sight the first day. The second day, she showed up. Despite a language barrier, there were smiles and attempts to communicate.

The next day, with work nearly done, she cooked jambalaya for the crew. The grandmother used the most valued gift of Native Americans: food. This expressed her deep gratitude.

Lawrence Hart, Cheyenne chief and Mennonite leader from Clinton, Oklahoma, chose to go to Houma specifically to serve MDS alongside the Houma Indians. On his return Lawrence reflected, "Too often we Native Americans have been on the receiving end. It was good to meet needs in the name of Christ. I fore- see greater involvement of our people in responding to needs of others. We have excellent vehicles to do this through MDS and MCC."

Are the shrimp ready? Lawrence Hart, Lyle Miller, and Robert Koehn, all from Okla., watch Robert Zehr check shrimp being prepared for a delicious feast.

Courtesy of Leroy and Ruth Miller

Below left: Making new friends from many places! From left: Steve Cheramie, local Native American pastor; Robert Zehr, Mennonite pastor from Des Allemands, La.; Julie Barth and Art Oswald from the Keystone Publishing Company of Shipshewana, Ind.— in the Live Oak Baptist Church fellowship hall at Point au Chiene, La.

Below: Steve Cheramie, a local Mennonite Native American pastor (center), sharing with MDSers about customs of Houma Indians.

Courtesy of Leroy and Ruth Miller

Courtesy of Leroy and Ruth Miller

CHAPTER SEVEN

The Red River Runs North

No man is an island,

entire of itself;

every man is a piece of
the continent,

a part of the main; . . .

any man's death
diminishes me

because I am involved
in mankind.

—John Donne[1]

I bind my soul this day

to the neighbor far
away,

and the stranger near
at hand,

in this town,
and in this land.

—Lauchlan M. Watt[2]

Mennonite Disaster Service is one of the few inter-Mennonite organizations that has remained binational (Canadian-U.S.) in structure and operation. Since its organizational beginning under MCC in 1955, MDS has always included Canadian representatives on its management board. While national issues have arisen over the years, the strong relationships derived from meaningful grassroots cooperative activity have always kept MDS from separating into national bodies.

As Region V, the MDS network in Canada has responded to disasters north of the border with the same energy and enthusiasm sent south with the thousands of volunteers who join cooperative efforts in the United States. The 1997 Red River flood response displays their ability to do creative programming and demonstrates the strength that MDS gains by our mutual partnership.

Red River Floods

Our Story—Pete and Marianne Friesen, as Told to Marj Heinrichs

Pete and Marianne Friesen with their four children, Roger, Courtney, Travis, and Josie, live in Halbstadt, Manitoba. On a clear day, they are in eyesight of the Canada-United States border. Thus the Friesens were among the first Canadians affected by the 1997 flood, which had already devastated their southern neighbors along the Red River in North Dakota and Minnesota.

As early as March 21, the first flood forecasts appeared for the Red River Valley and the hamlet of Halbstadt in the Rural Municipality of Rhineland. After an early April blizzard, the flood forecast was revised upward, expecting crest levels two to three feet higher than 1979, when severe flooding had wreaked havoc in the valley.

Bruce Hildebrand

Photo, page 84:
Dan Wiens stands
guard against rising
floodwaters assault-
ing his diked home
near St. Adolphe,
Man. In spring 1997
as the waters rose,
Dan was an MCC
volunteer in Haiti.
After hearing of the
flooding, he went
home. Joined by
other MCCers and
volunteers, Dan
saved his home
from the rising Red
River.

Far right: On May
1, 1997, the "Red
Sea" surrounds the
Pete and Marianne
Friesen home near
Halbstadt, Man.

Near right: It was
nearly two weeks
before Friesens
could start pumping
water out of their
basement so
cleanup could begin
several days later.

Like most Manitobans, Pete and Marianne started to pay attention. An earth ring dike, built after the 1979 disaster, protected their farm, but this time it might not be high enough.

By Sunday, April 20, Pete decided to take time from his job to aid the sandbagging. As the Red River rose, so too did the flood forecasts. By Thursday, it was predicted that protecting the Friesens' home would require a wall of sandbags up to nine feet high.

Marianne recalls sitting down to supper at the community hall when Pete asked organizers one more time about expected elevations and when work would start at their home: "One said we would need a dike eight and a half to nine feet high. They didn't think there was time to build a dike that high before the water came. They wanted to protect something they had a chance to save.

"Our appetites were gone. We took the kids home. We sat down at the table to talk: 'Now what? Where do we start? They said we had to be out by the end of the week.' Pete was frustrated: 'How can I just walk away from what I love?'"

Pete was not one to walk away from impending disaster. Five months earlier he had risked his life trying to save his youngest brother, Jim. An accident at Canamera Foods, a processing plant where both worked, had claimed the lives of Jim and a co-worker. Pete had not hesitated to enter the railroad tanker car where they had been overcome by nitrogen gas, but he too collapsed before others could lower oxygen to him.

Marianne and the four children were

driven to Winnipeg, where they anxiously awaited the outcome. Miraculously, Pete started to regain consciousness in the early evening. He spent one night in the Winnipeg hospital and one in the Altona hospital, then returned home the next day and to work two weeks later.

Though recovered physically, Pete felt helpless against the threatening floodwaters. He said, "I can't handle this. I'm not done dealing with Jim's death, never mind this."

Yet the flood was coming. Pete and Marianne would have to move. "When you know you don't have a lot of time, it doesn't take long to pack all your belongings," said Marianne. With the help of a few friends and relatives, the Friesens moved what they could upstairs into the bedrooms and took the biggest appliances and pieces of furniture to a relative's shed in Altona.

"While we were packing, we could see water on the American border. It happened in such a terrible hurry."

Courtesy of Marj Heinrichs

The Friesens left home Wednesday evening. The next morning they needed a boat to reach the house, and the basement was full of water. By Friday they were tying the boat to the banister in their entry. But flood predictions were high. The Friesens only had eight inches of water on the main floor. Sandbagging could have saved their home.

As the Friesens quickly discovered, eight inches or eight feet doesn't make much difference in damage caused by floodwaters

Courtesy of Marj Heinrichs

inside the home. The basement was completely destroyed, and the main floor would have to be gutted and rebuilt. It was May 11 before water could be pumped out of the basement.

Evacuated to Pete's mother's home near Altona, the Friesens were delighted to hear from MDS leader John Giesbrecht as soon as the waters receded. "He was fantastic," said Marianne. "He called and asked if there was anything they could do, and I said, 'Is there ever!' "

They coordinated a group of people to clean up as soon as they could drive to the house on May 15. Along with friends, neighbors, and MDS volunteers, the Friesens stripped and cleaned the basement and main floor.

Pete, still angry and bitter about the community decision not to sandbag his home, was glad to have strangers rather than local people cleaning up. "I know people expect I'll be more forgiving and understanding because of my accident and all the help we got. They think I'll be saying, 'It's fine.' But it's not."

It would be many weeks before he could forgive. But finally he did, and Pete can now say with joy, "It's forgiven and never to be brought up again. It's done." The love and generous spirit of volunteers helped bring Pete's gradual change of heart.

The Friesens moved a 23-foot construction trailer onto their yard. The children went back to school. Eventually Pete had to return to work. Rebuilding continued through spring and summer. The basement was destroyed and a new one built with Habitat for Humanity help.

Work was progressing, but Marianne was losing weight and unable to sleep. "We had all these bills and couldn't pay them," she said. "I'd get up and sit on the couch so Pete could sleep. I'd sit there and cry, thinking that after we worked so hard, it would all be taken. We couldn't keep this house, then go into town and face all those people we couldn't pay."

Eventually Marianne confided her fears to MDS coordinator John Giesbrecht. Once more MDS came to the rescue and gave Friesens bridge financing. They handed all their bills to MDS. When the Manitoba Disaster Relief funds started to arrive, the money went back to MDS. "That was wonderful," said Marianne. "MDS was here for us at the most crucial times."

Top: Debris piles up as the Friesen home is gutted. It was moved aside and a new foundation built. Then it was moved back.

Working Together
"Because MDSers are the experts in disaster relief, we're pleased to work alongside them in this whole thing. The shared resources are really valuable. Together we can do a lot more than we could separately." —Mary Williams, Executive Director, Winnipeg Habitat for Humanity

MDS Red River Manitoba Flood Response

	Volunteers	Volunteer Days
Mennonite Disaster Service	1,822	14,687
Christian Reformed World Relief	245	2,597
Manitoba Mercy Mission		3,795
Total (84.25 years of work for one person)		21,079

Houses or yards cleaned up:	802	
Reconstruction	minor: 28	major: 71
Complete rebuilds (new houses):	13	

Funding received to date: Can$2.2 million for bridge financing, homeowner grants, and general response. With funds revolving, over $3 million of financing was provided.

Grants to homeowners to date:	$370,905.14
Operating expenses, estimate:	$650,000.00
Raised by Flood of the Century calendar project:	$ 29,303.21

South of the Border

Top and bottom: Youth from Rockway Collegiate in Kitchener, Ont., came to help with flood cleanup near St. Adolphe, Man. Pictured are Jon Schmidt and Dave Bishop (top); and Krista Driedger, holding water-soaked books.

The record flooding of the Red River started in the United States. MDSers had a standing joke across the prairie border: Americans take the winter snow Canadians send south and melt it before sending it back north. With record snowfall on both sides during winter and spring 1997, there was plenty to melt and flood both sides. In Minnesota and North Dakota, crests in mid-April were more than 20 feet above flood stage some places. Hardest hit were Grand Forks, North Dakota, and East Grand Forks, Minnesota, where dikes gave way on April 17, flooding 75 percent of Grand Forks and over 90 percent of East Grand Forks. Total damage in the U.S., including major agricultural losses, was estimated at nearly U.S.$2 billion.

Local units and Region III MDS leaders attempted a significant response, based out of the Faith Mennonite Church in Fargo, North Dakota. Volunteers worked from Breckenridge to Grand Forks. Various factors led to closing the stateside project by late summer: bureaucratic rebuilding delays due to floodplain restrictions and levee relocations, major MDS efforts continuing on the Ohio River floods in Ohio and Kentucky, and the major Canada effort. MDS did return to Warren, Minnesota, in summer 1998 to rebuild several homes through its summer youth program.

Bruce Hildebrand

Manitoba Flood Facts

The flood of 1997 was unprecedented in recent history, but not the worst ever. From 1826 to 1965, the Red River Valley averaged one major flood every 25 to 30 years. But four major floods have come since then, in 1966, 1974, 1979, and 1997.

• In early May 1997, a 1,000-square-mile lake of muddy water, "the Red Sea," stretched along 70 miles between the U.S. border and Winnipeg. Of the 640,000 flooded acres, 450,000 are farmland. Nearly 28,000 people left their homes.

• Nearly 8,000 members of the Canadian military, the largest deployment since the Korean War, rolled into the valley in tanks and trucks. They worked alongside thousands of volunteers.

• Locally run flood command centers were joined by agencies such as Red Cross, Salvation Army, and Mennonite Disaster Service. Sandbag dikes were raised, food prepared, and homes opened for evacuees. Over 12 million sandbags were used in Manitoba.

• Nine ring-diked communities in the Red River Valley were saved. Hundreds of rural properties were not so lucky. More than 200 were eventually written off as unsalvageable. In the community of Ste. Agathe, floodwaters poured into the streets over the west-side railway tracks, leaving 475 people homeless.

• Winnipeg is protected by Duff's Ditch, a 29.4-mile floodway around the city's east side. However, the flood of 1997 still threatened over 100,000 city residents. The Brunkild Z-dike helped to save them. This massive 15-mile dike was hastily constructed by private contractors, government departments, and armed forces. They used 300 pieces of heavy machinery, mud, limestone, and even 3,000-pound sandbags. They completed the job in three days, working around the clock under phosphorous flares dropped by helicopters. Winnipegers also used 6.5 million sandbags for 14 dikes within city limits.

• On May 3, 1997, evacuees began to return home. By May 20 most valley residents had returned, though many stayed in other housing for months and even years before cleanup and rebuilding was complete.

Bruce Hildebrand

Courtesy of The Red River Valley Echo

Courtesy of Marj Heinrichs

Far left: Rosenort, Man., in the "Red Sea." At some places the Red River spread over flatlands of southern Manitoba for almost 30 miles. Large ring dikes protected the town and smaller dikes or sandbags defended rural dwellings.

Near left: A typical farm scene near Rosenort, using sandbags to try to save a house. Other farm buildings were usually left to the mercy of the water.

Below left: Canadian Armed Forces personnel approach the Orville and Jenni Kehler home near Rosenort, Man., at the height of the 1997 Red River floods. Many people and organizations banded together in responding to this record-breaking flood, proving that no one is an island, standing alone.

Courtesy of The Winnipeg Sun

Ring Dikes

A Better Way?

Canada and U.S. differ on flood control. Along the Mississippi, Red, and other U.S. rivers, extensive levee systems are intended to keep rivers and floodwaters within the banks. When these levees fail, towns and properties behind them are unprotected and major flooding occurs.

In Canada, a river is allowed to spread over the surrounding countryside, with towns and rural homes diked to keep out floodwaters. Despite the record levels of the 1997 floods, nine out of 10 communities in the floodplain were spared major flooding, and a majority of rural homes were saved.

A Canadian Difference: MDS Takes Lead Role in Red River Response

As the rising Red River headed north, MDS leaders in Manitoba began planning the largest MDS response ever in Canada. Abe Ens, MDS Region V director living in southern Manitoba, joined MDS Manitoba

The Painting Quartet

Four ladies, all over 60, spent about 200 person days painting 14 houses and using 255 gallons of paint in the Red River Valley recovery program. This included both new construction and major rebuilds. They drove over 10,000 kilometers (6,250 miles) without spending a night away from home. They usually took their lunches along to avoid wasting time going to a restaurant. They often sang while they worked, lifting people's spirits both in word and deed.

Left to right: Nettie Zacharias, Margaret Penner, Helen Ens, Sara Ens.

Courtesy of Abe Ens

leaders in urgent planning. Syd Reimer had served MDS for many years in various roles. Now he and his wife, Helen, were forced by rising waters to evacuate their Rosenort home.

Syd had also served as chair of the provincial government disaster board for 10 years and brought excellent connections to government and public officials. MDS was assigned to lead the overall disaster response effort. According to Syd, "The respect others hold for MDS and MCC is unbelievable. They trusted we would know how to do this." Despite being flooded out of his own home for weeks, Syd co-directed the response.

Abe Ens identifies unique characteristics of the MDS Manitoba response: "First, as we invited other agencies to meetings every Wednesday during the height of the cleanup, we became by default the 'interfaith' leader. Other organizations asked to work under our overall supervision, and many directed funds through our efforts. The Christian Reformed World Relief Committee (CRWRC) and Manitoba Mercy Mission organizations became valuable partners, directing their volunteers to our joint response efforts. Donations of food, tools, and finances came via the Red Cross, Salvation Army, churches, and many other organizations and businesses.

"From the start we decided that MDS needed to have at least one person involved in our effort for the duration of the project. So we hired a returning MCC volunteer, Paul Friesen, to be our assistant project director. This may be the only time MDS has hired a person for two years at the project level."

"We did another thing different," Abe recalls. "We knew the wheels of our government turn slowly and our building season is short. As we entered the rebuilding phase of the recovery, we agreed to do bridge financing. With funds we had received and major financial support from Red Cross and other agencies, we set up a revolving fund. Eligible persons could draw from it immediately to begin rebuilding. As they received funds from the government, they repaid our revolving fund. We were surprised that the government was so willing to let us assume this role of bridge financing. During the course of the project, we spent over Can$2.2 million from this fund."

Paul Friesen, the hired "volunteer" who coordinated the office and volunteer aspects of the project, remembers those hectic first days. Offices were established in the MCC building in Winnipeg. One phone line became four, including a toll-free 800 number, as hundreds of phone calls poured in. Hundreds of volunteers followed. MCC Manitoba and MCC Canada staff provided valuable help each morning with processing volunteers and assigning their tasks. As the flood subsided, satellite locations were established in Altona, Rosenort, and Otterburne. Each office had assessors who scouted out projects and coordinators who matched volunteers with work. During the first weeks of May, as many as 500 volunteers per day were involved in southern Manitoba. Volunteers came from all over Canada. Paul estimates that about 75 percent of them were from outside of Manitoba and about the same percentage were non-Mennonites.

The Border Shall Not Divide Us

The Birth of MDS North of the 49th Parallel

In 1955, MCC began coordinating the emerging MDS organization. Since MCC had representatives on its executive committee from Canada and the U.S., it made sense for the emerging grassroots disaster organization also to be binational. Edward Snyder of Ontario was appointed to the first MCC study committee for disaster relief. In the late 1950s, the Disaster Coordinating Committee asked C. Wilbert Loewen from Manitoba to be special assistant, visiting units in the U.S. and helping start units in Canada.

As a result of activity during the 1948 and 1950 Red River floods, a Manitoba MDS unit was formed in 1956. In 1955 the "Old" Mennonites in Alberta started a Mennonite Service Organization like their sister churches in Kansas. This later included other Mennonite groups and became Mennonite Disaster Service, Alberta. In 1955 Mennonites in Ontario responded to severe tornadoes in the London and Sarnia areas. By 1958, MDS was organized in Ontario. British Columbia started a unit in 1956, and Saskatchewan organized in 1959.

In 1962, MDS was organized with regions, whose directors served on the new MDS Section. Canada was divided into Region V (Ontario and east) and Region VI (Manitoba and west). Eddie Bearinger became director of Region V and C.

Gord Friesen

I had set a goal to work for compensation for 25 years, then volunteer for 25 years or as long as I could. So I made arrangements with my boss to retire in April 1997, but he kept me on till my replacement was on board in late June. I had planned to have six months to reflect and plan the future; it lasted two days!

My father [C. N. Friesen, longtime MDS leader] happened to be in Winnipeg and said, "Gord, they need somebody to do assessments in the valley. You can do that." So I hooked up with John Giesbrecht, who gave me a crash course, then went out with another party to do needs assessment. When I was asked to be project manager for the rebuilding phase, I agreed only till September. But a year later, I'm still working at it. I couldn't get away from it even if I wanted to.

One touching experience involved one of my first assessment cases, a young single father of two girls, ages two and four. He was suffering a double tragedy: in March 1997 his wife was killed in a car accident just outside their property, so he had quit his job to take care of the two girls. I'm not sure he was even into grieving the earlier loss when the flood hit and they lost their home in April. So they were natural clients. With help from CRWRC, we set a target to rebuild their house before school started. We were one week late. That home dedication was a moving experience.

The Dorge House

Leon and Lea Dorge lived in Ste. Agathe, a French-Catholic community, the only diked community completely flooded. The Dorges qualified for MDS home-rebuilding assistance. MDSers joined the extended family in a home dedication celebration on October 24, 1998.

MDS photo

Leon (front right with granddaughter on his lap) and Lea Dorge and their extended family celebrate at their house dedication on October 24, 1998. Paul Friesen (back left) and Gord Friesen (back right) played major roles in coordinating the MDS Red River flood response program.

MDS photo

Members of the Dorge family sing for MDSers at their house dedication. Their lyrics included an adapted popular song: "From this valley you say you are going, we will miss your bright eyes and sweet smile, and remember the Red River Valley, and the Dorges that love you so true."

Wilbert Loewen of Region VI. However, both Loewen and Bearinger favored a single Canadian region. After a short time, all of Canada became MDS Region V. Eddie Bearinger was their representative on the MDS Section from 1962 to 1980, followed by Syd Reimer (1980-1990) and Abe Ens (from 1990).

In 1974, MCC Canada was asked to send a representative to the binational MDS Section. In 1975 members-at-large were added to the MDS Section. Ruby Schmitt, active in the MDS Ontario unit, became the first woman on the Section. In 1984 the MDS bylaws were changed to give Canada one additional representative.

One MDS or Two?

Despite increased (yet still small minority) representation from Canada, a 1985 proposal was made in Canada to separate MDS Canada from MDS in the United States. Many inter-Mennonite and church organizations were reorganizing into more "national" bodies. This was part of a conscious move for Canadian Mennonites to gain a stronger voice in international and binational work. Other concerns included the issue of direct funding from Canada for the Akron MDS office and reducing Section meetings to one per year, to limit expenses. The proposal gained the "reluctant" acceptance and approval of MCC Canada in their 1986 annual meeting.

However, the MDS Binational Section in its 1986 meeting voiced "deep regrets" about this action. The MDS grassroots network across Canada, volunteers who rubbed shoulders and shoveled mud with sisters and brothers in the U.S. on almost every MDS project, also voiced opposition. In good Mennonite fashion, a committee was appointed to study the concerns.

Harold Koslowsky of MCC Canada reports: "As we spoke with people, there was a strong feeling that in the long term it would be to our benefit to stay part of a broader entity, that our strength would be in staying together as opposed to separation. We came back to MCC Canada and suggested that what was really needed was to strengthen the relationship rather than separate." The MCC Canada board accepted this and rescinded the previous action. MDS remained a binational organization.

Below: Canadians have always played a prominent role in the binational leadership of MDS, as in the 1982 MDS executive: (from left) Syd Reimer, chair, from Man.; Paul Longacre, treasurer, Pa.; Carl Nussbaum, Ind.; Ruby Schmitt, secretary, Ont.; John Jantzi, vice chair, Ore.; and Nelson Hostetter, executive coordinator, Akron, Pa.

Waldo Neufeld

Right: Canadian MDSers have often led projects south of the border. In 1972 Syd Reimer spent several weeks leading the MDS response in Rapid City, S.D. Here Syd (right) is in the Rapid City office with executive coordinator Nelson Hostetter.

MDS photo

A Presence Ministry Under Martial Law

Eddie Bearinger reports:

Soon after I got to Elmira, N.Y., the commandant of the National Guard told me, "Eddie, you got to give me some personnel. We're patrolling the food and water lines and had some near fights today. If I put more force in there, we're going to have problems."

I replied, "Well, sir, we came down here to do cleanup. I can't go along with that. We need our volunteers for our work."

He said, "Eddie, this is martial law. That's not a request. That's an order. Just give me two fellows with their MDS identification and their yellow helmets and have them walk up and down the line. That's all I'm asking: your presence."

So I picked two men, a young fellow not yet 20 and one of the oldest fellows there, in his seventies. I told them, "I'm not sure what you're getting into. Just do your thing."

That night they reported, "We had a whale of a time. We made a lot of new friends."

"Did you have any problems?"

"No. We walked up and down the lines and visited all day. People wanted to know why we were here."

Eddie reflects, "That commandant's faith in MDS was a lot stronger than my own."

The Red May Flow North, but the People Flow South

A key reason MDS did not follow the pattern of many organizations in dividing into national bodies was an uprising by grassroots MDSers. They wanted to make sure they could keep working together on disaster projects. Many more disasters occur in the United States. From MDS beginnings, the response there has depended heavily on hundreds and thousands of Canadian volunteers who have flowed south to serve neighbors in need.

After the widespread destruction of several 1972 disasters (chapter 4), Canadian leaders and volunteers supplied most of the response in the Rapid City (S.D.) and Corning/Elmira (N.Y.) projects. Syd Reimer responded to an appeal from Region III director, Marvin Hostetler, to help find a project director for Rapid City by going himself for 14 weeks. He drew on hundreds of fellow Manitobans and other Canadians to provide most of that project's volunteers.

In the East following Hurricane Agnes, Region V was encouraged to provide volunteers for the Corning/Elmira area. Region V director Eddie Bearinger remembers the call from Nelson Hostetter, MDS Akron, asking that he go to Elmira to set things up there. "I threw my boots in the car and away I went. When I got there, the Red Cross people said, 'We've been waiting all day for you; get in here! Here's your list.' It had a couple hundred names of people needing help—and I was alone! So I called back to Ruby [Schmitt, MDS contact in MCC Ontario], and we got things going fast.

Canadians Lead the Long-Term Brigade

On many projects, the majority of the long-term youth have been Canadian, and Canadian leaders have kept many an MDS project going. In the late 1970s, Joan Barkman, a Canadian voluntary service worker, served as the first administrative assistant, alongside Nelson Hostetter in the MDS Akron office. She assumed considerable responsibility for the early "youth squads" popular at the time. Joan remembers that often up to 75 percent of these teams were Canadian.

Carla Hunt, who has directed personnel placements since 1994, suggests that Canadians are several generations closer to their own refugee and migration experiences. That may remind them of the importance of serving others in crisis. She cautiously adds that the numbers and percentages from Canada are down in recent years and hopes they too are not losing that service vision.

Below: Since the start of MDS, volunteers from Canada have been going south to help their neighbors in the disaster-prone U.S. In 1959 these five men were among 40 from Man. who helped clean up after a tornado near Fargo, N.D.

MCC photo, Mennonite Church Archives

The Value of the MDS Binational Partnership

Without exception and from both sides of the border, MDS leaders and volunteers greatly value the MDS binational partnership:

Syd Reimer: "We believe MDS has provided a training place for our young people. We like to go south; it's partly climate. As Canadians, we're just much better off keeping this relationship with MDS in the United States. It gives us a purpose and some bragging rights that we send more people south than you send here."

Abe Ens: "Since the number of disasters happening stateside is much higher than in Canada, it really helps that our volunteers can go south and help. It keeps the MDS spirit alive and lets us provide opportunities for our constituency to serve with us rather than go with other agencies."

Eddie Bearinger: "I'm very gratified that there is no MDS U.S. and MDS Canada. I think it's a wonderful display of fellowship. Often on disaster projects, I've noticed a teenager working with a grandfather, an Amish man with a long-haired guy. That fellowship is being projected across the international border."

Harold Koslowsky: "The greatest value in a united MDS is the connection with so many wonderful people from all over North America. We meet and become friends with people from different denominations, backgrounds, and life experiences, in the intergenerational mix, working side by side on projects, talking around coffeepots."

Wilmer Leichty: "As Region IV director, we have depended heavily on Canadians to assist in our projects. They are able to respond quickly and provide valuable skilled volunteers."

Tom Smucker: "The cooperation of our two countries goes hand in hand with the cooperation of our many denominations. In MDS, a task-oriented organization, we can put together our common goals of serving Christ in disaster situations."

Disasters North of the Border

Don't Disasters Occur in Canada?

In 1996-98, the myth that disasters don't happen to our partners north of the border was shattered. In addition to the record-setting Red River floods in Manitoba, other provinces had significant disaster response activity during those years.

In Alberta, wildfires swept through Porcupine Hills near Granum on December 14, 1997. It affected 45 property owners, mostly ranchers losing homes, barns, corrals, hay, and hundreds of kilometers of fences. During spring and summer 1998, nearly 150 volunteers built two barns, framed in one house, and pounded posts for about 30 kilometers of fences. Herman Neufeld, Alberta MDS chairman at that time, remembers the close partnership that developed with the local community and the positive effects the project had on the community and Alberta MDS. One recipient said, "I can't wait until I can get this ranch back on its feet so I can go and help others."

In eastern Ontario, southwestern Quebec, and the northeastern U.S., the

Top: They're still going south, far south! All but three of these MDSers in P.R. in January 1999 are Canadians!

Middle: In 1987 a tornado struck the outskirts of Edmonton, Alta., spreading destruction and wiping out this trailer park on the northeast edge of town. MDS Alta. and Region V responded extensively, including field cleanup in rural areas.

Bottom: Volunteers from the MDS Ont. unit helped clean up after ice storms in eastern Ont. and Que. in January 1998. Thousands of people were without electricity for weeks, in Canada and in N.Y. Providing generators for farmers was a priority on both sides of the border.

Courtesy of Abe Ens

MDS photo

Courtesy of Orlan W. Martin

early January 1998 "ice storm of the century" paralyzed millions of people. Altogether it is estimated that more than five million people lost electricity, some for over a month. There were 35 storm-related deaths. The storm has been called the most destructive weather disaster in Canada's recorded history.

Farmers were especially hard hit. The MDS priority was to help rural areas on both sides of the border. A major contribution was providing generators, since electricity was crucial to dairy farm operations. In Canada, an estimated $7.8 million was lost in dumped milk, and many animals were destroyed.

The 1996 flooding in the Saguenay region of Quebec was instrumental in getting a native Quebecer as an MDS representative there. Abe Ens, regional director, and Keith Wagler, chair of the neighboring Ontario unit, joined French Canadian Mennonite pastors Jean-Victor Brosseau and Lyne Dufresne in visiting the region and initiating a response. The French Mennonite churches sent groups to the area for three weeks, assisting mostly in emergency relief efforts.

MAY 31 1985

TO COMMEMORATE THE MONUMENTAL TASK PERFORMED
BY THE

MENNONITE DISASTER RELIEF COMMITTEE

WHO CAME TO THE CITY OF BARRIE IN THE AFTERMATH OF THE TORNADO OF MAY, THIRTY FIRST, NINETEEN EIGHTY FIVE, TO FREELY ASSIST THIS COMMUNITY IN THE REMOVAL OF VAST AMOUNTS OF RESULTANT DEBRIS.

A MENNONITE WORKER PASSED THIS DOLLAR BILL TO A RED CROSS VOLUNTEER WITH THE COMMENT

WOULD YOU TAKE THIS PLEASE, I FOUND IT IN THE WRECKAGE"

"A FAITH BORN NOT OF WORDS, BUT OF DEEDS"

"* THE PEOPLE ARE THE CITY *"

Left: The respect and thanks are worth more than the dollar. Well done, good and faithful Canadian servants!

Courtesy of the Toronto Star/Ken Faught

Courtesy of the Toronto Star/Ken Faught

Above: Volunteers organized by MDS pitch in to help clean up debris and begin home repairs in Barrie, Ont., after the 1985 tornado.

Left: A thankful Barrie resident, Barbara Wilson, offers "free coffee and hugs" to workers assisting in cleanup of their devastated community.

95

CHAPTER EIGHT

Broadening Our Vision

In Christ there is no
East or West,

in him no South or North,

but one great fellowship
of love

throughout the whole
wide earth.

In him shall true hearts
ev'rywhere

their high communion find.

His service is the
golden cord

close binding humankind.

Join hands, then, people
of the faith,

whate'er your race may be.

All children of the
living God

are surely kin to me.

—John Oxenham[1]

Whom Do We Help? Decisions from Head and Heart

If MDS had gone "by the book," we might never have helped Don Warner. Cleaning fencerows is not priority work. But helping people regain hope is.

Disasters and the affected people are increasing; MDS cannot help all. Guidelines are needed. The MDS project manual states, "In the emergency or cleanup phase, MDS usually offers assistance without major evaluation of the victims' need or economic status."

In the repair or rebuilding phase, MDS provides help based on a more selective assessment of needs. MDS gives higher priority to helping the elderly, handicapped, widowed, single-parent families, those with low income, the uninsured or underinsured, or disadvantaged persons who cannot handle repairs or reconstruction on their own. Selecting whom MDS will help is one of the hardest jobs faced by project leaders. Volunteers like to help those in greatest need. But how does one bring hope to those like Don Warner who have more resources but are also hurting and have suffered great emotional loss?

Broadening our mandate and listening to the tugs of the heart and God's Spirit have led MDS into some of its most meaningful projects. This chapter captures some of those special stories.

Whom Do We Help? "Day of Disaster" records the story of MDSers who cleaned every flooded store on Main Street—except the liquor store. MDSers noticed the forlorn, forsaken attitude of the elderly couple who operated the store. Even though their need was pointed out, some refused to work there. Finally, a pastor and three men offered to help. When one of the men told his wife what he had done, she muttered sadly, "But, Papa, Papa . . ."

Left: Basil Marin (left), pastor of Family Mennonite Church in Los Angeles, and Steve Penner, director of MCC West Coast, view rubble left after the April 1992 riots in L.A.

MDS photo

Single moms like Tiffany rank high on the priority list for MDS help. On June 6, 1998, fire destroyed home and belongings of the Carter family: (from left) Tiffany, Kimberly, Christopher, and Kevin, near Geneva, Fla.

MDS photo

God's Angels—According to Don Warner

On March 27, 1994, tornadoes roared through northeast Alabama and northern Georgia. The media focused on the loss of life and destruction around Piedmont, Alabama, where 17 people died when Goshen United Methodist Church collapsed during their Palm Sunday service. Yet more people were killed and more property was damaged in Georgia than Alabama.

Don Warner, a retired postal service director, and his wife, Paulette, had recently moved to Pickens County, an hour north of Atlanta. Set to enjoy retirement, they were planning travels to children and grandchildren. But life was tragically interrupted that Palm Sunday. A tornado destroyed their home in Jasper and killed Paulette.

In shock, grief, and anger, Don stumbled through the next months. Pickens County had too many tragic memories for him. The children and grandchildren all lived in northeast Ohio—why not move closer? But how would he clean up the tangled trees and debris covering his property? Struggling alone, Don heard of the MDS team with headquarters in Jasper. He made contact. Since he was not going to rebuild and only needed assistance cleaning out his property, he was not sure if he qualified for help.

In Plain City, Ohio, the United Bethel Mennonite Church youth group was getting ready for their summer service week at the MDS site in Jasper. Thirty youth and sponsors left on June 12 for Georgia. The MDS field team led by project director Llewelyn Zehr had prepared jobs for them. By Tuesday evening their boundless energy, despite the heat, meant that more work needed to be lined up. MDS leaders made a quick call to Don Warner: "We'll have 10 people at your place tomorrow morning to help with cleanup."

Don recalls three surprises: that MDS would even help, that we would send 10 young people to work at the endless task, and that they did so much work in one day. By evening the property was almost cleared.

Friendships had formed between Don and his "angels," as he called them. He followed them back to the MDS center to tell his painful story to the whole group, to play games, to laugh for the first time since his wife's death three months earlier, and to plan to visit them after he moved to Ohio. He also promised that the next summer he would join them for their annual service work week.

Don's note of thanks was pinned on the MDS center wall: "Dear Friends, I've always believed in God and that he does answer prayers. But I have never seen him send so many angels at one time. Thank you for all your great assistance, especially the angels from Plain City, Ohio. Warmest regards, Don."

Jean Hampton

Youth from United Bethel Mennonite Church, Plain City, Ohio, teach Don Warner (back center) how to play Dutch Blitz. The youth, Don's "angels," assisted Don in property cleanup and in emotional recovery from losing his wife in a tornado near Jasper, Ga., in 1994.

From Ribbons of Smoke to Ribbons of Hope

Deacon Bobby Davis was standing in front of the newly built Mt. Zoar Baptist Church on dedication day, September 8, 1996, with 100 green ribbons fluttering across the entrance behind him. He watched an unending stream of people enter the churchyard. "We got enough to fill the

MDS photo

MDS photo

church three times already," he said with amazement. "I feel like shouting right here."

Eight months earlier, Deacon Davis, Pastor Arthur Coleman, and many others were in shock and tears as they found ribbons of smoke rising from the ashes of the charred remains of their small church in rural Green County, Alabama. Pastor Coleman remembers that night well: "On the evening of January 11, I was away. When I came home, my wife told me that Little Zion Baptist Church had burned down. The next morning the county sheriff's department called me and said Mt. Zoar had burned down. I said, no, I heard it was Little Zion. They said Mt. Zoar went down too. I drove 15 miles to the church. It was such a shock. There was still a little smoke coming from the debris, but it had burned the night before. Nobody knew what time of the night it had burned."

"Church Fires Rekindle Pain . . . Specter of Racism Rises with the Smoke."[2] During 1995 and 1996, newspaper headlines like this troubled many. Between January 1, 1995, and June 30, 1996, more than 60 African-American and multiracial churches across the U.S. were burned. The tragedy of these church burnings goes deep into the soul of rural southern communities. It may be just a little building, standing in a remote area, but when it burns, their hopes, dreams, and beliefs are also singed.

Nudged by Grassroots Supporters, MDS Responds

On January 19, 1996, the *Lancaster Intelligencer Journal* reported the burning of the Little Zion and Mt. Zoar churches in Alabama. A third church in the same

county, Mt. Zion, had burned less than a month earlier.

Marian Buckwalter of Lancaster wrote to Tobin Miller-Shearer, MCC U.S. Racism Awareness staff person: "I am saddened by the enclosed story from last Sunday's *Intel*. I have been wondering if Christians here could respond. Would it be appropriate for a group to travel to Alabama to express solidarity with this community by sharing in cleanup and hopefully in some rebuilding? I know MDS has more than enough to respond to, but is it reasonable to think a group could be pulled together? Would such a gesture be welcomed?"[3]

Tobin passed the letter on to the MDS staff with encouragement to consider some response. MDS Akron staff and MDS Region II leaders had been aware of the burnings and agreed to investigate. Ottis Mast and Duane Maust, MDS leaders from Mississippi, visited Greene County and met with pastors of the burned churches. Their report recommending an MDS response was taken to the Region II MDS meeting in Wisconsin. Those present said they would support such an effort. MDS leaders again met with church and community leaders, who invited MDS to rebuild the Mt. Zoar Baptist Church, the one with the least insurance and resources.

Copyright 1996, USA TODAY, reprinted with permission.

Top: Fire-scorched outer walls and rubble of Mt. Zoar Baptist Church after it burned on January 11, 1996—one of three African-American churches torched within a month in Greene County, Ala.

Bottom: By spring 1996, MDS investigators were in Greene County arranging MDS help for Mt. Zoar: (from left) Tom Smucker, field coordinator; Amos Miller, Region II director; Ottis Mast, Region II assistant director; Pastor Arthur Coleman of Mt. Zoar; and Deacon J. C. Smothers of nearby Little Zion Baptist Church, also destroyed.

99

Rising from the Ashes

By May, plans for rebuilding Mt. Zoar were under way. Amos Miller, MDS Region II director and a builder from Goshen, Indiana, worked with the church leaders and drew up plans for the new church. The MDS summer youth program would serve this project.

On May 21 the advance team arrived to set up camp. Since Mt. Zoar is in an isolated rural area, no local accommodations were available. MDS brought in two large mobile homes for the base of operations—kitchen, office, and lodging—supplemented by several smaller RVs. Preparation of the foundation began.

On June 16 the Pequea BIC youth group from Lancaster, Pennsylvania, arrived and construction started. Eight additional groups from as far away as Manitoba came, over 200 youth with sponsors. Skilled long-term leaders and tradespeople directed, but youth supplied most of the labor for the beautiful church.

Here are highlights from this unusual summer:

• Our newfound sisters and brothers at Mt. Zoar quickly became dear friends. We found new and meaningful ways to worship on Sunday morning. One evening each week they provided a special catfish and hush-puppy meal for the week's group, shared the story of their church, sang for us, and joined in hymns of praise.

• MDS has often been the focus of media attention, but we have never been so inundated with media personnel as we were at Mt. Zoar at Boligee. The MDS partnership with Mt. Zoar was one of the first to show actual building activity, so reporters flocked there. MDSers made the front page of *USA Today*, the national TV news, and dozens of other media reports. The CBS program *48 Hours* followed a Lancaster youth group from their homes to Boligee. Sometimes MDS leaders on-site felt the work could be done more easily with fewer reporters present. Early in the project, they named one person to handle public relations—an unusual assignment for an MDSer.

• The media attention did galvanize a tremendous response to the church burning and rebuilding effort. Government agencies were pressed to prevent more burnings and find arsonists. (Arson is one of the most difficult crimes to solve. As of late 1999, there was no proof that the Mt. Zoar Church fire was arson.)

• Christians and persons of all faiths responded generously to the need for rebuilding. They gave millions of dollars through many avenues for rebuilding over a hundred churches over the next several years.

• The MDS constituency was generous in financial support and in sending volunteers. Along with rebuilding the Mt. Zoar church, MDS helped with other community projects. An addition was built on another church and a roof replaced on a third. Four wheelchair ramps were built on private homes.

Ribbons of Hope

It quickly became clear that not everyone who wanted to respond to the tragedy of the church burnings could be used directly for rebuilding Mt. Zoar. A "Ribbon of Hope" project was developed in cooperation with MCC Racism

Top: In May an advance team poured the slab and prepared for the summer building program.

Middle: In June, the Pequea Brethren in Christ youth group arrived, eager to work. Guided by a long-term leadership team, they soon started putting the walls up.

Bottom: Every summer week, the Mt. Zoar church welcomed another youth group with a special catfish and hush-puppy meal.

Above: At midsummer, the church is framed. The Akron (Pa.) Mennonite youth were one of nine such groups that spent a week each at Mt. Zoar.

100

Awareness staff. It encouraged churches to find creative ways of using this opportunity for local racism awareness education as well as support for the church rebuilding project. A packet with suggested litanies and video resources was sent to interested churches. Many churches held services outside, sometimes with other congregations in the community, to demonstrate solidarity with those who had lost church buildings. A tithe of the rebuilding funds

sent to MDS was committed to MCC long-term antiracism efforts.

The Ribbon of Hope packet suggested that people send green ribbons signifying hope to the Mt. Zoar Baptist Church. By the September dedication, over a hundred ribbons of various shapes and sizes were proudly displayed at the church entrance.

God Was Good, and So Was MDS

On September 8, 1996, over 200 people filled the 120-seat sanctuary of the Mt. Zoar church to overflowing, with at least as many on the outside.[4] People sat and stood in the aisles, along the edges, and in the choir loft for the rollicking, 2½-hour service. MDS chair Eldon King observed, "This church stands as a monument to God's love, a monument to the power of God's grace, a monument to partnering among God's people."

Deacon Davis expressed thanks for "our Mennonites," saying, "This is not the Mount Zoar Baptist Church. This is the Mount Zoar Baptist and Mennonite Church." Thomas Gilmore, pastor of the First Baptist Church in Ensley, Alabama, was the dedication speaker. He proclaimed, "The person who torched this church didn't know about the Mennonite disaster teams.

What you do speaks so loudly. MDS says evil doesn't win in the end, that God's goodness rises above evil."

The concluding challenge Pastor Gilmore gave the Mount Zoar congregation speaks to us all. Recognizing the national and international attention given to Mt. Zoar (and MDS), he said, "You are no longer a little church. This world has been introduced to you, and you've got to be concerned about your brothers and sisters."

Pearl Sensenig

MDS photo

Left: An overflow crowd joined in the dedication after the church's completion in September. In February, after the MDS all-unit meeting in nearby Miss., MDSers shared in a Sunday worship service at Mt. Zoar. Deacon Bobby Davis welcomed them warmly.

Top: Amos Miller's wife, Wilma, joins Mt. Zoar members and other MDSers in planting a memorial tree for him in February 1997. Amos designed the church building and made several trips to work on the project. In fall 1996, Amos died of a heart attack. He had spent years in MDS leadership, as regional director, member of the board, and executive committee member.

Other Rebuildings

The Quakers led the rebuilding of the other two churches in Greene County. Additional church groups, many under coordination of the National Council of Churches, rebuilt more churches.

A Litany in a Time of Burning Churches

Leader: We thank you, O God,
People: for giving us songs angels cannot sing,
    for joy down in our souls,
    for amazing grace.
Leader: And we thank you, God,
People: for your church
    embodied in the praises, songs, and prayers
    of black women, men, and children.
Leader: Loving God, we thank you for the sanctuary
    the black church has been,
People: a place to learn the stories of your people,
    a place to heal from the wounds of racism,
    a place to be somebody.
Leader: God of us all, we pray for the congregations who
    have lost their buildings in the fire of hatred,
People: and yet,
    we rejoice with them, for we know the church is people,
    women and men, boys and girls,
    black and white, Hispanic, Asian, and Native American.
All: Let us come together in the spirit of fire,
    fire that tests,
    fire that purifies,
    like the flames at Pentecost,
    a sign of your Spirit moving
    among your people.
            —*Regina Shands Stoltzfus*

Stretching the Mandate: 50 Years of Practice

Those of us in current MDS leadership may have the tendency to think we are creative and pushing MDS to explore new boundaries. But the record shows that from the start MDSers have responded in unusual ways to special needs. Guidelines are just that; the leading of God's Spirit is more important.

Some may think that rebuilding the Mount Zoar Baptist Church was a new venture for MDS. Earlier records, including stories in *Day of Disaster,* suggest otherwise. During the civil rights disturbances of the 1960s, about 40 church buildings were

The Pilgrims of 1963

In 1708 Old Believer dissenters from the Russian Orthodox Church migrated south into Turkey, seeking religious freedom. Over two centuries later, again facing persecution, a group of 224 asked the Tolstoy Foundation to help them get to the U.S. Their last hurdle was adequate housing, and the best option at Seabrook Farms, New Jersey, did not meet sanitation codes.

Enter MDS. Carpenters replaced rotten boards. Painters transformed drab interiors with bright new paint. Crews cleared the grounds and built new sanitation units. Women gave the cabins a spick-and-span look to welcome refugee families from halfway around the world. The state inspector was amazed at the transformation of the camp, complete with 240 beds covered by MCC sheets and pillowcases, topped with towels and soap. The Old Believers arrived on June 5.

MCC photo

Citrus Freeze Results in Church Growth

In December 1998, a severe freeze destroyed 80 percent of the citrus crop in the rich San Joaquin Valley in central California. Over 80 percent of the farmworkers depending on the crop for their livelihood were left jobless and without money to buy food or pay bills.

The California MDS unit, led by chair Jim Clymer and in partnership with the Hispanic Caucus of Mennonite Churches, organized a food distribution and financial aid program. Members of nine churches in the Pacific District of Mennonite Brethren churches reached out to affected families. They invited them to church to hear the good news, then provided groceries.

Jose Elizondo, associate district minister for the Pacific District conference, led the response. Contributions solicited from California churches more than matched a $10,000 grant from the MDS binational office, providing resources to purchase food in bulk and prepare boxes for distribution each week for several months.

Elizondo claims James 2:14 as the basis for the ministry: "What good is it, my brothers, if a man claims to have faith but has no deeds?" As Jose puts it, "We could just be handing out groceries, but that would bring only temporary relief. Giving them Christ brings eternal relief." Attendance at several churches grew weekly, with conversions practically every week.

At the West Park Hispanic Mennonite Brethren Church, 57 persons in two weeks responded to the invitation to accept Christ. Four months earlier only 20 people attended the church. At the nearby new Raisin City MB Church, attendance climbed in four months from six to 52. "The church has really benefited from the response," claims Elizondo. "There will probably be some drop-off, but some will stay. Even if only one family stays, it is a gain. Seeds are being planted."

Members of the Iglesia El Buen Pastor Mennonite Brethren church in Orange Grove, Calif., assemble boxes of food for distribution to families left jobless because of the December 1998 citrus freeze in central Calif.

MDS photo

burned or bombed in Mississippi alone. As our answer to hate and prejudice in that troubled time, MDS volunteers helped rebuild five churches for blacks and two for Choctaw Indians. Other earlier projects illustrate going beyond the guidelines:

MDS photo

• 1952: MDSers from Kansas supplied additional volunteers to support an MCC service unit working at long-term flood rehabilitation projects in Kansas City.

• 1956: MDSers in British Columbia helped in preparing barracks and operating a clothing depot for thousands of Hungarian refugees migrating to Canada.

• 1965: MDSers worked at urban chronic housing needs in partnership with the Jeff-Vander-Lou organization in St. Louis, Mo.

• 1968: After the riots in Pittsburgh in 1968, MDS offered assistance to the United Black Front. After considerable discussion and learning to know each other, MDSers helped rebuild low-cost housing as well as teach the youth valuable skills.

• 1971: MDSers repaired public proper-ty on the mall near the Washington Monument after destructive demonstrations.

• 1972: Mennonite Native American leaders invited MDS to help reconstruction in the Pine Ridge, South Dakota, area, after the occupation and siege at Wounded Knee.

• 1981: The MDS network assisted MCC in gathering corn for the Horn of Africa, the first of many corn/grain drives for international relief.

• 1986: Haylift for southeastern U.S. Irvin Harms's work gathering hay earned him a spot on the Oprah Winfrey show.

• 1992: MDS helped rebuild six Amish barns burned by arson in central Pennsylvania's Big Valley; and helped persons affected by Los Angeles fires from riots following the Rodney King verdict.

Left: Paul Brubacher (center) commends Dean Kapenga (left) and Hank Balder on a load of hay sent from Hamilton, Mich. to Lebanon County, Pa., during severe drought in the eastern U.S. in summer 1999 (see nubbin, **top**). A major haylift from Mich. and other midwest states provided cattle feed for dairy farmers in the east. The MDS network has assisted in many haylifts/grain drives for drought and famine areas in North America and around the world.

MDS photo

MDS Response Thaws Ice on Main Street

In Arizona, the Hopi people had serious misgivings about an MDS project. Like typical Americans, the MDS unit started post-flood cleanup too fast. They neglected to clear all arrangements with the local chief.

Slowly the Native people began to trust them. One day the Hopis started helping MDS volunteers. Next they said, "Let us feed you a noon meal." Afterward everyone sat around chatting.

Then the chief in the Upper Village, who had been reserved about the project, said, "I'd like to take a picture for the *Hopi News.* You can take pictures too." Until then MDSers had been advised, "No cameras." Soon every man had his camera.

An experienced missionary commented, "I don't believe it. Six months ago in the middle of July, I could have skated down Main Street on the ice, the feelings were that cold. Now they have been reversed." Later the chief offered the MDS volunteers his pickup, including gas expense, to go to Phoenix.[5]

Tornadoes Hit Arkansas—Tressie's Story

The March 1, 1997, Arkansas Tornadoes During five hours on Saturday, March 1, 1997, 17 tornadoes cut a 260-mile path across Arkansas, killing 27 people and injuring 426. Several tornadoes stayed on the ground for over 50 miles. Eight of the tornadoes killed people; three were classified as violent—reaching F-4 or F-5 on the Fujita scale.

Saturday, March 1, 1997, was a warm, brooding day in Little Rock. Tressie B. Robierson felt troubled all day on her custodial job at the airport:

I felt a voice telling me all day, You should go home. I thought about punching out early but didn't have a good reason. My supervisor said, "Tressie, what's wrong with you today?" I said, "I just want to go home."

I went down to check out early but then waited till 3:30 as usual. I had planned to shop on the way home, but the voice kept saying, Go home, Tressie.

So I headed for home. At the little store near home, I put on my blinkers to turn in and get some things, but the voice said, Go home, Tressie. I turned the blinker off, pulled back into the traffic, and drove home.

My husband greeted me, "Well, you made it home, Tressie. I didn't think you were going to make it home today."

I said, "Why did you say that?"

He told me there were tornado warnings. As I went in, he sat down on the porch. I asked, "Why are you sitting there?

Tressie Robierson shares her story with Willie and Edna Miller as they sit outside the trailer that was the original MDS headquarters in College Station, Ark.

If the wind rises and you sit out here, you'll get blown away. Come along in. Let's close up the house."

It was dark and starting to rain hard. The curtains were blowing, and we got some windows closed. We were both in the living room when we heard this train coming. Since we do live next to the train track, we thought it was a train. But suddenly the house started to shake, so I hit the floor right by the front door. That's all I remember till it was over. The last I saw my husband, he was standing not far away.

I felt debris falling around me. The next thing I remember is being pinned and buried. I called for my husband but got no response. I'm not sure how long I lay there, how many times I called. I prayed and heard the same voice that had spoken all day: He doesn't hear you.

I kept calling for help. Finally I heard voices and called again. Rescue workers dug me out. I wasn't badly injured, but the emergency team wanted me to go to the hospital. I said, "Not till you find my husband."

Everyone was quiet.

I asked, "What's wrong?"

No one wanted to tell me, but then I saw something out in the yard. I thought, That looks like my husband's clothes, and tried to go that way.

They said, "Tressie, no, your husband is gone." I refused to go to the hospital until they took my husband's body away.

Tressie returned yet that day to live nearby with a daughter. In the small College Station suburb of Little Rock, three others had also been killed.

MDS began cleanup the next day under guidance of Willie Miller from the Arkansas MDS unit, who worked closely with local church and community organizations. College Station is an African-American community. MDSers were warmly welcomed and invited to begin a long-term rebuilding program. One of the first houses built was for Tressie Robierson.

In fall 1997, after Tressie's house was finished, she said to the long-term MDS team, "Now I have a nice house, and I'm all alone. You folks don't have very good lodging arrangements where you're staying. Why doesn't someone live with me?"

So that fall Melana Janzen from Ontario lived with Tressie. Then, from January to March, Henry and Pearl Dueck from Manitoba stayed with her. In addition, Tressie and others from the community provided lots of good food and often came and shared their stories and testimonies with MDS workers.

On March 1, 1998, one year after the tornado, special services were held at the Mt. Nebo African Methodist Episcopal Church, where MDSers worshiped while living in the community. Amid tears and hugs, Tressie and others gave testimony to what God had done for them in the past year.

Tressie recalled, "When I opened my home to you folks, others asked, 'Why are you letting those white folks live with you?'

"And I told them, 'After what they have done for me, how can I not invite them in? They are my sisters and brothers.' "

Tressie was not the only one shedding tears when MDSers closed the project and left. God had again brought hope, healing, and reconciliation from another disaster.

Vernon Miller

Breaking the Barriers of Race

To God Be the Glory, Great Things God Has Done

In March 1997, Willie Miller and his family were living in Harrison, Arkansas. He directed the 90-resident Hillcrest Nursing Home, run by Beachy Amish, and chaired the Arkansas MDS unit. So he had double concerns as he heard tornado warnings on Saturday, March 1. This is his story:

I remember walking outside. Everything was so dark. We just committed ourselves to the Lord. On Sunday morning we heard the first reports of tornadoes. I called other committee members; we divided up the area. I was to focus on Little Rock. As I drove out on Monday to investigate, I prayed that God would show me where to go. I drove right into College Station. As I walked through College Station, saw the destruction, met the people, and listened to their stories, I just felt in my heart, *This is where God wants us to be.*

By Tuesday, March 4, we had eight people from Harrison working in College Station. We had a good day helping people and making interesting contacts. Frank Kelly and Ronald Loren, community people, went around the community with us. I asked them, "Who can I talk to about coming in here and helping?" As we were walking, they said, "There he is." It was Pastor Hezekiah Stewart.

Hezekiah reminded me of Moses: he cared for the people. In the days that followed, I met often with Pastor Stewart and learned to know him as a brother in the Lord. We shared the same vision. As we helped people rebuild their homes, we were interested in rebuilding their lives as well and sharing the Lord Jesus Christ with them. We became workers together with God.

Thank You, Lord

Pastor Stewart helped us find a trailer to set up an office. The first night I stayed in the trailer, I noticed several bullet holes in the windows. I was scared. I made sure all the doors were locked, prayed for God's protection, and went to bed. The next morning I was looking for the keys to the trailer and found them outside, sticking in the lock. I said, "Thank you, Lord, for your protection." —Willie Miller, Harrison, Arkansas

---

Fishers of Shad

Pastor Hezekiah Stewart's story, as told to Russell Smucker:

Pastor Stewart says we MDS volunteers here in College Station are helping him fish for shad. We asked him to explain.

One time Hezekiah was feeling that his work was in vain. He took his feelings to God, and God told him to go fishing. He didn't know anything about fishing, but he got a line and tossed his hook and bait into the Arkansas River below College Station. All day he fished. He didn't catch a thing.

Late in the day he noticed there were thousands of fish near him, all sticking their mouths up out of the water. He realized the backwater where he was fishing had become isolated from the river; the oxygen was depleted, and the fish were dying. He grabbed a plastic bag, dipped several fish into the bag, and ran with them to the main part of the river. He put the fish into the fresh water. They revived and swam off.

Running back to where all those fish were gasping for air, he found two persons with sticks killing as many fish as they could. So there was Hezekiah, trying to save as many fish as he could while the other two were killing as many as they could. The fish were shad, and every sane fisherman in Arkansas will throw shad onto the bank to die. Then the rising Arkansas River poured fresh water into the backwater, and all the shad recovered and swam away.

That was how Hezekiah found his vocation, to save people society considers as useless as shad. He says God has brought us MDSers here to College Station to help him save them.

Pastor Hezekiah Stewart shares his vision of "fishing for men" with MDSer Henry Dueck.

Carl Hiebert

Along the Road to Rebuilding

In addition to working with Pastor Stewart and his Watershed community program, MDS partnered with several other organizations in the rebuilding program. State Representative Wilma Walker, president of the Progressive League, helped generate more resources to support MDS. She said, "You cannot beat the kind of cooperation we got. FEMA and the volunteer agencies have been fantastic."

Austin Porter Jr. is a lawyer living in College Station. His father, Austin Porter Sr., was out of town when the tornado hit but had his house destroyed. His uncle, living next door, was killed. Yet Austin Sr. said, "I think the storm has been a blessing. A lot of businesses and homes are better than they were before the storm. I'd like to say that my brother and the people who died have made a way for us to have life more abundantly."

Both Porters reflected on the racial history of their larger area. They remember school segregation and white business people using white privileges to take advantage of African-Americans. College Station itself, never incorporated into Little Rock, had fewer resources for sewers and other services. Yet they could not recall a single racial incident in College Station, even though there has been an element of distrust.

Austin Jr. remembers, "The Mennonites coming in left a lasting impression on the people of this community. Before the storm, a lot of people would have said there are no good white people around. Now we can see there are white people who have heart. They came in without fanfare, to work, not to be on TV."

By late August five houses had been rebuilt. Vernon Miller, MDS Region III director, joined Willie Miller and the MDS project team in the dedication service. Along with local recipients and community members, a surprise attendee was James Lee Witt, director of FEMA, from Washington, D.C.

Each family received their house keys, a Bible, and a blessing on their house. Director Witt later told a conference of disaster leaders that attending the dedication service was a highlight of his years as director of FEMA.

MDS rebuilding in College Station continued through several phases, often after an emotional appeal from Pastor Hezekiah Stewart. They would work at finding more funding so more people could be helped. Various local organizations contributed resources to keep the project going, and MDS continued rebuilding in College Station for nearly two years.

Right: Bill Mast of Oklahoma City puts his drywall skills to good use in constructing new homes in College Station, Ark.

Below: Willie Miller, project coordinator at College Station, presents owners of the first five rebuilt homes with Bibles and house keys, at Mt. Nebo church. Behind Willie on right is James Lee Witt, director of FEMA.

Wilbur Litwiller

Carl Hiebert

When the Fishing Is Good, It's Hard to Quit

It's hard to determine what makes a project special, but clearly College Station became so for MDSers. Almost everyone who served longer-term found it hard to leave newfound friends.

Russell and Linda Smucker, an Ohio teacher-librarian couple on leave, spent January-March 1998 at College Station. Russell let MDS Akron see his weekly journals to family and friends. On January 11, five days after arriving, he reported, "We're living in a small RV that's semi-functioning. The AC outlets work. No furnace, no lights, leaks in the water line, leaks in the roof. Linda and I are stubborn campers."

After talking about College Station and the interesting folks he met, he wrote, "Mostly Linda and I are frustrated. We don't know what we're doing here. But we're doing our best to make ourselves useful. I'm discovering how unhandy I am."

Only two months later, Russell felt the need to send a special letter of thanks to his "Brothers and Sisters at Mt. Nebo A.M.E. Church." He shared that letter with them at the special services held March 1, 1998, to commemorate the one-year anniversary of the tornado. He thanked them for the many gifts they had given him, including hospitality, gratitude, joy, and dependence on God. "We Mennonites came to share our building gifts with you, and you have shared your riches of faith with us. I believe we have had the better of the exchange. Thank you so much."

Henry and Pearl Dueck from Bossevein, Manitoba, served as project leaders at College Station for several months, living with Tressie Robierson in her home, built by MDSers. Pearl reflects, "For me, the highlight was to stay with Tressie in her home. The longer we stayed, the more she opened up about different situations, and the more we got to understand her. Hopefully the same happened for her."

Henry spoke for MDS at a special thank-you service one year after the tornadoes: "On behalf of all the volunteers working with Mennonite Disaster Service, I want to thank you for your friendliness and hospitality to us. We may have come as strangers among you, but as we worked among you, we became friends. Your smiles, warm greetings, handshakes, and hugs have made us feel part of your community. Your tokens of love spoke volumes to us: sweet potato pies, hot water cornbread, barbecued ribs, greens, and much more. You will always have a warm spot in our hearts. It's going to be hard to say good-bye."

Carl Hiebert

MDS photo

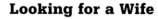

Looking for a Wife

The first house MDS completed was for 93-year-old Emmanuel Benton. He was so proud of his new home that he let it be known he was now looking for a wife! When Kid Henry Williams (above), only 87, also got one of the first homes and heard that Manuel was looking for a wife, he thought maybe he would need to start looking, too.

Left: Emmanuel Benton, 93 years young, shares his pleasure in his new home with Vernon Miller, MDS Region III director.

After 40 Years, Some Healing Comes!

What They've Gone Through
One of the highlights I had working here was learning more about African-American culture, and then visiting the Civil Rights Museum in Memphis. It starts to give us a sense of what they have gone through. I like worshiping in the African-American churches. —Ryan Hildebrand, Port Rowan, Ont.

Right: Elizabeth Eckford reflects back to being one of nine students who bravely integrated Little Rock High School in 1957. MDSers worked for Elizabeth, and she shared her story with them.

In the fall of 1957, nine young black students under federal troop protection integrated Little Rock Central High School against the wishes of Governor Faubus and most of the people of Little Rock. Elizabeth Eckford was one of the students who faced the jeers and hatred of unruly crowds as they entered the school, the first blacks to do so. Eckford's picture is most often shown to illustrate those stories; she was featured on the cover of *Life*. It was reported that when she went home that first day, she could wring spittle out of her dress.

During fall 1997, a variety of services were planned to commemorate the 40th anniversary of the Little Rock integration effort. MDSers participated in some of the events. President Clinton went back to Little Rock, and eight of the nine students who braved the mobs in 1957 came together again. Elizabeth Eckford, the only one of the nine who remains in Little Rock, still suffers from the emotional impact of the 1957 event.

Pastor Hezekiah Stewart of Mt. Nebo Church in College Station became acquainted with Elizabeth Eckford during the 1997 remembrances and discovered that her home needed repair. He asked if he could bring MDSers to help; reluctantly she agreed. The damage was not from tornadoes, yet MDSers felt called to help heal the old wounds. At first Elizabeth was fearful about white people working in her house, and MDSers did so only with Pastor Stewart or another community person present. Before long, she welcomed MDSers without escorts. Later she said, "Come anytime. If I'm away, here is where you'll find the key!"

In March 1998 MDS held a project leader's training workshop at College Station. One noon Elizabeth Eckford had lunch with us and shared her thanks to MDS, not only for physical work on her house but for help in trusting whites: "You are the first white people who have come to help me and allowed me to retain my own dignity." She had questions about Mennonites, who we are, and why we serve others as we do. She thanked us over and over for helping to restore her emotional well-being.

Thank you, College Station MDSers, for going the extra mile, and showing that miracles of healing can still happen 40 years later.

Carl Hiebert

Will Counts, in the *Arkansas Democrat*

Mending Fences

Forty years after Hazel Bryan angrily followed Elizabeth Eckford into Little Rock High School, the two met again in front of the school. The meeting was quietly arranged by Will Counts, the same photographer who took the earlier picture.

Bryan, now Hazel Massery, is the only white person who has publicly come forward and apologized for the hatred directed at blacks during the segregation crisis.

Will Counts

Photos from the Birmingham Project

Left: Gracie Brown (90) in the kitchen of her new MDS home.

Left: Hattie McCamble (center), her daughter, Margaret (left), and Pam Denlinger talk on the porch of Hattie's new home.

Carl Hiebert

Carl Hiebert

Above and left: Before and after— Dan Jones in front of his shanty and later on the steps of his new MDS home.

Carl Hiebert

Carl Hiebert

109

CHAPTER NINE

Dear God, It Hurts

Carry each other's burdens,

and in this way you will fulfill the law of Christ.

—Paul, in Galatians 6:2

O God . . . Come Here!

This was not a usual day.
The great storm had passed,
   and business had not returned to normal.
Eight o'clock rush hour did not come.
   The construction worker,
      the pharmacist,
         the convenience store clerk,
           the executive,
             the technician,
               the school teacher,
                 and the office clerk did not go to work;
  nor did the yellow bus pick up the uniformed children.
On this day . . .
   those whose acquaintance had not gone beyond the wave
      or the casual "hello"
         became intimate . . .
   by common experience.
With landmarks gone, homes crushed, and geography rearranged,
   the routine was not done today.
Instead . . .
   There were conversations in the street.
      Hugs replaced the usual handshakes.

MDS photo

And tears came without shame.
Grateful hearts were saddened by the awareness of injury
   . . . and even death.
With landmarks gone and homes blown away,
   bewildered children,
         uncharacteristically quiet,
         searched the faces of their parents
               for some indication of what might be real now.
   Nothing had prepared the parents to explain this to them.

Photo, page 110: A man watches the remains of his home burn after the Palm Sunday tornado in northern Indiana.

Explanations were not meaningful . . .
   and soon gave way to silence.
         Arms slipped around the children
         without thought
               and delivered some comfort.

Prayers were shortened to
   Oh God, . . . Come here.
   Hallelujah.
   Thank you, Jesus.
This was not a usual day.
The great storm had passed,
   and business
         had not returned to normal.
A new sense of community was being born.
                  —*Paul Unruh, September 29, 1998*

B earing each other's burdens" (as in Gal. 6:2) has been the MDS scriptural motto since our beginning. Following disasters, these burdens are more than physical and material loss. MDSers have always recognized the crucial need for listening ministries. As in the churches from which we come, some of us are better listeners and some are better doers. This chapter is dedicated to every MDSer who has taken the time to listen and aid crucial emotional healing in the recovery from loss and pain.

Stories of Pain and Healing

"Please Call Right Away"

Pam Denlinger and her husband, Dean, have led many MDS projects, including one at Gainesville, Georgia. Pam's story:

Our car was covered in red Georgia dust. MDS leaders would visit us the next day. I popped into the MDS office before hitting the car wash and found an urgent message from Jenny. "Pam, please call right away." Jenny hadn't called for over a month; "right away" seemed serious.

The March 20, 1998, tornado that hit near Gainesville had destroyed the house trailer of Jenny, Peter, and their granddaughter Erin. They weren't physically injured. But the shock of losing everything, plus finding a neighbor and a baby dead in their front yard, had taken its toll. Jumping through hoops to get disaster assistance had left them depressed. Finally they had given up on government help.

Jenny had moved her family into a new trailer, even though it frightened her. When she answered the phone, she was sobbing. Between sobs, she told of a porch that hadn't been built (Peter couldn't do it), her daughter's biopsy just that morning, her sister's recent cancer surgery, Peter's poor health (with a liver transplant), and worries about Erin. Since our construction foreman had to look over the porch project, we went out to visit.

They had been in their new trailer over a month. Peter had set the four porch posts but couldn't complete the project. They climbed in and out of their trailer, using concrete blocks. Jenny couldn't stop crying even though we promised to work on the porch the next day. Something else was needed.

Suddenly I heard an inner voice say, *Invite her to the worship service.* It was Wednesday evening, and our volunteer youth group from the Agape Fellowship in Williamsport, Pennsylvania, had planned the service. I'm not one who seeks out these situations, but this seemed a definite "salvation appointment," in the words of a speaker at our church. He explained that God puts us in these situations for a reason; all we have to do is open our mouths. So I did.

Jenny and Erin came back with us. During the prayer time, several people lifted up Jenny and her concerns. Afterward, the visiting pastor's wife and I sat down to talk with her. We encouraged her to unburden herself of everything, assuring her that nothing she was struggling with would shock us. We talked a long time. We learned about hopes for her granddaughter that weren't going to come true, sorrow over her daughter's sickness, and the unreasonably high expectations she was placing on herself to solve all these problems. We tried to help her let go of them one by one. Mostly though, we just listened.

Listening is what I spend most of my MDS time doing. There are times a touch or hug is called for, but sometimes all that is left to do is just to cry along with the disaster survivor. We have cried together over everything from facing a move back into a trailer to the loss of an only child. Most of the time, I am prepared for it, but every once in a while, it just happens.

Suddenly I heard an inner voice say, "Invite her to the worship service."

"Please Dig My Grave"

Irvin Harms, longtime MDS leader from Moundridge, Kansas, shares his story:

We were in Brandenburg, Kentucky [right after the 1974 super tornado outbreak]. We took a group in a bus, 50 of us, loading it to the gills. When we got there, nothing was ready for us. We went block by block, searching for people, helping find and bury the dead.

Then the mayor came to me: "Irv, I've got a job for you. Out in the country is a guy who says he's going to kill himself." We were staying with a Methodist preacher, so we went together. We found a really confused man. The preacher was quite a talker. Then he finished and I started. The guy wouldn't say anything for a long time. Finally he said, "Yeah, you can help me. Right over there you can dig my grave; I'm going to die. I want to die."

I started bawling. I turned around and cried like a baby. No one said anything. I looked up and the preacher was bawling. We just stood there crying, both of us.

Finally the guy said, "You really do care, don't you? You really care."

I said, "Sure we do. We'll do anything for you."

"Would you build me a shed for my tobacco barn?"

I said, "Sure, we will."

As we left, I told the preacher I wasn't sure if the Mennonites would go for this. But we had promised him, so we built him a tobacco barn.

Left: Kid Henry Williams, who lost his home to a tornado, shares his story with Henry Dueck outside his new home, built by MDS in College Station, Ark.

BENTON MENNONITE
CHURCH LIBRARY
15350 CR 44
GOSHEN, IN 46526

Be a Sensitive Listener

MDS photo

Above: Paul Unruh, Newton, Kan., represents Mennonite Health Association on the MDS board.

Below: Alonzo Crain, recipient of a new home built by MDS at College Station, Ark., confers with MDS volunteer Nik Tymoszewicz from St. Catharines, Ont.

The MDS brochure "A Message to Our Volunteers" states the purpose of MDS and lists ministries of "*listening*, cleanup, repair, and reconstruction" as examples of giving the "cup of cold water." Before talking about work assignments, that brochure suggests these guidelines, underscoring the importance of relationships in MDS work:

• Do everything you can to preserve the sufferer's dignity and sense of worth. Remember the truth, "It is easier to give than to receive." Respect personal property and rights of ownership.

• Be a sensitive listener. Don't be judgmental. Grief is a natural reaction to loss, even the loss of possessions. Be friendly and optimistic, but not so lighthearted as to imply the situation is not serious. Be careful about giving simple answers to the very complex confusion and grief that follow disaster. Treat the disaster victims as equals.

Carl Hiebert

Always Responding to the Whole Person

Early leaders in Kansas in 1954 developed a "Do's and Don'ts" list for MDS volunteers. Among the "Do's" is the following: "Take time to visit with those you are helping. The boost in morale and the spiritual help you can give is worth more than the work you can do. (This doesn't mean you should not work; you came to work.)"

During a 1955 MDSers training school session in Hesston, Kansas, H. B. Schmidt spoke on "Effective Witnessing." He stressed, "Remember that people suffer in disaster as well as buildings, property, and livestock. A 15-minute break for personal contact with the people may be as much appreciated as two hours of work."

Through the years MDS has continued an emphasis on assisting with emotional recovery of those affected by disaster. Cooperative MDS-MMHS [Mennonite Mental Health Services] workshops were conducted for the following purposes: To sensitize MDSers to the importance of being patient listeners to disaster victims, to become more concerned about needs other than material and physical, to invite professional staff persons to be part of the process in disaster situations, and to enable and train resource persons.

On project locations, MDSers always welcome the opportunity to meet the people they are helping. Many project leaders arrange for local persons to come in one evening during the week to eat and fellowship with volunteers and share their stories. At MDS all-unit meetings, the most likely remembered input is the sharing, often emotional, by persons MDS has helped.

Chapter 6 tells of a recent intentional partnership with Mennonite Health Services (that includes earlier MMHS agencies). MDSers with special training in mental health services have been part of response teams in several major disaster response efforts since Hurricane Andrew, such as 1993 Midwest floods, 1998 tornadoes in Birmingham, and 1999 tornadoes in Oklahoma and Kansas. Their input at project training workshops or all-unit meeting workshops is also valued and well-received.

Since 1994, Paul Unruh, a trained mental health professional at Prairie View (Mental Health Center), Newton, Kansas, has volunteered many weeks at MDS project sites. He guides the heightened MDS concern for the total needs of those in crisis. At our request, he wrote the following to encourage all of us to listen more effectively to stories of pain and healing. In doing so, we help bring hope and recovery to broken spirits and dreams.

Jon Warren

114

Contributing to the Mental Health of Disaster Survivors

Paul Unruh

The most significant contribution MDS makes toward the emotional recovery of disaster survivors is simply to repair what has been damaged and to rebuild what has been destroyed.

To storm survivors who have lost their homes and also the security and sense of well-being invested in those homes, the sight of cleanup, restoration, or rebuilding is hard to describe. Such acts of repairing and rebuilding alone lift spirits toward restoration and wholeness! It is difficult to overstate the meaning experienced by a storm survivor who sees a group of volunteers repairing or rebuilding what was destroyed. The storm may have taken only a few seconds to occur, but the repair task seems so overwhelming.

Imagine what it is like for the homeowner and/or family to see a new house being built on a new foundation after enduring months of difficulties, struggles with financing, and repeated doubts that it would ever happen. Now, before their very eyes, it is happening! We need not hear their words. We can read people's faces when they say to themselves, and sometimes each other, "Oh, it can be done! . . . People will help. . . . Maybe I dare to hope after all!" Such powerful birthing of hope cannot occur until disaster survivors let go of the despair they have been feeling, sometimes for a long time.

In the community wracked by disaster, hope is contagious. Many times MDSers have witnessed what happens in the community when the first hammer rings out. The faces of specific homeowners light up. Members of the entire community are invited to lift their heads and see what can be done. In such moments, the collective spirit of the community may be revitalized.

The second most significant contribution of MDS is volunteers' readiness for actively listening to the disaster stories.

Many volunteers are adept at asking permission-giving questions: "Where were you when the tornado struck?" "Where were you when the water rose?" "What did you do with your children?" "How did you bear the strain?"

All human beings, especially survivors of disaster, tragedy, or trauma, have a right to tell their stories, a right to have other human beings hear their stories and a right to have their stories believed. *Storytelling heals!*

Most survivors of disaster and trauma recover with the help of their natural social support network. Because of the enormity of the cleanup and rebuilding or repairing tasks, MDS workers have the privilege of briefly becoming part of that social support network.

Third, a few survivors are so traumatized that they need professional help.

Sometimes MDSers with mental health training can assess the needs of disaster survivors and refer them to appropriate mental health facilities and services in their community. Disaster victims and their families may not recognize their need for such services. Frequently it takes only a well-directed question or comment to get the survivor to acknowledge need and seek suitable help.

In initial phases of a disaster, field workers from community mental health facilities, the Red Cross, and other agencies offer counseling. When emergency and cleanup phases end, those field services may no longer be available. MDSers with mental health skills help fill the void.

After disaster, survivors may be vulnerable and open to accepting services. Often survivors acknowledge being near the end of their emotional rope and ready to accept professional help if available. In addition to referrals, the MDSer with mental health or pastoral skills can walk through physical or emotional difficulties with survivors such as Susan or Larry.

Susan, her mother, Jane, and her son, David, fled to the closet as the storm approached. The tornado removed everything above the first floor and hurled them into the backyard. All survived, though Susan and her mother were hospitalized for several days. At a community information meeting, a pastor introduced Susan to the MDS mental health worker and explained that Susan had been unable to visit her house since the storm. He wondered whether the MDSer would be willing to accompany Susan for the first visit.

As they walked toward her house, Susan explained that she had not slept in

Building Natural Bridges
All MDSers, whether builders or workers with mental health skills, must do their work in such a way that it builds natural bridges between the disaster survivors and other persons and resources in their local community. MDSers must never work in such a way that survivors become dependent on MDS and thus again are traumatized when MDSers leave the survivor's community. MDS must always strengthen survivors' connections to their own community. —Paul Unruh

Left: Jerry Klassen (left) and Wes Heinrichs listen to the stories of Jack and Lois Howard, whose home was damaged by the Northridge 1994 earthquake.

Many times MDSers have witnessed what happens in the community when the first hammer rings out. The faces of specific homeowners light up. Members of the entire community are invited to lift their heads and see what can be done.

the nine days since the tornado. "Every time I close my eyes, the old images and sounds of the storm come back, and I have to wake up." She spoke of emotional exhaustion and despair. As they walked the property, Susan stared at the lot next door: "I don't understand it. All three of us survived, and she died." After this first walk to her house, Susan slept for the first time since the tornado hit.

Larry moved slowly when the MDS/mental health worker met him for the first time on the street, three days after the tornado. He spoke in short, broken phrases. His eyes couldn't focus on any-thing for more than seconds. He was often tearful. He worked in scattered style. On that first visit, he talked about surviving the storm and what it was like not know-ing whether his son in the other room had survived. In days that followed, during five-minute encounters, he often wondered why he had survived and others had not.

The MDSer noted that each day his speech became more coherent and his work more productive. By the end of the second week, when MDS volunteers offered to help finish the roof repair he had begun, he graciously accepted. As the volunteers began working, he burst into tears of sorrow, joy, and relief. He later acknowledged that healing had come through those brief conversations day after day "right here on the street where I live, in front of my damaged house."

Such stories are visible and encouraging. MDSers work at simple little human con-nections: acknowledging persons as well as their pains and dilemmas or connecting them with local services. This is parallel to cleaning up the mess, repairing the roof, nailing the siding, painting the interior. God calls some to clean up, some to build, some to talk and refer—and special ones to listen while they build!

MDS photo

Overcoming Fear

Joanne (not her real name) was in her home when the F-5 tornado devastated her house and other near-by houses. After the storm, she came out of her basement with a flashlight and couldn't find her living room, bedroom, or bathroom. Eventually she found one or two neighbors. They comforted each other as well as they could until rescue workers arrived.

Since the disaster was widespread and they were uninjured, they were left to care for each other until day-light. As the early morning sunlight revealed the scope of the disaster, she discovered the bodies of several neighbors lying in the street.

By midday, her daughter was allowed to take Joanne to her home for awhile. The ordeal of the storm, and especially of seeing the neigh-bors' bodies, was traumatic; Joanne didn't return home for days.

In following weeks, Joanne couldn't make decisions. She repeatedly cried. Sleep was interrupted by images of physical destruction and death.

With the help of her daughter and the staff of recovery agencies, she eventually filled out forms to qualify for Red Cross and FEMA funds. When those funds were pooled with her meager insurance money, Joanne had enough to buy materials for a modest new home, but not enough for labor. Her depression worsened.

Then Joanne learned that MDS volunteer labor would stretch her funds and make rebuilding possible. She responded with disbelief and more depression. Eventually the package of resources was put togeth-er. She attended groundbreaking for her new home and moved in when it was built.

Months later, an interviewer found a happy and healthy older adult, enjoying her surroundings. When asked how she recovered from trauma and depression, Joanne replied, "First, they built this home for me. But while they built it, I talked with the 'angels,' those volunteers that came week after week. Every week it was a new set of volunteers. But they all were angels, because they came and worked on my house and listened to me talk.

"Sometimes I know I interfered with their work, because I talked so much. We never met before, but they really cared and really listened. Each week the van brought a new load of angels to build my house. They lis-tened to my stories. I don't know when it happened, but one day I real-ized I was better."

When asked if her life was differ-ent than it was a year earlier, she replied, "Yes. Now I'm not afraid. I survived the storm and have seen the worst. I no longer live in fear."

With a chuckle she described a storm in the area two weeks before. Everyone else on her block went to the downtown storm shelter. "I just went to my basement. It was safe down there."

Joanne's granddaughter, living with her at the time, said that after the tornado, "Grandma is different now. She is more calm. She is not tense and nervous anymore."

Joanne added, "Now I go to church again, and it has meaning again, like it did a long time ago. I had lost that meaning, but the angels, the volunteers, helped me find my faith again."

Joanne survived the trauma of the tornado. After traumatization, disori-entation, and immobilization, she recovered and become healthier than before. She did this without profes-sional help, by engaging friends, neighbors, and volunteers in conver-sation.

—Paul Unruh

Steve Wiest

Dreams for the Future—to Benefit All

MDS welcomes more persons with listening/pastoral/mental health skills to join field teams in responding wholistically to those traumatized by disaster. Drawing on recent MDS experience, Tom Smucker and Carla Hunt of the MDS Akron staff, with Paul Unruh and Joe Steiner, trained mental health counselors, share their insights.

Paul: MDS has a long history and has fulfilled its tasks well. As the disaster and recovery process became more complicated, MDS adapted. When my father did MDS work in the early 1950s, there was a little announcement at church. Next day a bunch of folks showed up and did what was needed. Now there are many other actors on the disaster scene. Red Cross and FEMA are two major ones. Now it takes a lot more coordination. Dealing with more regulations is much more complicated these days.

Tom: In one disaster we were helping people decide whether to bulldoze their house. They were really uptight. We helped them discern what the money was for—housing or temporary repairs? We'd call FEMA and get answers for their questions. Next day they'd come back totally different, relaxed, knowing where they were. We hadn't pounded a nail yet, but what we knew or helped them learn really helped.

Carla: We need to do more advocacy. Some of our people come with those skills, and we want to use them. Women, like Pam Denlinger, often bring such gifts. Just getting out in the neighborhood and sharing, getting someone to talk on their

level—this is part of the healing process.

Paul: Over the years we've added different roles to MDS teams—project directors, construction foremen, persons with electrical or plumbing skills. Then we needed office workers with computer skills, and we developed a role for investigators. Now we're adding MDSers with special training in mental health or crisis intervention skills. These people can see how survivors are doing and, if necessary, give or obtain help.

Joe: Some people are specialists in rehabbing houses. We think of ourselves as specialists in helping people having an extra rough time. For example, someone told me about a family having a difficult time. When I talked with them, I learned that the husband had a heart attack three days before, his brother had died the day before, and the tornado had gone through about two weeks earlier. They were really struggling. I spent about an hour and a half with them. They thanked me profusely, then thanked other MDSers helping them sort through red tape to get money to rebuild.

Top left: Women wait outside their Hurricane Hugo-damaged home for help from someone—maybe you?

Bottom left: Ron Busker surveys damage to his family's things after the 1995 floods in Calif. Aid with physical recovery often helps to heal emotions and bring new hope.

Below: Joe Steiner and Paul Unruh survey widespread damage in the Del City, Okla., area after the May 1999 tornadoes. MDS workers with mental health skills help link MDS to people and organizations with special needs.

MDS photo

Paul: This is quite different from the traditional mental health setting. We seldom work in an office. It's more important to go where people are; that's where they like to talk about their struggle. We begin with work boots and jeans, just like other MDSers. It's important for the community to view us as MDSers. We want the regular work of MDS to be central and front stage; MDSers with mental skills are an addition.

Carla: In working with Paul and Joe, we make sure they come in first as MDSers. Then the mental health side fits under that umbrella. I've seen that happening. It's been a good experience.

Paul: One of my long-term beliefs about MDS is that the way we've done business has always contributed to the health and mental health of disaster survivors. That tangible vision of a person coming to restore what's broken on my house brings hope and is one of the most important aspects of recovery. We're interested in

bringing in a few MDSers with training to do a little more.

Tom: We want to expand this to invite pastors to an unusual adventure in ministry. With the MDS board's approval, we have a vision for developing a "Pastor of the Week" program. Pastors would also go to disaster sites as MDSers and work as needed but have two additional assignments. We'd like them to provide addition-

al spiritual ministries at long-term MDS locations, beyond what busy project leaders can do. This might include devotions and Bible studies as well as spiritual support for MDSers.

In addition, they would use skills of counseling and listening to help disaster victims. We think their special gifts of ministry and sharing of Christ's love will help bring healing to those experiencing grief and loss.

Send Your Pastor to an MDS Project Pastors and/or churches interested in learning more about the "Pastor of the Week" program should contact MDS Akron for more information.

Near right: MDS puts a priority on meeting the spiritual needs of MDS volunteers working in disaster settings and of those affected by the disaster. Pastors, bringing needed gifts, are encouraged to spend a week with their church members in MDS activity.

Far right: Children's lives are torn apart by disaster. They may be forgotten in the scramble for survival and recovery. Some groups like the Cooperative Childcare of the Church of the Brethren assist children after disasters. After Hurricane Andrew, a caring clown provides a lighter moment for a young girl in the Homestead, Fla., tent city.

MDS photo

Mike Hostetler

118

Our Testimony, . . . Listening to Awesome Stories

Pam and Dean Denlinger of Cincinnati, Ohio, are members of Cincinnati Mennonite Fellowship. Dean recently retired from law practice. Pam is a stay-at-home mom who has done much local volunteering. This made them available for service they had always wanted to do when a 1997 call came from MDS.

Dean: The Cincinnati floods of 1997 got us involved. We were immediately attending meetings, helping get the project located, and making a lot of contacts.

Pam: The first three MDS people we met were Randy Short, Paul Brubacher, and Dan Bontrager. They are masters of delegating work. Once they saw that Dean and I were interested, they didn't hesitate to bring us on board, even though this was our first time. That gave us a good opportunity to view MDS. Both of us were ready to do something major for the church. Would it be MDS or not?

Being part of this project from beginning to end taught us how much actual involvement with disaster victims there was, with no bureaucracy between them and us. We also saw that donated dollars were directed right to the victims, right to the relief. We wanted to be involved with this kind of organization.

Dean: During that time we received calls from about every type of Anabaptist there is, including Old Order Mennonites, Holdeman Mennonites, and Old German Baptists. It was gratifying to see just about every branch of Anabaptists engaged manually and spiritually.

[Dean then attended a project leader's workshop. Next the Denlingers were asked to lead the Gainesville, Georgia, tornado response project in March 1998.]

Pam: This was the first time we were at a disaster site so early. We had many meetings with survivors as we walked with them toward recovery. I'll always remember their awesome stories of the

Lord's protection and of life-changing experiences. Several survivors helped with MDS work. We learned that not every survivor is restored and that we need to make ongoing contacts even after we leave, especially if we were the first MDSers there and were privileged to walk with survivors through their emotional recovery.

Dean: Our involvement in MDS has provided a focus for everything we've been studying at church over the years. I feel this is such a plain duty, as taught by the New Testament. I sense that MDS is doing the right things—no question about it.

Pam: When we reread the Bible now, it's interesting to have a different perspective. Passages about love and brotherhood and recognizing my neighbor take on an entirely different meaning when we have gone beyond our comfortable neighborhood. We will never read those texts in the same way. We hope our MDS life is just beginning.

Far left: MDS office staff like Dean Denlinger provide a listening ear as people call or drop by to apply for assistance.

Near left: Bernetta Hunter and Pam Denlinger enjoy each other's company at the Oakridge, Ala., project in early 1999.

Carl Hiebert

Carl Hiebert

Photos by Carl Hiebert

CHAPTER TEN

Give of the Strength of Your Youth

Don't let anyone look down on you because you are young,

but set an example for the believers

in speech, in life, in love, in faith and in purity.

—*Paul, in 1 Timothy 4:12*

Give of your best to the master,

Give of the strength of your youth.

—*Howard B. Grose*

There is something in youth always looking for a challenge, for meaning, and for adventure. In MDS, they can find all three. Build a house—or a church. Listen to people who survived traumatic experiences—and know you are part of their recovery. Travel to California, Puerto Rico, the Deep South—and experience other cultures. This chapter is dedicated to each one who has served on a project leadership team hosting MDS youth groups, thus providing growth experiences for the next generation of MDS and church leaders.

I'll Take a Youth Group . . . Anytime

Dan Bontrager

I was a crew leader during the Hurricane Hugo project in South Carolina beginning December 1989. There I had my first experience with a youth group. It was a hot day, and we had a roof to put on. I showed them the project. I told them to wet the shingles with a hose so they wouldn't tear so easily.

When I got back two hours later, they had two water hoses. They were squirting water at each other. They had the roof all wet. I was upset, ready to pull my hair out. I sat in my truck to calm down and get my thoughts together: *Well, I guess the sheeting will dry, it's hot, and they're having a ball.*

Margie Hess

Above: Give us the strength and excitement of our youth. This almost all-woman crew (one guy in center) from the Pequea Brethren in Christ youth group celebrates putting on a roof in one day!

121

Photos, page 120: Youth . . . looking for a challenge, for meaning, for adventure! In MDS they find all three.

Right: Summers can be hot. A youth from Ontario finds a way to cool off in the Alabama heat.

Today, after working through that and many other experiences with youth, I'd take a youth group any day. I had Amish youth do plumbing under a house in South Carolina. I've taken youth and plumbed and wired the interior of a house. There are always youth who catch on to how to do something and lead the rest.

In Shepherdsville, Kentucky, I had two girls from a youth group do plumbing. The inspector came out, looked at it, and passed it. I told him two girls had done that. He looked at it again. "That's a better job than some of my craftsmen do."

So youth can do about anything. But you have to remember you're not paying them. You have to make it fun. And you'll get the job done. I'll take a youth group any day over someone who doesn't listen.

MDS Needs Youth

During summer 1999, MDS worked at long-term recovery programs in Puerto Rico (from Hurricane Georges); Birmingham (spring 1998 tornadoes), and Oklahoma and Kansas (April 1999 tornadoes). Youth groups from over 20 churches did most of the work at all four projects. According to MDS Akron personnel coordinator Carla Hunt, "It's difficult to get summer volunteers. When you have a summer like this with four or five major projects going, it would be hard to get the work done without the youth."

Youth have been a part of MDS since its beginning—even before it was MDS! Two young adult Sunday school classes had the vision for MDS in the first place. In the

A Tribute to Dan Bontrager

Dan with his wife, Pollyanna, spent 11 months in South Carolina after Hurricane Hugo. In the next five years, they spent over half their time in voluntary service, most of it with MDS. Pollyanna died in May 1996. In 1997 Dan returned to MDS project leadership till cancer claimed his life in June 1999. God took a faithful servant home.

In January 1999, at Gulfport, Mississippi, youth advisor Dave Weaver recognized Dan Bontrager for his work with their youth group in a 1991 Louisiana flood recovery project.

At first the kids were a little scared of Dan, Dave reported; they thought he was grumpy. But Dan took the kids under his wing. He took them with him grocery shopping. By the weekend, he was full of compliments for the nasty, grubby work they had done. In one house they had found a snake and live crawfish in the wall. Dan made a point of thanking everyone for hard work. From then on, Dan was a firm believer in the value of youth to MDS.

Dan Bontrager stands with Miss Lilly at her home repaired by MDS after the 1997 floods near Shepherdsville, Ky.

MDS photo

Carl Hiebert

first recorded official project of the emerging Mennonite Service Organization (Kansas, May 17, 1951), coordinator John Diller reports that among the second group of 35 persons sent to help with the Wichita flooding were "a number of students."

Day of Disaster reports that 42 students traveled to South Sioux City, Nebraska, in 1953 to help with flood cleanup. One said, "Many of us who volunteered had often longed for the privilege of doing specific voluntary service. We eagerly took advantage of the call given to us."

Youth also joined the 1972 flood response program in Rapid City, South Dakota. Of the 1,500 volunteers who registered, 50 percent were under age 25. On the basis of that experience, MDS Summer Youth Squads were organized in following summers and generated tremendous interest and response.

Traveling Youth Squads became more prevalent in the next decade (1975-85). A group of six to eight youth with a leadership couple would work together for six to 12 months, traveling from place to place,

responding to disaster activity.

Sandy (Weaver) Yoder was secretary in the MDS Akron office for 12 years, beginning in 1980. She joined a traveling youth squad for a three-month service break. "I felt like my years with MDS were an education all their own. It was my eye-opener to the larger Mennonite world . . . and beyond. I have good memories of experiences, of people we've helped, of places I traveled. Now I'm married to a pastor, and those MDS years are really valuable in understanding issues in the wider Mennonite setting."

MDS still depends heavily on long-termers, both youth and adults. These two-to-six-month volunteers become the backbone of project leadership teams. Youth often become crew leaders, gaining quick experience in a wide variety of skills and leadership responsibilities. Persons who serve long-term have most or all expenses paid and receive a monthly allowance. Interested persons may request further information and application forms from MDS Akron or their nearest MDS office.

> **Summer Youth Squads**
>
> **1973**
> 77 volunteers
>
> **1974**
> 59 volunteers
>
> **1975**
> 62 volunteers

Below left: Nelson Hostetter gives a 1975 youth squad orientation at Akron, Pa., before they head for project locations.

Below: Sandy (Weaver) Yoder worked in the MDS Akron office for 12 years and also served three months as part of an MDS youth squad.

MDS photo

MDS photo

123

A New Direction for MDS Youth Programs

Top right: After seven years of service weeks with MDS, the Laws youth group knows how to roof a house, as in Birmingham, Ala., in 1998.

In summer 1990, a new version of the youth program was launched at the South Carolina Hurricane Hugo project. A leadership couple and several long-term young adults provided on-site leadership for church youth groups who wanted to spend a week in service. Youth groups with adult advisers rotated in and out on a weekly basis. The program provided a meaningful service experience for hundreds of youth and a crucial volunteer resource for MDS.

Positive response from the 1990 summer participants and calls from groups like Oklahoma (sidebar) told MDS this was a program to continue. MDS returned to South Carolina in 1991 for another youth program, skipped 1992, went to Homestead (Fla.) for its 1993 program, and has continued each summer (chart).

Longing for the Privilege of Service

Youth groups who experience MDS summer service keep coming back for more! In addition to the Oklahoma group, others have become regulars. Youth from the Laws Conservative Mennonite Church at Greenwood, Delaware, and the Pequea Brethren in Christ Church near Lancaster, Pennsylvania, went to the 1993

Courtesy of Dan Yutzy

Ohio Lad Meets Oklahoma Cowgirl

In July 1984 I joined an MDS traveling youth squad at work in a flood project in Alabama. Shortly afterward a young woman from Hydro, Oklahoma, was added to the group.

Marilyn Shantz arrived wearing cowboy boots that were an interesting shade of blue. She seemed eager to get to a phone and call a male acquaintance back home. Later our group was transferred to South Carolina; the urge to call Oklahoma faded, and the boots gathered dust in the closet.

Marilyn was a tireless worker, fun to be around. Everyone admired her ability to sing. I was keen to be involved in whatever she was doing, and we became good friends.

After Christmas our group split up and Marilyn went to finish her studies at Goshen College. We kept in touch. After I finished my term with MDS, I moved to Goshen to find work. Soon after Marilyn graduated, we were married.

Now we have two wonderful little girls

Courtesy of Duane and Marilyn Yoder

and are working with MCC in Akron, Pennsylvania. I spent over a year in MDS. Even if I hadn't found a wife, I would look back on it as one of the best times of my life. I'll never forget what a great experience it was and what tremendous people I met.
—*Duane Yoder, formerly from West Liberty, Ohio*

An MDS family: Marilyn Shantz, Hydro, Okla., met Duane Yoder, West Liberty, Ohio, while serving with an MDS youth squad. Later, while in service with MCC at Akron, Pa., their family includes Hannah (left) and Julia.

Summer Youth Programs

Year	Place	Groups	Participants
1990	Charleston, S.C.	7	140
1991	James Island, S.C.	7	100 +
1993	Homestead, Fla.	11	227
	Franklin, La.	13	357
1994	Des Moines, Iowa	4	64
	Hannibal, Mo.	5	126
	Homestead, Fla.	1	29
	Jasper, Ga.	3	82
	Keithsburg, Ill.	1	45
	Americus, Ga.	1	33
1995	Whiton, Ala.	9	120
1996	Boligee, Ala.	9	240
	St. Thomas, U.S.V.I.	3	59
	Louisville, Ky.	1	45
1997	Yuba City, Calif.	5	94
	New Richmond, Ohio	2	50
	Shepherdsville/ Cane Valley, Ky.	5	125
1998	Warren, Minn.	3	75
	Birmingham, Ala.	4	90
	Gainesville, Ga.	6	123
	Waynesboro, Tenn.	5	79
1999	Puerto Rico	4	115
	Birmingham, Ala.	7	150
	Guthrie, Okla.	6	175
	Augusta, Kan.	5	110

MDS photo

Homestead project and have served in MDS every year since. Both groups held reunions to reminisce and record reflections, such as these:

Laws Youth Group

Service weeks: 1993 Homestead, Fla.; 1994 Hannibal, Mo.; 1995 Whiton, Ala.; 1996 Williamsport, Pa.; 1997 Shepherdsville, Ky.; 1998-99 Birmingham, Ala.

Daniel Yutzy, Coordinator: I remember preparing for the first trip and wondering how wise it actually was. As I look back, I've seen a lot of growth in these young people over the past six years. I've seen much spiritual growth and enthusiasm for God and working for people different from us. I see it as a cross-cultural experience that has helped our young people learn to know people from a different viewpoint.

Kathleen: It's really helpful to get out of our own community and see someone going through a different type of struggle than we've experienced at home. We can't really identify with people unless we go and begin to see what they've gone through. I think it gave me a heart of compassion.

Bethany: One of the biggest things I've learned through MDS trips is not to take the necessities of everyday life for granted and to realize that they're all God's gifts that tomorrow may be gone. Never let your love for other people go unspoken, because you never know when someone you love may be gone, or you could be gone.

April: We girls had a special time in Birmingham. On Monday night we had a time of revival among the girls. We were up till early in the morning, just worshiping together and drawing closer to God and to each other. The next day we were exhausted, but it was worth it.

Sara: The revival was partly because I had doubts about salvation, and I was confused. They encouraged me to make a

commitment again, and I did. It was just like "whew!" because I felt good. It was fantastic.

Joni: Our motto is "Work hard when you work and play hard when you play." All of my MDS trips have been learning experiences, and I would go back and do them all over again if I had a chance. I don't know where we're going this year, and I don't care. When those vans pull out, Lord willing, I'll be with them because Uncle Daniel has proved that work can be fun. I will always be grateful for the sacrifices he has made to make it possible for us to go.

Bottom left: Youth give up a precious week of summer and see joy in the faces of Charlene Beck and her children, Warren, Minn., as their MDS groups finish a house for the family after the Red River floods.

MDS Service, Oklahoma Style

For many years the Oklahoma MDS unit sponsored a service week. Youth from all over the state traveled by bus together to whatever project state leaders could line up. Sometimes this was an MDS project and at times other endeavors. Dean and Grace Schantz started this project in 1975. Dwight and Luella Unruh, who remained involved in this project for over 20 years, soon joined them. The Unruhs remember that youth could keep going as long as they were not married, so some went for seven years or more. It became "family" and bonded the Oklahoma church youth. As highlights, they recall hymn sings that led to many programs in other churches, the traditional talent-night program, couples who met on these trips and later married, and especially times when youth made decisions to follow Christ.

Luella and Dwight Unruh enjoy cake provided by the Oklahoma youth group in recognition of their 20 years of leadership in service projects with the youth squad.

Courtesy of Paula Schmidt

Pequea Brethren in Christ Youth Group

Service weeks: 1993 Homestead, Fla.; 1994 Americus, Ga.; 1995 Whiton, Ala.; 1996 Boligee, Ala.; 1997 Yuba City, Calif.; 1998 Waynesboro, Tenn.; 1999 Puerto Rico.

Dan Houck, Coordinator: From a pastor's and youth leader's perspective, the meaningful things happening on a trip relate to what's going on in the lives of the youths. They are stretched and grow and do things they earlier never thought they could do. That's part of the excitement. The youths go home feeling, *Well, I've really made a contribution here. I was part of something important. I helped somebody, and I built something.* It does wonders for them as individuals and for the group.

Marge: In California I was put on an all-girl roofing crew. It turned out great. The best part for me was using the talent I already have, just being friendly and caring. While everyone else was sweating up on the roof, I spent almost two hours with the lady whose house we were roofing, sitting under a tree just to be there for her. During the week I got really close to her. I didn't have to be good with a hammer and could use the gifts that God had already given me.

Ruth: We can get so caught up in our little world and then go off and see a bigger picture. God uses us to touch lives. One trip changed the course of my life. Never in a million years did I think I would be sitting here as a youth advisor. But here I am.

Brian: Each year when I go, it helps put life in perspective. Living here in Lancaster, it's prosperous and easy to say, "I need this; I want that." On a trip we see what people have lost and how happy they are with the little they have. That helps put things in perspective. We come home and realize we don't really need what we thought we did.

Marge: Sometimes it feels good just to be noticed. Last year I spent the whole week at one job site, helping put up a house for a young family. We got to respect them and they us. When we left, Terry, the father, came to the van and said, "I want you to know that you're the nicest people we have ever met." I just wanted to cry. He said other people offered help and brought their beer and bad language. "But you guys are different. You work as a team. There's no swearing, no yelling at each other." We don't go to be heroes; we go to help those in need. Then it gets turned around and we're the heroes, though we're only there to do our jobs.

Jay: I could go to the seashore for a week, spend lots of money, get sunburned, come home, and feel that I've accomplished nothing. But with MDS, I can go for a week to another area, get sunburned, and come home feeling physically tired but spiritually refreshed because I made a contribution to someone's life. That's a more meaningful vacation than any I could take elsewhere.

Top right: Laura Landis, a Central Christian High School student, puts finishing touches on a roof in P.R. during her January 1999 interterm service.

Israel Finds One More Use for Duct Tape

We were tearing off a metal roof. They had the ridge cap off, and I was sitting on the ridge. It didn't take me long to realize I had cut my pants clear around. We were out in the middle of nowhere. We couldn't think what to do to fix these sorry pants.

Someone had a roll of duct tape, so I took it, ran for the barn, and taped up my pants. I got too much on and could hardly walk. Kinda sticky, too.

Tap, Tap, What's That?

One year the girls were put on a house to tear it down. The roof was steep. We were told, "If you have time, you can tear the tin off the roof."

When Norma Jean was pulling off the ridge cap, we heard this "tap, tap, tap."

We asked, "What's wrong?"

She said, "Oh, I hit a hornet's nest, and as they come out, I'm nailing them!"

On the way home we had a praise service that no one had been hurt.

Right: Getting there is half the fun. One vanload of Pequea BIC youth packs for one of their seven summers in MDS service.

Dan Houck

126

MDS photo

Student Groups Are Welcome, Too

Many of our church high schools and colleges encourage students to participate in service experiences, including MDS. During vacations or for day-experiences when the disaster is close, serving with MDS becomes a meaningful part of an education.

Dennis Landis led Central Christian High School (Kidron, Ohio) students on a January 1999 service experience in Puerto Rico. He sent a thank-you letter to MDS Akron, which helped make arrangements: "I had a great bunch of students. We could have just done a choir tour with them. At first they were better singers than carpenters. At the end, they were still better singers than carpenters, but they did show great improvement in their nail-hammering skills. We sang at church Sunday, at the hospital, at the school, and on the job site. There's nothing like a bunch of blonde high school girls singing on a roof to attract attention.

"MDS provided an opportunity students will never forget. Students were introduced to an important part of the church's mission. I affirm MDS for recognizing that the cultural and relational aspects of this work are just as important as the physical work—maybe more."

In fall 1997, four Goshen (Ind.) College students gave up fall break to work at the MDS tornado project in College Station, Arkansas. They joined the MDS long-term team and a group of Amish men. Karla Hernadez, a student from Tegucigalpa, Honduras, wrote, "There was a big mix of people. We had an African-American family, the Amish men, and people from different states, Canada, Indonesia, and Honduras.

Courtesy of Dennis Landis

Harold Voth, MDS project leader, commented, "The students got the Amish interested in their families, homes, education, and how they decided to come to College Station. The Amish men got the students interested in singing."

Hernadez recalled a touching moment: "One night an African-American woman [from College Station] was talking about the tornado and losing her home and husband. The older Amish man beside her took her hand and said, 'I understand.' He had lost his wife in an accident. They were two very different people who found they had something in common. To me, seeing that is seeing God."[1]

Rhoda Lehman

Bottom left: While on MDS assignment in P.R. in January 1999, Central Christian High (Kidron, Ohio) students sing in the local school and repair roofs damaged by Hurricane Georges.

Left: No youth MDSer who served in summer 1995 at the Whiton, Ala., project will forget Euclid Rains, a blind man. Euclid and his wife, Nell, spent time with each youth group. His stories, interest in everyone, and amazing abilities challenged all who met him.

Send the Adults, Too

At Pequea Brethren in Christ Church, the youth work hard during the year to raise money for mission week. In 1997 they decided they would go to Yuba City (Calif.) and knew it would take a lot of money. They raised nearly $14,000, over their goal by $2,000.

Meanwhile, this excitement over service was rubbing off on the adults. A group decided to take a vacation week and work on the Detroit tornado project. The youth were so impressed by the adults' commitment, and so thankful for the way God had provided for their financial needs, that they voted to pay for the adults' transportation costs!

Generation X has received a lot of bad press. Here at Pequea, Generation X stands for Generation of Excellence. I'm proud of our teens. They're not only the church of tomorrow; these guys and gals are busy being the church today. —Pastor Dan Houck

We'd Like to Go; How Do We Go About It?

Where Do We Send Them?

Carla Hunt, MDS personnel coordinator, says that each year brings more queries from youth groups about the summer program, though it has never been advertised. In 1998, over 50 groups inquired about it and 18 served. What issues does the summer program face? Can it be expanded? Where can MDS find leadership teams?

First, Carla explains, any interested group must be willing to meet the guidelines for the summer youth program (below). Second, any group must be patient about scheduling and location of

Above: Carla Hunt

Below Right: Students from Rockway Collegiate in Kitchener, Ont., tackle cleanup in Ste. Adolphe, Man., after 1998 Red River flood.

MDS photo

their service week. MDS responds to the most recent and urgent needs but has no control over where and when disasters happen! Sometimes long-term planning is possible; other times groups may be asked to change at the last minute.

The MDS board recognizes the importance of the youth program and has given the summer program high priority. For Akron staff, the biggest challenge is finding project leadership teams. Each location, sometimes four or more, should have an on-site team of four to six long-termers to plan and run the program. This includes director, construction foreman, cook, office manager, and people to help with planning special spiritual, educational, and recreational activities for the youth. "It's not a lack of youth," Carla says, "but it's a struggle to have enough committed long-term adult leaders year after year. We're thankful for the special leaders we have who take time to work with the youth. We need more of them."

"Finally," Carla reflects, "I pray every year that it will be clear where we can send the groups. Each year we're on edge, wondering if this will all work out. I start getting calls before Christmas: 'Where will we be going this year?' I know it helps planning to know as early as possible, but groups need to be flexible. Those that can't may need to look for other kinds of projects. We wish disasters wouldn't happen, but they usually do. I've never had to cancel a group yet. Change locations? Lots of times!"

On the Home Front

In the local church, youth advisers may grow weary of the endless planning for MDS involvement. While less expensive than some short-term mission programs and/or conferences, it still takes many fundraisers to cover travel and other costs. Wilf and Margaret Unrau from Grunthal, Manitoba, arranged for their youth group to travel all the way to Whiton, Alabama, in 1995 for its first service experience.

MDS Summer Youth Program Guidelines

1. **Group size:** usually limited to 20-30, including adult sponsors.

2. **Adult-youth ratio:** one adult for every 3-4 youth, half the adults with construction skills.

3. **Age:** high school or older.

4. **Food/lodging:** provided while on site. Donations of food or finances welcome.

5. **Dress:** for work safety and modesty, as requested in brochure "Serving Together."

6. **Transportation:** group arranges and pays travel to and from location.

7. **Arrival/departure and schedule:** arrive Sunday evening or Monday morning; leave Friday evening or Saturday morning. One afternoon off for sightseeing, etc. Evenings for recreation, local culture, and Bible study. Further information, brochure, and medical information are available from MDS Akron.

Bruce Hildebrand

Carl Hiebert

Carl Hiebert

Virgil Kauffman

"We had a vision: let's take the kids. They had never gone any place before. A lot of kids signed up. A tour bus took us down, 30 hours on the road."

Wilf remembers trying to explain to parents, "'We want to take your kids on an MDS trip. We don't know where.' The actual location shifted three times. At monthly meetings we talked about the trip, issues we might face, behavior guidelines, and getting them psyched up for the trip. Even this preparation was team building.

"The week went well; the kids really enjoyed themselves. They got a different view of 'Who is my neighbor?' It bound the group together. I'm thrilled to have been able in a small way to touch their lives and get them thinking of others more than just me, myself, and I. I'm pleased three of the youth went out later in the long-term program.

"On our way home, the bus broke down. On a Sunday, we were left sitting in Chicago. When we were almost home, I said, 'I don't think I'll ever do this again.' I got tired. It was a lot of responsibility, quite stressful. I'm glad it was only a week. But I had to admit it was neat. To give the kids a big hug when they left because of the week we'd had, that meant a whole lot to me."

Wilf did help the group organize a trip the next year to Boligee, Alabama, but could not go himself because of Margaret's pregnancy.

Top left: On MDS projects, youth have learned new skills that may be useful in careers.

Middle left: Many hands make light work. A youth group spreads top-soil around the Mt. Zoar church in the blazing hot Ala. sun.

Bottom left: Simone Dalia of the St. Johns school youth group from Ont. paints a porch swing for a family at the Birmingham, Ala., project.

Called to Service

Courtesy of Stella Toews

Many youth like Stella Toews give MDS a boost in the office because they know computers.

In fall 1997 I felt God calling me beyond what I was doing in Steinbach. I needed to leave my comfort zone. I was interested in volunteer work, so I contacted MCC. They sent me a package with various options.

I had heard of MDS when Wilf Unrau organized our youth groups to go to Alabama in 1994-95. Four siblings had gone and had positive experiences. I wrote to Carla at MDS Akron for information, applied, and after a long wait was accepted.

Two weeks before I was scheduled to leave for MDS service, I was told I would be going to Sanford, Florida. Six months in Florida! I could hardly believe it. I applied for office work but soon found out that MDS volunteers do many other jobs in addition to what they were "hired" to do. I didn't know there were so many kinds of wood and nails! Cooking for 30 people by myself was also a life-changing experience. Thank goodness, I came from a family of 11.

It did not matter what the task, God would always give me the strength to do it, and not just the physical strength. The support and encouragement from the group helped me through many days.

Our project director, Virgil Kauffman, would often say that MDS is not just to help the storm victim, but also for the volunteers. I have never experienced God working in my life like that before, nor have I ever matured or grown as much spiritually. After I returned home, I was baptized in May of 1999 and four of my new MDS friends came to Steinbach to add to the celebration.

I am very thankful for the friends I have made and the opportunity to serve God and others. I'm looking forward to doing it again. —*Stella Toews*

MDS, Mennonite Dating Service

These photo stories illustrate a few of the couples who met while working with MDS. Thousands of youth came together over the years. God's Spirit and personal chemistry led some to make lifelong commitments to each other. "Bless'd be the tie that binds our hearts in Christian love!" (John Fawcett).

Courtesy of John Miller

Love blooms in Calif., too. Daniel Epp from Aldergrove, B.C., and Cindy Miller from Reedley, Calif., met while working on the earthquake project in Coalinga, Calif. They now live in Aldergrove.

Courtesy of Ted and Elinor Shattuck

Elinor Miller became administrative assistant in the MDS Akron office in 1992. She learned to know Ted Shattuck, an MDS project director in Homestead, Fla. After their marriage, they served together in Homestead in the Nehemiah program.

Tied by Hugo, Tested by Andrew

What made me think of service was growing up with a VS unit here at our church. That's how my mom and dad (Kathleen and David) came to Homestead. That really affected my life as I grew up, so I wanted to serve in some way. My grandfather (Wellington Moyer) was MDS coordinator in North Carolina, so I heard about Hurricane Hugo and arrived in Moncks Corner in September 1990. Two weeks after I got there, this young woman from Pennsylvania showed up.
—*Doug Hartzler, Homestead, Fla.*

I arrived in Moncks Corner on September 24. I saw Doug and thought "This is a guy I'm going to have to watch out for." At first he seemed arrogant to me. He had this southern laid-back style. Watching out for him lasted about a day, then I watched for him. We dated. The older MDS leaders kept an eye on us, and they moved him to James Island for a while.
—*Rhonda Halteman, Shippensburg, Pa.*

Doug and Rhonda both served six months in South Carolina. When the project closed in spring 1991, they returned to Homestead and Shippensburg respectively, for a little while. They were engaged in September 1991 and married in April 1992.

They bought a house, fixed it up, and settled in Homestead. Five months later, Hurricane Andrew roared through. Their house suffered less damage than many, likely because they had just put on a new roof. Their home was one of the few with a working phone that MDS leaders used extensively.

Rhonda reflects, "It's ironic how hurricanes have shaped our lives. Via Hurricane Hugo, I met my spouse. Then Hurricane Andrew changed our lives forever. We should have named our first boy Hugo or Andrew."

"For me," Doug recalls, "each event was a spiritual high point of my life. Especially with Hugo, I was coming back into the church. Working side by side with Christians every day was a significant part of my spiritual growth. When MDS came [to Homestead] and set up at the church, we had meals together. We gathered as a church, an extended church. We felt the community, being part of the body of Christ.

Doug and Rhonda agree, "We want to go back into MDS someday, when the kids are older.

What we've experienced we definitely want to pass on to them, the value of being able to give what we have."

An MDS couple found each other serving in MDS after Hurricane Hugo in S.C., then moved to Homestead, Fla., and coped with Hurricane Andrew! Doug and Rhonda Hartzler with sons Cole and Ben, in front of their home.

MDS photo

Canadian Relief Worker Arrested

A man who apparently thought he bought a souvenir at an Alabama war memorial was arrested Sunday when he tried to board an airplane here with a hand grenade. Greg Toews, a Canadian doing hurricane relief work in south Louisiana, seem baffled when he was arrested. Toews, of Steinbach, Manitoba, said the grenade in his outgoing airplane luggage was a souvenir, and the story, at first glance, appeared to be true. 'He doesn't seem to be a serious threat,' said Assistant U.S. Attorney General Gerald Bertinot."
—The Advocate, *Baton Rouge, La., April 5, 1993*

Greg: I had just completed my MDS assignment working at the Hurricane Andrew project location in Franklin, Louisiana. On April 2, three long-term volunteers had graciously provided company for me in going to the U.S.S. Alabama battleship memorial in Mobile, Alabama. I always had an avid interest in military history, and it had been a dream of mine to see the U.S.S. Alabama. At the souvenir shop, I bought a replica World War II hand grenade, quite realistic in appearance.

I was scheduled to fly home early on the morning of April 4. The ride to the airport was a time of mixed emotions: I was sad about leaving close friends at Franklin. I realize these feelings don't justify sloppy and haphazard packing of my duffel bag, but it's a convenient excuse. An alarm clock with a cord lying near a grenade does appear as a battery-powered explosive device on a security monitor screen—trust me, they showed it to me. Strangely enough, the security guards were not satisfied with my explanation.

Two policemen appeared in seconds. "What's your name? What is that device? Do you think you can get away with this?"

They had me standing against the wall in a jiffy, hands up. I was placed under arrest, complete with reading me my rights. Suddenly the gravity of my situation struck me. I was in the custody of a hostile police force in a foreign country, having unknowingly committed an act of terrorism. I was separated from Janice Enns, the MDS volunteer who had brought me to the airport.

Soon the FBI, which assumes jurisdiction of offenses at U.S. airports, took over the case, again reading me my rights and asking questions. They had contacted Canadian authorities and MDS in Franklin to verify my story. I was surprised at how many of the questions revolved around MDS, Mennonites, religion, and pacifism. I could see how my collecting of "military toys" could appear as a discrepancy to the FBI.

I spent most of the afternoon waiting for the police, FBI, and district attorney to determine my fate. At first optimistic about being released, my hopes evaporated as I was transferred to the Lafayette Correctional Center.

I was allowed one phone call, which I used to call my parents at home. I was handcuffed, photographed, fingerprinted, dressed in prison clothes, and taken to a jail cell. Words can't adequately express my feelings. I wasn't really afraid for my safety, but I had a feeling of profound loneliness and isolation.

After two or three hours in the cell, a guard told me to grab my stuff, follow him, and get into my street clothes. I was soon at the front door, signing papers, free to go!

I called the attorney general, who said that when the judge saw the "grenade," she said to let me out. No charges would be filed; I would have no criminal record. Amazing as it was to me, I was a free man!

The reunion back in Franklin with my friends was filled with laughter, tears, and hugs, just what I needed on being released from jail. Two days later with a replaced ticket, I headed home. The trip was uneventful, but not till I passed through Canadian customs did I stop looking over my shoulder.

Since then I've heard nothing about the incident and have flown through the U.S. many times. The only "problem" is my family and friends, who are still laughing and reminding me, "Don't carry any bombs on the plane."

Carl Hiebert

Steve Gossen, St. Catharines, Ont., takes a short break to play his "guitar" on the project at College Station, Ark.

Carl Hiebert

Above: Break time during the Birmingham Project.

Right: Two from the Pequea BIC youth group add an artistic touch to lighten the spackling task.

Go Borrow a Dolly

Our youth group was gutting a house, clearing out everything—stoves, refrigerators, whatever. Up and down the street, other MDS groups were doing the same. We needed a dolly to move a stove out. We asked Dennis to go to one of the houses where MDSers were working and see if he could borrow a dolly. We thought he knew what a dolly was.

He came back shortly and handed Dave a dollar, saying, "Here's your dollar."

We asked, "What's that for?"

He said, "I don't know. You said go get a dollar, so I did."

We said, "No, we want a dolly."

Then we tried to figure out how he got a dollar. He had gone a couple of houses down to where some Beachy Amish were working and asked one of the guys for a dollar.

They asked, "What do you need that for?"

He said, "I don't know; they told me to get a dollar."

They had no idea why he needed it, but they gave him a dollar anyway; we were impressed! He later exchanged the dollar for a dolly . . . and a good laugh.
—*Dave and Sue Weaver, youth advisors, Gulfhaven Mennonite Church, Gulfport, Mississippi; Franklin, Louisiana, Hurricane Andrew project*

Debra, Lili, and Jenn's Bad Hair Day

In Shepherdsville, Kentucky, three of us girls were told to paint a barn and shed. They said this was water-based paint, so it would wash off.

Lili and I looked at each other and said, "Let's get Jenn."

With paint all over us, we gave her a big hug and patted her head. Then she retaliated. So we were all painted up—and the homeowner came home. He had been having doubts about letting the youths onto his farm, and we were thinking, *Oh, no!*

He put his arm around his wife as they were looking at our work and said, "Didn't I tell you they would do a good job?" We almost died.

The next day we were determined to do the best job we could. We were good, not getting paint on anything. He brought us one can of oil-based paint instead of water-based. We mixed them together and got something that looked like cottage cheese. We were ready to cry and told him, "We're sorry. It's ruined. We didn't mean to."

He said, "That's all right. Take the farm truck and gather up debris in the field."

So we went to pick up boards and stuff they had put on piles. The truck had a bad brake and accelerator problem. They didn't work together. So we ran the truck into a telephone pole. We only got one light bent out of shape, but we were ready to cry again.

When his wife came home, we said, "Look what we did to the truck."

She just laughed at us. Yet Jenn remembers this as her worst day ever on an MDS project.
—*Laws youth group, Greenwood, Del.*

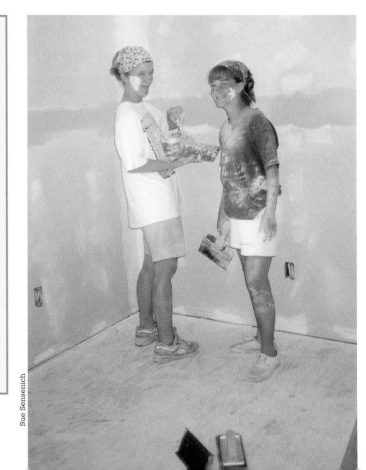
Sue Sensenich

MDS photo

Youth Are the Future of MDS

For Marisa, the Future Is Now

On May 13, 1999, Marisa Doncevic held a microphone toward Bill Mast in Mulhall, Oklahoma, as the video camera hummed. Videographer Jim Bowman and Marisa were in the middle of a sea of devastation caused by the May 3 tornadoes that ravaged Oklahoma and Kansas, killing 43 people. They were on their first videotaping trip to produce a new video about MDS for its 50th anniversary in 2000.

How did this energetic young woman find herself in the middle of MDS history? According to Marisa, "My first experience with MDS was in 1993, the summer before my senior year in high school. I was sixteen, and my sister and I were invited to go to the MDS project in Homestead, Florida, with a friend's youth group.

"That was my first experience doing that type of service, and it was great. I put up drywall and shingled a roof. I had never done that before. As a youth, it made me feel good to know the project directors trusted that I, as well as the other youth, could do that work. They didn't give us easy work just because we were young. They had confidence in us.

"Two summers later my sister and I organized a trip for our church, Springfield Mennonite, to the MDS flood project in Albany, Georgia. Then two years later we served again with MDS, in Cane Valley, Kentucky. The two trips really bonded us. I had attended Springfield all my life and

knew the people, but the MDS trips took us outside the church scene and united us in a different setting. Young and old were working together, encouraging, helping, laughing.

"It really bonded our whole church, even those who didn't go. After our week of service, we'd come back, do our Sunday morning presentation, and show pictures of the week. That brought excitement to our church, especially older people who couldn't go but were able to experience it through our stories. The kids too young to go now look forward to when they can go.

"Looking back, it's neat to see how God drew me into MDS. It was a last-minute decision to go to Homestead. Now I'm at the center of it all. In the summer of 1997, I started a student internship with MCC; my desk was right next to the MDS office. During that time, I did some writing for MDS. Later that year, I was asked to consider the job soon to open in the MDS office. I graduated from college and started working with MDS a week later. That small taste of service the Lord gave me as a youth was so powerful I couldn't imagine not doing it again. It was a spark that is now flaming."

Growing New Volunteers

It's not just the fact that the youth are the church of tomorrow, but that there is a lot of growing happening. They see different parts of the world. Not everything is like Lancaster County, Ohio, Indiana, or Manitoba.

We saw a lot of growing, spiritually and emotionally. I don't think there is a job youth won't try. We need to keep new volunteers coming. The youth program is one of the best ways to do that. —Virgil Kauffman, project director

Top left: Bill Mast, Okla. MDS unit chair, and Marisa Doncevic survey the damage caused by the May 1999 tornadoes near Del City, Okla.

Bottom left: Marisa Doncevic (right) with two of her youth group friends, on her first MDS project in Homestead, Fla., in August 1993. After other MDS experiences, Marisa graduated from university and used her major to became the communications coordinator for MDS staff at the Akron headquarters.

Courtesy of Marisa Doncevic

133

Carl Hiebert

Right: Youth throw wood on a burn pile at Birmingham.

J. D. Kuepfer

Right: Jane Kuepfer dreams of the good things that happen when youth get involved in MDS. She and her husband, J. D., served as youth program coordinators on the church rebuilding project in Boligee, Ala. Jane was then elected to the MDS board to represent youth in MDS.

In the complicated world in which today's youth are maturing, MDS is doing something that needs to be done and is right. Through MDS young people can respond to Christ's call to do something positive and constructive with their lives and to help build God's kingdom in this fragile and fallen world. There is a sense of being part of a miracle, . . . and it's fun. —Jane Kuepfer, MDS board member

What Did You Do to My Son?

On our return home, we rented a gym to show slides and tell our stories. A lot of people had generously contributed to our trip, and we wanted to thank them.

We were surprised how many people came out. Russell's mom said, "What have you done to Russell?"

I said, "I don't know. Why?"

She replied, "He came into the kitchen last night and did dishes without saying a thing. I'm thinking, 'That's not the Russell I know.'"

Steve's dad came to me and said, "I have to shake your hand. You've done an incredible job with Steven; he's a new guy."

I think that is a result of people whose lives touched him, and people's lives he was able to touch in the week we were gone. It's amazing—the last day we were in Whiton, he got real moody because he didn't want to go home! —Wilf Unrau

Your Young Men Shall See Visions

Once Nathan Koslowsky predicted, "I'm going to be the youngest MDS project director." In summer 1999, at the age of 24, he may have realized that dream as he and his wife, Danielle, began serving as leaders in the Kansas flood-tornado recovery project. MDS has often given young persons a chance to prove themselves. For Nathan, that may be twice true.

Nathan's roots lie deep in the Mennonite church and service tradition. Yet like many young adults, after high school he wandered through some deep valleys. Nathan reflects, "I worked at several jobs, trying to get money to live the good life, and during that time I met Danielle.

"Once while working as a roofer, I fell off a ladder and landed on concrete steps. I thought I was paralyzed and prayed to God for mercy, to let me walk again. I didn't have a bruise, a definite miracle from God. But my lifestyle didn't change. I moved around, then back with my parents. I tried school, but that just didn't cut it.

"Philosophy class did get me thinking about God. I had an urge to go into the wilderness, but my parents and Danielle begged me to reconsider. My parents spoke about MDS; I can look back now and see this as God's calling.

"So, here is MDS, a chance to get away and do something. I wasn't as sincere as I needed to be. I had deep questions about God and what his purpose was for me and other Christians. I didn't care where I was going. I was sent to Yuba City, California.

"While I served in California, Danielle stayed in Winnipeg and attended school. With many prayers from my family and church, both Danielle and I came to realize our need for God. I started rediscovering what my parents had taught me all along. I'm thankful for that upbringing. MDS gave me the opportunity to leave all behind, step out in faith, and let God work through me.

"I remember my first impressions of MDS. I felt like I was at a permanent family reunion—and there was no one my age. I was young enough to be everyone's grandson. That was tough. I wanted to be treated like an adult—yet I was a grandson. But I was also taken in and loved unconditionally.

"Summer came around. We had these youth groups coming in. I think God was showing me some of the gifts he had given me. I felt comfortable with the kids; I could relate to them more. My sense of self-worth just skyrocketed when I had a group of kids and got to teach them something. This leveled the playing field and opened up communication on various topics. The dinner conversation was a highlight, just the love that was shown.

"We went to different churches, but for some reason the Salvation Army church clicked. It was totally different from the one where I grew up, but I felt welcomed and comfortable. Then I became involved in their youth program. After my MDS term was over, I was invited to come and work here as their youth minister."

Back home, Danielle was traveling much the same route Nathan had earlier. She was studying, reading and questioning, "Who is God? What's the point in all this?" Separated from Nathan, she learned to rely on God and had an opportunity to use her God-given abilities and grow as a leader. According to Nathan, "It was really cool how God worked things out." They agreed to get married and return to Yuba City, where Nathan began as youth minister for the Salvation Army. Nathan says, "MDS was a tremendous experience that changed my life forever."

Danielle and Nathan Koslowsky in front of the MDS headquarters in Augusta, Kan., where they led the MDS summer service program.

In spring 1999 Nathan and Danielle responded to the call from MDS. They agreed to lead the summer youth program in Augusta, Kansas. After a brief and intense orientation, they welcomed their first youth group the week of June 29. Danielle wrote, "This week was a wonderful experience. Our first youth group was independent, skilled, and workaholics. The volunteers were pleased with the opportunity to meet with the clients and see how joyful they were even in times of loss. Everyone was touched in some way. Most received hugs."

She commented that they were still waiting for local organizations to list more work for the next week: "We're confident that the good Lord will provide as needed."

As the Teacher says, "Remember your Creator in the days of your youth." —Ecclesiastes 12:1

CHAPTER ELEVEN

New Paradigms:
A Changing World

Serenity Prayer

God grant me the

*Serenity to accept the
things I cannot change,*

*Courage to change the
things I can, and*

*Wisdom to know the
difference.*

Reinhold Niebuhr

When I wrote this chapter in summer 1999, my dad, Oren Detweiler of Fairview, Michigan, was approaching age 102. The first author in our family, he wrote a book about his family homesteading in Michigan when he was nine years old. Last summer we reminisced about changes he has seen during his lifetime. If he had lived four more months, he would have lived in three centuries.

He said that when they moved to Michigan in the early 1900s, one had to ride many miles by horseback to reach a telegraph station and send messages to family in Ohio. I took the laptop computer, had him peck out a short note, and sent it by e-mail to his children, grandchildren, and great-grandchildren. In hours we had responses from several states and provinces. This chapter is dedicated to Pop, who lived with change, embraced it, and passed on to many of us his spirit of adventure and commitment to serving others.

A Changing World

This book is written to record 50 years of Mennonite Disaster Service activity. In God s time, 50 years is but a tick of the clock. Yet changes that have happened since MDS was born in 1950 make the present world hardly recognizable from a 1950s vantage point. In 1995 at the MDS All-Unit Meeting in Saskatoon, Saskatchewan, Edgar Stoesz, longtime MCC/church leader, gave the keynote address. Excerpts follow:

The Changing and the Eternal

We live in a time of rapid change. No generation has been called on to process so much change in the course of one lifetime. The world in which we live hardly resembles the world into which we were born. The education we received is only remotely relevant to what is expected of us now.

Photo, page 136:
What lies ahead?
How do we keep up
with all the
changes? Is there
really global warm-
ing? Are disasters
on the increase?
What does this
mean for MDS? This
photo is from
Nicaragua.

Most of us were here before—

TV	ballpoint pens	credit cards
penicillin	photocopiers	McDonalds
VCRs	space flights	e-mail

We thought grass was what cows graze on. We thought hardware was hammers and chisels. We thought bunnies were small rabbits. We thought gay meant to be happy. Oh, did we turn our eyes when we learned the new meaning! As the Pennsylvania Dutchman said, "*Ei-yi-yi-yi-yi.*"

"Change," says Alvin Toffler in his book *Future Shock*, "is avalanching on our heads. It cascades on us with such force we hardly feel life any more. We are numbed by it." We would like to return to the world we grew up in, only to discover it no longer exists, and we experience "future shock."

Yet here we are. We have survived. On good days we even feel optimistic about the future. "But surely," we mumble to ourselves, "now things will level off, and we can invite our grandchildren to help us catch up by teaching us how to use this new technology." No, to the contrary! We are on the threshold of unimaginable sci-entific change, driven by what some are calling artificial intelligence. Change won't wait for us to catch up.

Much of this change is associated with the computer. Some people wear more comput-ing power around their wrists than existed in the whole world before 1950. We live in the Information Age, having passed through

A whole new picture defining how we think about disaster response has burst on us. Those who see it will be players. Those who don't won't know what happened.

the Agricultural Age and the Industrial Age. The TV and now the computer are swamp-ing us with information. One issue of *The New York Times* contains more informa-tion than was available to the average per-son in a seventeenth-century lifetime.

Demographics are also changing our world. In our lifetime the world's popula-tion has increased from two billion to six billion. By 2050 it is expected to reach 10 billion. That has staggering, mind-boggling implications for the human race. What will people eat? How will that many find shel-ter? How do we relate to this from a Christian perspective? —*Edgar Stoesz*

The Changing Disaster World

Disaster agencies are more affected by these changes than most organizations. Places with the fastest population growth are often areas at high risk of disaster, such as California and Florida. In the information age, disasters are instant media events. Often reporters are in the middle of a storm, broadcasting live so we can see what's hap-pening. Even a "small" disaster may make the evening TV news or the morning paper.

When Hurricane Andrew hit south Florida and then Louisiana in August 1992, the disaster world changed forever. Andrew caused unprecedented damage and triggered an unprecedented response. Over 200 disaster agencies, many founded spon-taneously to join the action, descended on south Florida. Media appeals inundated emergency responders with acres of used clothing and other supplies, often left in the open to broil under the sun or be drenched by the next downpour.

During the long-term Hurricane

Andrew response, members of the National Voluntary Organizations Active in Disaster (NVOAD) gathered to reflect on and evaluate our efforts. Monte Sahlin, at that time national executive director of Adventist Community Services, gave an inspiring address, "Paradigm Shift." With his permission, excerpts follow.

Paradigm Shifts

Sahlin begins by defining "paradigm shift" as follows: A non-evolutionary change. A change that involves a leap. There may be no logical continuity between where we were and where we are. He illustrates the need for vision during times of change with the following story:

In the 1940s the Santa Fe Railroad was offered the purchase of a little fledgling company called Trans World Airlines (TWA). They could buy the whole thing for a pittance. The board of directors said, "We don't know if this new technology is going to pay off. It's just a fad. We're in the railroad business."

Santa Fe went bankrupt. TWA made millions and became an industry leader. What if the board had said, "We're in the transportation business. How can trans-portation best be provided?"

Sahlin identified several things that hap-pened following Hurricane Andrew that have led to significant changes for disaster agencies. First, one-and-a-half million peo-ple were evacuated. The Civil War was the last event to make that many people homeless in the United States.

Second, there was a great change in the role of the military. They helped to make

Virgil Kauffman

order out of chaos, organize food distribution, and build an emergency tent city. In any major disaster, they will be permanent players; relief organizations need to learn how to work with them.

Third, information systems were woven into the disaster response more than ever before. A daily Red Cross fax updated interagency information. Many agencies used 800 numbers to provide information and gather support.

Sahlin described four major paradigm shifts affecting volunteer agencies:

• A change from pyramid organizational structures to flat network organizations interconnected by the need to know and the ability to contribute information.

• Information as the primary source of value instead of wealth and power.

• A shift from nationally based organizations to local participatory organizations. People want to participate on a personal level. They don't trust large organizations and don't want to be put in some bureaucratic system.

• A movement from specialized, particular knowledge or skill to a broad cross-disciplinary focus. It is less important to know how to do mass feeding (or construction) than to understand how chaotic systems reassert themselves toward order.

Sahlin concludes, "I may be wrong, but I have a distinct feeling that disaster relief will never be the same after Andrew. Partly because Andrew connected with a lot of pieces that were already out there, sprouting in the shadows. Partly because disaster relief has been ripe for a paradigm shift. A whole new picture defining how we think about disaster response has burst on us. Those who see it will be players. Those who don't won't know what happened."

More Disasters: Global Warming?

In January 1996 a massive blizzard marched up the Eastern Seaboard, muffled the hills of Virginia, covered cars, and shut down Washington, Philadelphia, New York, and Boston. Firefighters used metal detectors to locate hydrants. Tempers rose, roofs collapsed, schools closed, shovels sold out, and commuter trains stopped. With the storm well predicted, stores in the nation's capital sold out of bread, milk, and toilet paper. For once, hoarding paid off. Six days after the storm, parts of Washington were still unplowed.

Days later, temperatures rose sharply. Heavy rain fell on melting snow, causing severe floods in several states. The toll from the blizzard and flooding over the affected area claimed 187 lives and cost over $3 billion in damages.

The January 22, 1996, *Newsweek* cover reads "The Hot Zone—Blizzards, Floods, & Hurricanes: Blame Global Warming." Using the January blizzard as background, *Newsweek* had a story and pictorial map on weather extremes and a possible cause—global warming. It quotes James E. Hansen, director of NASA's Goddard Institute for Space Studies: "As you get global warming, you should see an increase in the extremes of the weather cycles—droughts and floods and heavy precipitation."

Statistics show we are facing more disasters that are affecting more people. Some blame global warming—and want us to consider our responsibility for it. Others point to the scriptural possibility that we are nearing the end times as described in Revelation. Others note that there have always been variations in weather patterns over the years and suggest we are simply in a high frequency cycle. A table showing three decades (1960-89) of recorded annual disaster events in the world, prepared by the Swedish Red Cross, shows an increase in number of events each decade for each type of disaster—floods, storms, earthquakes, and droughts. When the turbulent 1990s are added to that graph, the lines will surely go off the paper!

In 1995 alone, says the *Newsweek* article, the U.S. had 1,011 tornadoes, the second most active season recorded. July brought a record heat wave, killing over 800 people. Then came a hurricane season with 19 named storms, second only to the record 21 in 1933. California had floods; Mexico, the coldest weather in 25 years; Siberia, a five-degree increase in average temperature. Extremes abounded.

Left: Population is rapidly increasing in disaster-prone areas. During the 1990s, the U.S. has endured five disasters with the greatest property damage ever. MDSers have to cope with many regulations when rebuilding in places like Detroit (tornado in 1997) or south Fla. after Hurricane Andrew.

139

Change Around Us

MDS is not facing these forces of change alone. Other disaster agencies have felt the pressure of unprecedented disaster activity and have made organizational changes to respond adequately, struggling to find resources needed to make the changes.

NVOAD became the forum for discussion and ferment during the 1990s. After Hurricane Camille in 1969, various disaster agencies agreed that cooperation would be easier if we had an organization linking major disaster responders. In 1970 NVOAD was founded. MDS, the American Red Cross, and five other organizations were charter members. NVOAD's goal was to improve communication and cooperation for the benefit of disaster victims.

By 1999 this organization included over 30 disaster organizations. It remains mainly a forum for discussion and coordination of agenda of mutual interest. Recently a widespread movement has created VOADs (Voluntary Organizations Active in Disaster) at the state level. As of 1999, there were 49 state VOADs. These organizations are defined by the "Three Cs":

• Communication: disseminating information through electronic mechanisms, newsletters, an organizational directory, research and demonstration, case studies, and critique.

• Cooperation: creating a climate for cooperation at all levels (including grass-roots) and providing information.

• Coordination: coordinating policy among member organizations and serving as a liaison, advocate, and national voice.

In the changing post-Hurricane Andrew disaster world, NVOAD was a forum for discussing two issues that demanded debate and action by national agencies. Agencies gave major attention to managing donated goods and services and sharing client information while respecting privacy laws. Cooperative efforts between NVOAD and the Federal Emergency Management Agency (FEMA) brought new directions for working at these ongoing problems.

Elizabeth Dole, president of the American Red Cross, expressed the spirit of these cooperative efforts well in 1992 at the NVOAD annual meeting: "Given the pressures our organizations face, it is absolutely essential that we renounce turf issues and devote ourselves to working closer and more efficiently. Meetings such as this one are vitally important to keeping the lines of communication open, and in developing a better understanding of each other's capabilities. Maximizing our resources by avoiding duplication will ensure that those we serve receive the highest quality, most effective, and most efficient services."

During those years of organizational change, MDS renewed its formal agreement with the American Red Cross (ARC) and wrote new partnership agreements with the Salvation Army and FEMA. MDS continues to work with ARC at many locations and often works at long-term recovery programs with the Salvation Army. Stronger government involvement in overall disaster recovery activity, including special partnership

Vernon Miller

Above: Responding to disasters requires understanding and cooperating with many other agencies. This sign on a home built by MDS in Ark. illustrates the multiple partners needed to complete the project.

This house was built through the love of Jesus Christ and
The Mennonite Disaster Service
United Way of Arkansas
Federal Emergency Management Agency
U.S. Corps of Engineers
Red Cross
National Guard of Arkansas
A project of Watershed, Inc.

Right: MDS has been a part of National Voluntary Organizations Active in Disaster (NVOAD) since its formation in 1970. This 1998 board photo shows (from left, in back) John Gavin, Adventist Community Services; Bill Dell, Points of Light Foundation; Chris Rebstock, America's Second Harvest; Jerry Collins, American Red Cross; Micky Caison, Southern Baptist Disaster Services; Major David Dalberg, The Salvation Army; (in front) Lowell Detweiler, Mennonite Disaster Service, president; Rino Aldregheti, executive secretary; Jane Gallegher, Catholic Charities, treasurer; Rich Augsburger, Church World Service; and Mark Publow, World Vision, vice president.

NVOAD Information

NVOAD offers an excellent website that provides information on its own activities. It also provides links to all of its member organizations. Find NVOAD at www.nvoad.org.

Courtesy of FEMA

programs in several Caribbean island projects, has suggested the need for new models and agreements for working with FEMA.

Monte Sahlin reflects, "The volunteer agencies, MDS, and all the NVOAD members represent something unique and good about America. Beyond the fact that they mobilize millions of dollars worth of aid (cash, in-kind donations, and donated time and services), they provide a key role in bringing emotional and spiritual healing to families and communities that can never be duplicated by government services.

"I have the utmost respect for the MDS volunteers I have seen working at hundreds of disaster sites over the years. MDS is to be commended for being willing to work under the most difficult circumstances—and always seeking to serve the poorest, the most marginalized and forgotten."

MDS photo

Change Within

In 1971 Nelson Hostetter became the first full-time executive coordinator of MDS. From 1971 till 1993, MDS had fewer than two full-time staff and was considered a section (department) of MCC. Since beginning under the MCC umbrella in 1955, it had always had its own board, also called "the MDS Section." On several occasions during these years, the question of "who's in charge" (MCC or the MDS Section) needed to be clarified. Staff were considered MCC employees, and the budget needed approval of MCC (in later years, MCC U.S.). However, the MDS supporting constituency usually designated enough direct funding for MDS to meet its budget.

Separation from MCC

In 1991 MCC obtained a legal audit for itself and all related agencies. Among other actions, this audit committee recommended legal separation of MDS from MCC. The most significant reason was the necessity to create a legal shield between MCC and MDS. Legal experts considered MDS activity to be at high risk of legal action,

MDS photo

though no lawsuit had ever been filed against MDS. Since MDS had its own board with basic responsibility for the MDS program, there would be more clarity and less legal and financial risk if MDS became separately incorporated.

MCC Executive Committee and the MDS Section approved that recommendation. In February 1993 MDS became a separately incorporated nonprofit organization. The MDS Section became the board, separate bank accounts and tax-exempt numbers were obtained, and staff became MDS employees. By written contract, MDS still obtained many services from MCC, including rented office space and mail, financial, and computer services.

The separation from MCC brought both planned and unforeseen changes. Overall, the new direction was a positive step, stretching staff and board into more independent and responsible activity. We did our own budgeting and fundraising when necessary. We had more freedom for movement and change. When we wanted a computer or voice mail, we got it! We had fewer meetings to attend and reports to write. But we also had more paperwork, our own insurance policies, audits, and legal issues to clarify. Although the separation was at MCC's request, it was most helpful to MDS. The ongoing MDS-MCC relationship remains positive and of benefit to both organizations.

Growing Up and on Our Own

MDS soon felt the pressure of simultaneously working through the unending 1992-1994 disasters and the new organizational changes. During those years, responding to

Costly Disasters

The United States has sustained 37 weather-related disasters over 19 years (1980-98) in which overall damages and costs reached or exceeded $1 billion. Of these, 31 occurred in the past 10 years.

Far left: From 1950, MDS has partnered with the American Red Cross, as here in rebuilding a house for Mattie Chandler after the 1997 tornadoes in Birmingham, Ala.

Near left: Martin Sommers, MDS project leader at Homestead, Fla., confers with Major David Worthy of the Salvation Army on joint efforts. MDS has a cooperative agreement with TSA.

several of the largest disasters in U.S. history, including Hurricane Andrew (1992) and the massive Mississippi basin floods (1993), stretched MDS. Feeling the crunch, staff asked for help. A part-time secretary, Phyllis Miller, joined the two staff in place, Lowell Detweiler and Elinor Miller.

A Task Force on the Future of MDS recommended program changes and additional staffing. The executive and board approved the recommendations and began a search for an assistant coordinator.

The search group recommended that

MDS move toward a staff team. A trio of part-time staff were added, each bringing expertise. Rick Augsburger, with excellent communication and computer skills, helped jump-start the team into the information age. Tom Smucker brought expertise in field programs and helped cover the multitude of project activities. Don Snyder, a volunteer, brought his wealth of administrative experience and over the years spent many months helping carry the load at Akron headquarters. This team approach proved valuable in keeping MDS viable during a time of change. Later Art Smucker and Wilbur Litwiller also accepted roles in the team.

The MDS board and staff met at Camp Luz near Kidron, Ohio, in fall 1994, to wrestle with implications of changes taking place outside and inside MDS. Edgar Stoesz, author of *Doing Good Better*, a manual for board members of nonprofit organizations, led a positive discussion of future directions for MDS. Under the able leadership of the board chair, Eldon King, the group looked creatively at the new picture and how to make MDS an effective player in years to come.

Given the external changes and complexities in the disaster response world, several priorities were identified. They are listed here along with implementation steps taken over the last five years.

Priorities for the Future

• **Pre-disaster preparedness.** *MDS will prepare and train its network for more effective disaster response efforts.* MDS has increased the numbers of leadership-training workshops and educational activities for units and volunteers. MDS staff and leaders have traveled throughout the MDS regional and unit network to strengthen readiness for disaster response. At various levels, MDS has added vehicles, stocked tool trailers, and prepared self-contained first-response vehicles with kitchen and office equipment, computers, and other items for prompt response to the next disaster.

• **Disaster investigation and cleanup.** *MDS will strengthen its investigative network and participate in immediate cleanup efforts as needed.* Dozens of organizations now arrive on a disaster scene immediately. Many work at cleanup activity, for many years an MDS stronghold. Through its local or regional network, MDS tries to place investigators at all disaster sites immediately. MDS still provides cleanup assistance when needed and especially seeks places of need outside the headlines, where particular populations are overlooked.

• **Long-term reconstruction and recovery.** *MDS will increase its efforts to participate in long-term recovery efforts, often staying at disaster locations long after most disaster responders have left.* Recognizing the complexity of long-term recovery programs, MDS has encouraged a leadership team approach for administering project activity. It is providing additional training for project leadership teams. MDS participates with local communities in special housing programs that may go beyond normal disaster response efforts (chapter 8). New methods of financing long-term recovery programs need to be explored, such as the bridge financing used to speed up rebuilding in the Red River flood project in Manitoba.

• **Advocacy and counseling.** *MDS will*

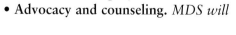

commit itself to a more wholistic response to disaster survivors. In both emergency and recovery efforts, MDS is preparing its teams to provide advocacy, casework management, and counseling as those it serves face the complex tangles of disaster recovery. When possible, MDS adds to field teams persons who understand the increased red tape of disaster assistance and those who can help meet emotional and psychological needs of disaster survivors (chapter 9).

• **Communications and the Information Age.** *MDS will avail itself of appropriate technology to be an active participant in the information age.* Both Akron headquarters and major disaster locations have computers for work and communication needs. MDS has both internal and external communication networks as well as access to disaster information on the World Wide Web. MDS gives a biweekly update to the network via fax or e-mail. For the latest reports, call 1-800-241-8111 or consult the MDS web page www.menno-disaster-service.org.

MDS photo

Amid Change, There Is the Eternal

Edgar Stoesz, in his presentation on change quoted earlier, gives words of encouragement and perspective.

Stoesz identifies some eternal truths that have not changed and are important for MDS to remember.

• God has put in the human spirit the desire and need to be useful, to live for something beyond ourselves. We all want to participate in meaningful and fulfilling work. MDS provides that opportunity.

• The hunger for love will never change. After visiting the United States, Mother Teresa said, "I have seen the starving of the world, but in your country I have seen an even greater hunger, and that is the hunger to be loved. No place in all my travels have I seen the loneliness as I have seen in the poverty of affluence in America." Love is necessary for survival, especially after times of crisis.

• God's word to us never changes. "Jesus replied: 'Love the Lord your God with all your heart and with all your soul and with all your mind.' This is the first and greatest commandment. And the second is like it: 'Love your neighbor as yourself' " (Matt. 22:37-39).

Stoesz concludes with an affirmation and a challenge. "I have no doubt that MDS would have disappeared long ago if your love for the neighbor were not grounded in your love for God and your desire to serve him. Mucking out basements quickly becomes tiresome for those who are not driven by a deeper motive. What has sustained MDS through the mud and the disorganization that is an inevitable part of a disaster response is, I have no doubt, your love for God and your love for the people you have come to serve.

"We should not assume that this will go on indefinitely. Just because MDS has done it for 45 [now 50] years is no guarantee for the future. Organizations die, and new ones are born. Some organizations lose vision and therefore the right to exist. They get lazy and no longer perform the functions for which they were called into existence. The dynamic of change does not escape MDS. You, too, need to continually strive to adjust; to rise to new challenges."

Jean Hampton

Change is inevitable. Yet through all the changing scenes of time, there are some eternal truths around which we can orient our lives. None is more beautiful and inclusive than the promise God gave to Noah, "As long as the earth endures, seedtime and harvest, cold and heat, summer and winter, day and night will never cease" (Gen. 8:22).
—Edgar Stoesz

Left: Computer classes are standard in leadership training, to help MDSers keep up with the information age.

Why Do You Keep Serving?
You couldn't pay me enough to do this job, but I wouldn't take anything in the world for all the experiences I've had and the friendships we've made.
—Marlin Gingerich, longtime MDS project leader

Left: Marlin and Nancy Gingerich from Riverside, Iowa, enjoy a break at a MDS leadership workshop, College Station, Ark., March 1998. They have served as project leaders over the past 15 years.

CHAPTER TWELVE

How MDS Works After Disaster Strikes

Carl Hiebert

> *Many Gifts*
>
> *A body has many members,*
>
> *Yet all work in unity.*
>
> *The church is the body of Christ:*
>
> *His arms, ears, and eyes, hands and feet.*
>
> *There are many gifts but the same Spirit,*
>
> *There are many works, but the same God,*
>
> *And the Spirit gives each as it chooses,*
>
> *Praise the Lord. Praise God.*
>
> —*Patricia Shelly,[1] based on 1 Corinthians 12*

Sometimes we all wonder how MDS works! Landis Hershey, Region I director for 17 years, commented, "MDS was one of the most unorganized organizations that really worked well. When people were put on the spot, they produced." Many are amazed at what MDS has done over the years, especially when they hear that until 1993 MDS never had more than two salaried staff. This appropriately assigns credit for this MDS reputation to the grassroots network of thousands of volunteers who serve each year.

Using several 1998 disasters as case studies, this chapter illustrates how MDS operates.

Setting the Stage: A 1998 Retrospect

On February 12-14, 1998, the annual board meeting and the MDS all-unit Meeting were held in Calgary, Canada. Over 600 people gathered to carry out MDS business, share stories of disaster response efforts, and enjoy the warm hospitality of Alberta hosts. At both board and all-unit meetings, *transition* was the buzz word. Eldon King completed his six-year term as MDS chair, and Paul Brubacher was elected to take his place. Recognition was given to Lowell Detweiler for 12 years as MDS executive coordinator. Tom Smucker was welcomed as incoming coordinator. Carla Hunt was promoted to assistant coordinator. Marisa Doncevic was introduced as the new administrative assistant, replacing Marilyn Godshalk.

MDS photo

Eldon King (left) and Lowell Detweiler were made honorary Calgarians at the MDS All-Unit Meeting in Calgary, Alta., in February 1998. King was completing six years as board chair and Detweiler 12 years as executive coordinator.

The MDS Akron Binational Staff team (September 1999)

• Tom Smucker, executive coordinator, responsible for overall planning and direction, leads the MDS Akron team as they work with regional and unit leaders. He works with MDS board, executive committee, and board chair on policy issues; and represents MDS to other disaster agencies.

• Carla Hunt, assistant coordinator, helps with administrative tasks and field visits. She is responsible for MDS personnel coordination, working with long-term volunteer placement and the summer youth program. She is involved in planning and facilitating leadership workshops.

• Marisa Doncevic, communications coordinator, leads in writing news service articles, midmonth and quarterly newsletters, brochures, and other publicity items. She coordinates office tasks: reports, mailings, fax updates, web page, and project manuals.

Other staff team members, working on a part-time or volunteer basis, include—

• Wilbur Litwiller, who from Iowa assists the team as field consultant.

• Ginny Sauder and Glenda Hollinger, who work part-time in the Akron office at filing, data input, and other clerical tasks.

• Art Smucker, who from Indiana or Florida shares computer skills as computer consultant.

• Don Snyder, who helps with special projects or administrative backup, from Akron or in the field.

1998: A Busy Beginning for a New Team

The year 1997 had seen above-average MDS activity. The binational annual report listed 13 projects with nearly 4,500 volunteers providing over 27,500 days of service. By far the largest of these was the Red River flood response (chapter 7). Three 1997 projects carried over into 1998: the Red River response in Manitoba and Minnesota; rebuilding after a tornado in College Station, Arkansas; and a fascinating spring project in Alberta responding to late 1997 wild fires.

Despite many prayers for a quiet 1998 transition year, disasters began early and came regularly. The first two disasters occurred in the East. There were severe ice storms in New York, New England, Quebec, and Ontario, then tornadoes in Florida. The New York MDS unit made a remarkable response to dairy farmers in northern New York, providing over 80 generators for milking cows while the electricity was out for weeks. MDSers in Ontario and Quebec helped in eastern Ontario and southern Quebec. The tornado project in Sanford, Florida, became long-term and was compounded when summer wildfires burned dozens of homes, some within miles of where MDSers were rebuilding after the tornadoes.

MDS Begins at the Grassroots

From its beginnings in 1950, MDS has been structured with local units as the organizational building blocks. The MDS bylaws state, "Local units are the basic operational entities that respond to disasters. . . . Each local unit has the primary responsibility for disaster response in its geographic boundaries." Each unit is "expected in its capacity . . . to respond to calls from the regional director or executive coordinator to help in other programs." (See list of MDS units on page 180 and regional map on page 181.)

MDS responds to disasters from single-family fires to hurricanes. In many situations the local church will provide volunteers for small MDS-type needs, such as a neighbor-helping-neighbor response, often without invoking the MDS label. Depending on size and strength, the local unit will tackle the next level of needed response. Resources of the regional and binational network are dedicated to larger responses.

Case studies of several 1998 disasters illustrate these levels of response.

Photo, page 150: Do we need to bring our own tools? No, it is in here somewhere.

Right: The current team leading MDS into the new century includes (from left, in back) Tom Smucker, executive coordinator; Glenda Hollinger, part-time administrative secretary; Wilbur Litwiller, part-time field consultant; (in front) Carla Hunt, assistant coordinator; Marisa Doncevic, communications coordinator; and Ginny Sauder, part-time administrative secretary.

MDS photo

Then spring tornadoes followed week after week, with MDS setting up major project efforts in Gainesville, Georgia; Birmingham, Alabama; Waynesboro, Tennessee; and Salisbury, Pennsylvania. There was excellent local response from the MDS network to other locations including South Dakota, Minnesota, Michigan, Pennsylvania, and New York. In the fall, Hurricanes Georges and Mitch topped off an above-average fall hurricane season.

The new staff team hit the ground running. Included in the response was another excellent summer youth program; over 400 youth and sponsors from 20 churches served at four project locations.

MCC photo by Pearl Sensenig

Tornadoes? Not in the Mountains!

"Never saw anything like it" was the repeated refrain in the stunned Amish and Mennonite community of Casselman Valley, nestled in the Allegheny Mountains of western Pennsylvania.[2] Most residents of Salisbury and the farming community of Somerset County had never seen a tornado. Then in two days, four tornadoes tore through. The first struck on Sunday evening, May 31, 1998, followed by three more on Tuesday evening, June 2. Those storms were part of a larger system that caused tornadoes to seven counties in Pennsylvania and severe storm damage to many others.

As these storms crisscrossed Casselman Valley, several farm families were hit twice, a disaster oddity. The Sunday evening tornado hit the town of Salisbury and surrounding areas. The Tuesday tornadoes mostly cut through farm communities. About 90 homes were damaged or destroyed along a 10-mile path. On the farms, many barns and other buildings were destroyed, but most houses escaped. Despite widespread destruction, only one fatality was directly related to the storm.

Twice in Two Days

Bill and Sylvia Mast, members of the Oak Dale Mennonite Church, have a 640-acre dairy farm about a mile east of Salisbury. On Sunday evening they had finished evening chores when the first tornado hit. Emerging from the basement, they found 15 windows broken, some siding torn off, and roof shingles gone from their house, but other buildings fared worse.

Wind and a toppled silo had badly damaged the barn. Neighbors helped get out as many cows as they could; Masts lost four. More helpers arrived and worked till 3:30 a.m. hooking up a generator for the morning milking. The next morning volunteers arrived as early as 5:00 and by 7:30 were milking cows. Then the massive cleanup began. On the home farm and a neighboring rented farm, 15 farm buildings had been damaged or destroyed.

Amid the Tuesday evening rebuilding came warnings of a second round of storms. About 30 persons helping on the Mast farm joined them in the basement. "This time," Bill remembers, "I didn't make fun of Sylvia for being worried." The tornadoes on Tuesday night tore off the buildings tin that had been replaced after Sunday's storm, destroyed a heifer barn farther uphill, and mangled the timber stand. The Masts lost over half of 4,400 sugar maple trees they had been tapping. Foresters estimated the timber loss as greater than the building loss.

Twice in One Night

The Sam and Katie Beiler family farm a mile or so north of Salisbury escaped the Sunday storms. As the Tuesday storms approached, Sam was helping at a neighbor's farm. Warned by a neighbor, Katie huddled with her children in the basement as the storm pounded overhead. Through a cellar window they watched tin peel off the barn roof and trees break. In the eerie quiet that followed, they went outside to find branches everywhere, part of the barn sides gone, and the equipment shed moved five feet off its foundation.

Left: Bill and Sylvia Mast and their children in front of their barn as MDSers repair it after the Salisbury-area tornadoes of May-June 1998.

We are thankful to God that none of us, or the people that helped here, were hurt. We are also grateful for all the people who helped with cleanup and rebuilding, and for the food that was prepared day after day. —*Bill and Sylvia Mast*

In the two hours before the next storms, Sam made it home through blocked roads and downed power lines in time to inspect the damage and join his family in the basement. In the gathering darkness, they prayed as windows broke and debris flew. The barn went down, floor and all, pinning horses and cows.

Neighbors arrived and throughout the night moved beams and freed cows, a mission accomplished by 3:30 a.m. In the morning the cows were moved to nearby farms for milking, and rebuilding started.

The MDS Response

The western Pennsylvania and Maryland MDS unit covers most of the western half of Pennsylvania, the western panhandle of Maryland, and a few northern counties of West Virginia. To handle that vast territory, the unit is divided into subunits, including the Casselman Valley subunit where the tornadoes occurred. At the time of this project, Menno Yoder was subunit director and Raymond Yoder secretary-treasurer. Philip Bender was cochair of the larger unit and lived in the area. These three formed the leadership team for this project response and gave many weeks of time to it.

On Sunday evening Menno Yoder was at Mountain View Church near Salisbury. He and others watched the tornado veer

from the church and pass on the other side of a hill less than a half mile away. They could see debris swirling as it hit various farms and headed for Salisbury. Menno immediately went into town, where he was a member of the volunteer fire department, and helped with emergency work.

By next morning MDS had volunteers at work in several locations. With fire departments and outside volunteers focusing on Salisbury, MDS leaders targeted rural areas. The first priority was helping dairy farmers milk cows, then beginning the massive cleanup. Following the Tuesday night tornadoes, new assessments needed to be made and volunteers directed to new locations.

Headquarters were soon set up at Mountain View Church, centrally located in the disaster area. There incoming volunteers reported to MDS leaders, who assigned them where most needed. In cooperation with the Red Cross and other agencies, a feeding center was also established there to pack lunches for volunteers and prepare the evening meals workers ate before returning home.

In a few days, word had spread. Volunteers were coming in from other parts of the unit in Johnstown and Belleville. Joining them were volunteers from Lancaster, Pennsylvania, and other areas. In most cases people came just for the day or stayed with families, so no lodging facility was needed.

Many Amish joined the major task of barn raisings. Often one barn per day was raised somewhere in the valley. The Lancaster unit MDS bus made 17 trips to Casselman Valley, leaving Lancaster at 1:30

a.m. to be there for an early start. After a long day's work, they often didn't reach home till midnight. Altogether, over 10,000 volunteer days were coordinated by MDS.

During the project, Paul Brubacher, regional director, and Tom Smucker, binational coordinator, had frequent contact and made several visits to the project site. Funds from outside sources were added to those coming to the local community so more projects could be completed.

As the project was nearing closure three months after the tornado, local MDS leaders reflected. Menno remembers, "There was a Joe Beiler from the Oakdale congregation who said he prayed that the Lord would open the doors in Salisbury for witnessing and relating to people. He said he then not only opened the doors, he opened the windows and took off the roofs. Now they just can't thank us enough."

"One challenge," Philip Bender says, "was when people didn't call to let us know they were coming. One day we had a bus here and had most workers lined up with jobs. Then here came a van we didn't know was arriving. So we found a place for them. By that time, here came another van. I think

Courtesy of Floyd Yoder

Right: Local unit leaders Phil Bender (left) and Menno Yoder did an excellent job of taking requests for assistance and matching them with hundreds of volunteers.

we had three like that in one day.

"That made it hard for the women providing the meals as well. Many people didn't even come to the church to register. One day we prepared lunches for the 300 MDS volunteers and drivers took them to farms at noon. Soon they were back for more lunches; there were actually over 500 for lunch that day."

Raymond Yoder said, "It's been kind of a whirlwind, but good. Probably one of the most thrilling experiences was when we didn't know how a job would get done or who would do it, and the Lord provided somebody with the right skill."

Building Hope in Birmingham

On Wednesday evening, April 8, 1998, intense storms hit four southern states. They dealt their cruelest blow to the small suburban towns on the northeast edge of Birmingham, Alabama. A 22-mile path of destruction from an F-5 tornado with winds over 260 miles per hour left 34 per-

MDS photo

When I looked around, I knew we had a lot of work to do, but we didn't really know how to help the people. . . . When I met Paul Unruh, he told me he was with the Mennonites, and they had come to help us. It was just like a miracle that came from God. —Pastor Bernice Mahan

sons dead in that area alone. Vice President Gore visited and called it the "most powerful tornado ever known in that part of the country." Even veteran MDS leader Ottis Mast shook his head and said, "I've not seen one this bad before."

As Pastor Bernice Mahan surveyed her Oakridge community (West Ensley) the day after the storm, she saw buildings in street after street flattened. Her own home was gone. One street over, a neighbor had been killed. "When I looked around," she said, "I knew we had a lot of work to do, but we didn't really know how to help the people. Then one day somebody told me about Paul [Unruh]. When I met him, he told me he was with the Mennonites, and they had come to help us. It was just like a miracle that came from God. I know God can do all things, but I know it was a miracle to have him send them to the Oakridge community."

Miracle, the Leading of God's Spirit, or Good Hard Work?

The story of how this "miracle" happened is an excellent example of God's Spirit leading MDS at all network levels in responding to a major disaster. As news of the tornadoes became known on Thursday, regional director Ottis Mast got in touch with Roland Stutzman, MDS contact person at Southside Mennonite Fellowship in Birmingham. Roland did preliminary

investigating and reported to Ottis, "This is a big one, and I'd like you to help." Ottis called the Akron office to share this information and his plan to go to Birmingham on Friday morning.

On Friday Ottis and Roland thoroughly investigated the tornado path. It was clear that MDS was needed. But where in the miles of destruction should they begin? Southside Pastor Steve Longenecker knew local pastors through involvement in area prison ministry. He called Pastor T. L. Lewis at a church in Pratt City, an affected community. Pastor Lewis immediately asked Steve to go with him on a community tour. When Steve joined Pastor Lewis, he had already lined up four other African-American pastors. They appealed to MDS for help, so it was becoming obvious where to begin.

Again Ottis reported findings to MDS Akron and to the Alabama unit chair, Michael Martin. Michael joined them for additional investigation on Saturday. The Red Cross noted a need for mental health workers, so the Akron office asked Paul Unruh, MDS board member and mental health volunteer, if he was available. Local volunteers from the Birmingham area also began cleanup. They offered a large home, formerly used as their church, for MDS volunteers.

More Saturday investigations confirmed the need for a major response. MDS still

Left: Ottis Mast, Region II director (left), and Roland Stutzman, local congregational contact at the Southside Mennonite Fellowship in Birmingham, Ala., tackle some cleanup as they investigate the April 8, 1998, tornadoes in the Birmingham area.

felt led to the African-American community. They were not receiving as much publicity and attention as other suburbs. Ottis Mast appealed for surrounding units to send volunteers on Monday morning. Paul Unruh cleared his schedule and headed for Birmingham on Sunday. God was at work!

On Sunday a member who lived in Oakridge challenged Pastor T. L. Lewis for talking only about Pratt City when Oakridge was much worse. The pastor and the deacons toured Oakridge that afternoon and agreed it was devastated. When Paul Unruh and Wilbur Litwiller contacted Pastor Lewis early that week, he gave them an Oakridge tour. They met community leaders like Pastor Mahan and Fan Bailey, president of the Neighborhood Association, who welcomed MDS. By midweek MDS volunteers from Tennessee were busy clearing trees and debris and covering roofs in Oakridge.

That week God also led Paul Unruh's work assignment. Though a mental health

professional, he had not been certified for Red Cross counseling. This freed him to give more time to MDS program setup. He and Roland Stutzman made connections to keep incoming volunteers at work. Paul has said (chapter 8) that his own involvement in the community—running a chain saw and talking with people on the streets— was likely a more effective form of counseling than sitting in an office. He developed many relationships that placed MDS in a strategic position for the long haul.

The Search for Long-Term Facilities

From the beginning, MDS saw this as a long-term project. Over 1,100 homes were destroyed or badly damaged in Jefferson County alone. With excellent early contacts in needy communities, Tom Smucker, representing the Akron office, was soon on-site to help with further planning. To provide longer-term leadership, two couples who had been serving at a flood project in southern Alabama were transferred to Birmingham. A youth group from Delaware was on-site by the first week of May, with other volunteers coming from throughout Region II.

The house provided by the Southside Fellowship was great for initial lodging. But it was far from the disaster site and was committed to Eastern Mennonite Mission teams for the summer. This forced a search for other headquarters.

One day, MDS office manager Mary Oesch called Roland Stutzman for help in tracking referrals passed on to MDS. Even in good times, it was difficult to find places in the area. With signs and land-

marks gone, local guides like Roland were crucial. Roland asked another Southside member, Gary Bonham, a Birmingham business owner, to help track down some places. While helping, Gary heard of the MDS search for headquarters. He invited us to set up on five acres he owned in west Birmingham.

Setting up headquarters was a challenge Ottis Mast liked. Soon two large mobile homes were brought in to serve as base for lodging, kitchen, and office. Water, electricity, and phone were available, and a septic system was installed. A deck built between the two mobile homes was covered by a tarp and became a dining area for large groups; later it was enclosed and

Below: Make Do Somehow (MDS) operating at the Birmingham project: an area between two mobile homes was enclosed to be a dining "hall" for large groups.

Carl Hiebert

Carl Hiebert

used year-round. A new portable shower unit just built by Region II MDSers in Indiana was called south. MDS brought in the large tool trailer and made utility connections for other mobile units. Soon a well-organized headquarters was functioning right in the area of our work.

MDS certainly used those headquarters. Youth groups came during the summer of 1998. MDS committed to working with Red Cross on an initial rebuilding of 10 homes, then more. Fall became winter, and snowbird volunteers arrived in large numbers. New leadership teams gave extended blocks of time. An anonymous organization liked the work MDS was doing and gave a major grant. The work continued

into spring, with additional youth groups through summer 1999. Over 1,200 volunteers served at Birmingham, many coming back for a second or third time. Why?

People Are Key

What makes a volunteer want to come back? Good food? A decent bed or mattress on the floor? A long ride to an unknown place? Meeting new people? Meaningful work? All the above, but mostly people—the people you work with and for.

Bob and Doreen

Bob and Doreen Rempel drove all the way from Alberta to spend two months helping in Birmingham during fall 1998. Bob worked as a handyman, sometimes as a crew leader. Doreen was head cook. A year earlier they had spent a month in the Yuba City, California, flood project. Why did they come again?

Bob reflects, "We've enjoyed the work groups, especially the Amish. We had a lot of fun with them. I liked meeting the local people. Every time I can, I grab one on the road and start asking questions. They're always so happy, so appreciative. We've gone to three or four black churches and really enjoyed that."

Doreen quickly adds, "Meeting friends, this has become family to us. This was my first experience cooking [for large groups]. I was nervous about doing it, but I'm glad I did. The cook gets rewarded with a lot of 'thank yous.' I'd do it again. We'll feel sad going home because we've had such a good experience."

Tim and Jamie

Tim Charles and Jamie Alderfer were two young men from Pennsylvania who signed up for three and six months respectively, as part of the long-term team for fall 1998. Jamie says, "The MDS representative in my church encouraged me to come; I'm glad he did. I like the work, meeting people you are working for, building relationships with them, earning their trust."

"The highlights for me," Tim adds, "are hearing the different stories of miracles that happened during the disaster. I've really enjoyed it down here. I love meeting the local people, going to their churches, listening to their style of worship. Then in the evenings, it's nice being around people from all over the United States and Canada, playing games, and talking with them. I wasn't sure I was qualified for all the responsibilities I was given, but it turned out all right."

When asked if they would recommend MDS to other younger folks, both answered a resounding "yes."

Doreen and Jerry

Doreen and Jerry Klassen from Burns Lake, British Columbia, were project leaders at Birmingham in fall 1998. They think this was "about their 10th assignment during the past 10 years." They reflected on both tough and good assignments. What makes a good one?

"There has to be meaningful work," Jerry suggests. "It can be menial, but it has to be meaningful. Volunteers need to feel they're improving the situation. And contact with community people is important. The bottom line is that our volunteers

The MDS representative in my church encouraged me to come; I'm glad he did. I like the work, meeting people you are working for, building relationships with them, earning their trust.

Left: If volunteers come all this way to work, feed them well!

151

If I were doing this for pay, I likely wouldn't be here. I need a channel for serving the Lord. I've found that in MDS. What I contribute out here in the field is so minute compared to what I receive.

have to be respected for donating time."

Doreen's role on MDS projects has often been running the office and acting as hostess. She admits, "Sometime I have to be tugged to go again. I'm a homebody. But I go and enjoy it once I get here and see the need. I like to go to project sites and work when I can. I like to be busy. Even if I don't go out, I can contribute here too. And we've found some really good friends."

So why are they back for the 10th or maybe 11th time? Jerry reflects, "If I were doing this for pay, I likely wouldn't be here. I need a channel for serving the Lord. I've found that in MDS. What I contribute out here in the field is so minute compared to what I receive.

"We meet such good people. Just in the three weeks we've been here, 50 people have come to work. And I've met at least that many in the community. Today I can drive into people's yards, holler at them, and they'll come out, and we can talk. Dan Jones will tell you again just how to bore those holes in the coal mine and set off the powder. I need a place to serve. MDS has given that to me."

The Cookie Lady

Pam Denlinger: We inherited the role of "Cookie Lady." We aren't sure who was the first one. When my husband, Dean, and I arrived to direct the Birmingham project in January 1999, Louise Schrock was that month's Cookie Lady.

The Cookie Lady at the Birmingham project was the cook, assisted by one of her weekly volunteers. Each day they brought coffee and a snack to the work

sites. Birmingham is not the first or only project to do this; the difference may be how this came to be viewed by the Oakridge community.

In summer, water joined coffee and fresh fruit on the coffee truck. When cold weather came, hot cocoa was added. Fresh-baked cookies were the mainstays, but in January, Fridays were designated "cinnamon-roll days." Word got around the neighborhood. Soon not just MDS workers and homeowners were being fed off the tailgate; neighbors also showed up midmorning at the work site to talk and wait for the Cookie Lady.

MDS was reaching out to the community with a smile, a cup of coffee, and a cookie. Conversations flowed freely. People shared problems and hardships that MDSers could address or quietly refer to a

caseworker. Equally important, our kitchen staff made friends with people we were serving and gained new insights. This was teamwork at its best.

We learn something new on every project. Now we know how important Cookie Ladies are.

Ottis Mast Says

We can learn a lot from the storm survivors. Their faith: that's what they want to talk about. Could we have that type of faith if we lose all our possessions, had them scattered by the winds? Your keepsakes and treasures, all destroyed? I think we can learn from them. They still have faith. And I marvel at how accepting they are of us, total strangers, coming in to help. Would I accept that? We can learn a lot from them.

Right: "The cookie lady" provides a welcome break for volunteers and locals at the project near Birmingham. Breaks help MDSers build relationships with community residents.

Carl Hiebert

A Month in the Life of MDS Staff— Including Georges

To illustrate the work of the MDS Akron office, this case study will mix the response to Hurricane Georges with other network activity planned by a busy staff during September and October 1998.

Fall 1998 and the MDS Planning and Response Cycle

As Hurricane Georges appeared in the Atlantic and headed for the Caribbean, MDS staff were catching their breath from a hectic summer and planning for the year ahead. For several years, an annual staff retreat for long-range planning had been held in the fall. The 1998 retreat was scheduled for September 20-22 at Laurelville Mennonite Church Center in western Pennsylvania.

With a hurricane on the way, should staff go ahead with the retreat? Yes, they

MDS photo

decided; the time together is crucial for annual planning. We can find ways to monitor Georges from Laurelville, even without TV and Internet access. So Tom, Carla, Marisa, Wilbur, Don, and Art (with Eldon and Lowell part of the time) spent Sunday through Tuesday in retreat.

What do staff do when on retreat? Work mostly, though sharing and prayer time, eating and walks are important team-building activities. With new team members and new roles for others, executive coordinator Tom Smucker stated, "The most important thing is to have staff all together in one room at one time. MDS needs to be on one page. This is the best way to do it."

Hurricane Georges Aims at Puerto Rico and the Caribbean

While staff met, Georges was gaining strength as it sped west toward the Leeward Islands. By Sunday, September 20, it had reached category 3 status, with winds up to 120 miles per hour. It tore through the small island of St. Kitts and took direct aim at Puerto Rico.

Wavering between a category 2 and 3 storm, it bore down on Puerto Rico on Tuesday. From Laurelville, Tom Smucker contacted Julio Vincenty, MDS unit leader in Puerto Rico. Julio reported, "Preparations on the island are going well. We think we can ride this one out in good shape."

Wednesday, September 23

Back in the Akron office, staff were eagerly watching the news and waiting for that phone call from Julio in Puerto Rico. Amid widespread destruction, Julio man-

aged to reconnect his own phone line and get the call through to Akron. He reported that the entire island of Puerto Rico had experienced major damage. Georges was described as the worst hurricane in 60 years. Julio said, "You can point your finger anywhere on the island and find destruction. It is terrible. All the roads are blocked. We couldn't get farther than 10 miles, and the damage kept getting worse."

At Julio's invitation, Tom made immediate plans to go to Puerto Rico Friday. Julio's contacts with the Federal Emergency Management Agency (FEMA) led to MDS focusing on the mountains surrounding Aibonito, in south-central Puerto Rico, one of the hardest-hit areas. This included LaPlata, Cayey, Coamo, and Barranquitas, places populated by Puerto Rican Mennonites.

After the report from Puerto Rico, MDS staff shifted into high gear. Marisa issued a fax update to churches and the MDS network, over 360 locations. Information was placed on the MDS web page; on Mennolink, an Internet communications network; and on the MDS telephone number (1-800-241-8111), where anyone can obtain the latest from MDS.

With the first call from Puerto Rico, MDS knew that the small unit in Puerto Rico (from only 11 churches) would need outside help to respond to the ravages of Georges. MDS Akron and Region I leaders consulted and responded. MDS asked for and received financial and volunteer support from the binational network.

While MDS was responding in Puerto Rico, Hurricane Georges crossed the small

Left: MDS leaders in P.R. (from left) Isasis Martinez, Julio Vincenty, and Enrique Ortiz check out a generator, needed after Hurricane Georges left much of P.R. without power and roofs.

Four at One Time!

On September 26 the National Hurricane Center announced that there were four hurricanes in the Atlantic Ocean, the most at one time since 1893. Thankfully Ivan, Jeanne, and Karl did not hit land.

Georges Floods the Gulf Coast

Georges finally sputtered ashore over Biloxi, Mississippi, with heaviest rains east in the Florida panhandle. Michael Martin, MDS Alabama/Northwest Florida unit chair who lives in Crestview, Florida, remembers that after about 30 inches of rain in 24 hours, Crestview became an island. The resulting floods caused more damage than the winds.

Ottis Mast as regional director, and Wilbur Litwiller, field consultant representing MDS Akron, joined Michael in the investigation. It was agreed the local unit would take the lead in responding to needs in Mobile and other locations and call on the region as needed.

Betania Mennonite School lost part of its roof but still sheltered homeless families, then was headquarters for MDS recovery efforts.

strait to unleash its fury on the Dominican Republic. Winds and heavy rains leveled hundreds of thousands of homes there, with later reports claiming more than 200 people killed. After losing some of its punch over the land, Georges packed winds and water to kill over 150 in neighboring Haiti.

Thursday, September 24

Hurricane Georges made a more direct hit on northeast Cuba than expected and headed for the Florida Keys.

Additional reports detailed catastrophic damage in the Dominican Republic. The MCC Latin America department consulted with MDS staff about involvement there. Paul Brubacher represented MDS on an MCC team going to the Dominican Republic the following week.

With media broadcasting the devastation, Akron was receiving phone calls asking if MDS would be sending volunteers. Puerto Rico said the local infrastructure (travel, housing, water, electricity) was so damaged it was unlikely volunteers should enter for two weeks. Lists were made of volunteers available.

Friday, September 25

Hurricane Georges went directly over Key West with moderate damage, then headed into the Gulf of Mexico.

Tom met Julio Vincenty in Puerto Rico. They checked in with FEMA, Salvation Army, American Red Cross, and other agencies for the latest damage assessment. The agencies estimated over 100,000 families affected and over 40,000 with homes destroyed.

Saturday, September 26

In Puerto Rico, Julio and Tom went inland to the mountainous area, winding their way around downed power lines and mudslides. The pair finally made it to the Betania Mennonite School, which was badly damaged but sheltering homeless families. They met pastors and other church leaders who reported that one Mennonite church had been destroyed, along with homes of many church members.

Sunday, September 27

Investigation in Puerto Rico continued with tours of many communities. The cement houses were usually intact except for roof damage, but the frame homes were badly damaged or destroyed. Some houses could be repaired immediately if funds and materials were available. The Betania school was hit hard, but there was a possibility of housing MDS volunteers in one of the buildings.

Monday, September 28

In Puerto Rico, Julio Vincenty and Tom Smucker finished their investigation and called Akron. Julio said, "The main problem is transportation: you need four-wheel-drive trucks to get through. We visited five to six Mennonite churches in the mountains. They had just built a new church in Botijas; the wind blew it apart. They built it with their own hands. It took three months. They built it with heart and soul—and all that's left is their tears."

Tom stated, "MDS will send volunteers as soon as some infrastructure is restored.

The local MDS persons are doing the best they can under tough conditions. I ask that you pray for our brothers and sisters in these weeks of hardship."

September 29-October 2 Project Leadership Workshop, Georgia

For fifty years, the MDS problem most often identified has been the need for more trained and experienced project leaders. Each year staff hold two or three leadership workshops. When possible, these workshops are held on project sites, so the 1998 fall workshop was in Gainesville, Georgia. A spring tornado had devastated the community, and MDS volunteers had been serving there since April.

Pam and Dean Denlinger, local project leaders, hosted the group of 30: experienced leaders; new candidates; and unit, regional, and binational staff. Highlights were vivid stories from the Gainesville community, plus Julio Vincenty with his account of Hurricane Georges in Puerto Rico.

Project leaders have many tasks, such as deciding whom to help, lining up work, providing food and accommodations, and helping volunteers have meaningful experiences. They need emotional energy to support those they meet daily who depend on them to help make decisions. Paul Unruh was the resource person for the group discussion on helping others find emotional healing while learning how to take care of ourselves to avoid burnout (chapter 9). Prospective new leaders attending the workshop were enthusiastic and committed to go on sites already during the coming winter.

Oct. 2-3 MDS Executive Committee, Project Site, Georgia

Each February the MDS board meets at the all-unit meeting and other times as needed. Between board meetings, MDS staff receive direction from the executive committee, a seven-member group meeting another two or three times per year. One meeting each year is usually held at a disaster location, so the fall meeting was piggybacked onto the workshop in Gainesville, Georgia. Paul Brubacher, MDS chair, led the group through a full agenda, including program updates, the proposed 1999 budget, and discussion of proposed bylaws to have a permanent nominating committee and a board member term limit of 12 years.

The Long Road to Recovery

Insured losses in the Caribbean and the U.S. from Hurricane Georges reached $2.5 billion, the fourth costliest hurricane to date. Total charges against insurance would have been much higher if damage had been fully covered, but in the Caribbean only about 30 percent of households have insurance. The significant damage, plus interest in supporting the local unit/church in responding to needs in the Mennonite communities, led MDS to continue its Puerto Rico program for over a year.

Reconstruction projects in the hurricane-prone Caribbean islands, where MDS has often been called, bring special challenges. One cannot just drive MDS vehicles and tool trailers to Puerto Rico. Getting such equipment there after a hurricane is difficult. Usually building supplies

The Deadly Trail of Georges

A deadly storm, Georges killed an estimated 400 persons along its path. Hardest hit was the Dominican Republic with over 200 deaths and Haiti with 150. In Puerto Rico, 11 persons were killed and $2 billion damage was reported, with 30,000 homes destroyed and another 60,000 damaged. In the mountains and on the south side of the island, strong winds destroyed or damaged about 30-40 Mennonite homes.

Spanish-Speaking Mason?

MDS Akron wants a list of persons fluent in Spanish and/or with good masonry skills for special Caribbean/international assignments. Contact MDS at 1018 Main St., Akron, PA 17501.

Left: Tom Smucker and Carla Hunt (foreground right) lead a discussion at a project leader's workshop in College Station, Ark., in March 1998.

Jean Hampton

Left: MDS board members are briefed by MDS project leaders Wilbur Lentz and Marlin Gingerich (far right) as they meet at the project in S.C. after Hurricane Hugo in 1990.

MDS photo

155

are in short supply, and transporting them to rural mountainous communities is another challenge. Most buildings are reinforced concrete or cement block. Rebuilding to meet hurricane-proof guide-

Important Meetings

As if a staff retreat, Hurricane Georges, a project leader's workshop, an executive committee meeting, and some smaller disasters weren't enough to keep staff busy for a month, fall is also regional meeting time. Each region calls units together for annual meetings. Four such meetings are held in the fall.

MDS Akron staff need to be represented at these important meetings. To round out the month's work, Tom Smucker headed for the Region I meeting in Greenwood, Delaware, the weekend of October 16-17. Carla Hunt went to the Region V meeting in St. Catharines, Ontario.

Recognition, affirmation, and training of the MDS network is a priority: its members make MDS happen. Throughout the year, MDS staff often participate in annual meetings held by local units as well.

Not every month is this hectic. With more disasters and people hurting, it's hard to say no. Pray for MDS staff and network leaders. Show your support by joining the MDS team!

lines poses yet another challenge; masons are always in demand. The number of MDS volunteers fluent in Spanish is also limited, yet Spanish, while not essential for all, is a must for some.

Unless a volunteer agrees to give two months or more as part of the long-term leadership team or is asked to go by MDS Akron for a special assignment, they need to pay their own transportation. Despite the expense in getting to Puerto Rico, many volunteers came forward. Over 250 served in Puerto Rico in the first year of the project, including four youth groups during summer 1999.

Merle Sommers, who had earlier taught school in Puerto Rico, served as MDS coordinator for the project. His language skills and knowledge of Puerto Rico were

extremely valuable and helped strengthen the partnership with the Puerto Rican Mennonites. Despite the difficulties mentioned above, Sommers says the MDS presence in Puerto Rico has been rewarding:

"We have been so warmly received by people here and are affirmed that what we do is really important to them. People are amazed at what we do. The fact that volunteers would actually pay to come here to work for nothing blows their minds. When I tell them we don't charge for labor, their faces light up like Christmas trees. That's been the fun part of it."

Other Project Activity

While Hurricane Georges claimed the headlines and much staff time, other projects were not forgotten. During that month, project leadership changes were taking place in the Gainesville and Birmingham projects. Headquarters staff or regional leaders try to spend time on site during leadership transitions.

The people of Texas said, "Don't forget us!" Flooding in Texas was severe. Region III and binational leaders spent much time investigating and trying to set up a response program. In any flood response program, weeks or even months may be needed to clear bureaucratic channels so people know where they can rebuild and what assistance they will get. Many of the rules are useful, but persons waiting for assistance are caught in long periods of uncertainty. Their pain and frustration is keenly felt by MDS leaders trying to set up recovery programs. Not till January 1999 was MDS able to begin a small flood recovery program in the San Antonio area.

Then There Was Mitch!

Mennonite Central Committee (MCC) led the Hurricane Mitch response. Over 50,000 hurricane relief kits (buckets), each with a Spanish Bible added, were sent to Honduras and Nicaragua. MCC personnel joined local Mennonites and other relief organizations in emergency and long-term rebuilding efforts.

MDS did not have direct program responsibility for Hurricane Mitch response since it did not affect the United States or its territories in the Caribbean. However, the MCC switchboard was swamped with thousands of phone calls. Since many are unsure who does what on the Mennonite disaster scene, MDS staff also received many calls and helped answer questions or redirected calls.

Without question, 1998 brought more than its share of disasters and suffering to millions of people in North America and around the world. But also without question, 1998 brought an unprecedented sharing

of "the cup of cold water" by so many people in so many ways. "To God be the glory, great things [God] has done!" (Fanny J. Crosby).

A family enjoys their sturdy home erected with MCC assistance after Hurricane Mitch, and a bag of MCC food.

MCC photo by Tony Siemens

Virgil Kauffman

MDS photo

156

Reaching Mennonite Disaster Service

The MDS binational office is at 1018 Main Street, Akron, Pennsylvania. Visitors are welcome. MDS invites your suggestions, questions, prayer, and volunteer and financial support. Contact channels: MDS, 1018 Main St., Akron, PA 17501. Phone: 717-859-2210. Fax: 717-859-4910. Information: 800-241-8111. Web page: www.menno-disaster-service.org. In Canada: MDS, 134 Plaza Drive, Winnipeg, MB R3T 5K9. Phone: 204-261-6381. Fax: 204-269-9875.

Unit Life

Left: Is this legal, a man in an MDS kitchen? Yes, and more are welcome! Barry Murphy from Sellersville, Pa., makes his famous chocolate pie for MDSers to enjoy.

MDS photo

Left: MDS project leadership teams on location guide the activity, as in P.R. in fall 1998: (from left) Merle Sommers, project coordinator; Jean Hampton, head cook; a client in Coamo who received assistance from MDS; Sue Kathler, office manager; and Fred Kathler, project director.

Below left: With the dishes done, MDSers can play games. Leaders at a 1996 workshop in Alderson, W.V., squeeze in a game of dominoes between sessions.

Below: An evening hymn sing or a sing-along, as led by (from left) Egon Hofer, Ann and Wes Heinrichs, adds to the enjoyment of making new friends.

Paul Brubacher

Egon Hofer

Far left: The bunkhouse for those who slept—or tried to—at the MDS headquarters in Rapid City, S.D., in the 1972 flood recovery project. Facilities vary greatly.

157

CHAPTER THIRTEEN

On Doing Good Better

Therefore, since we are surrounded by such a great cloud of witnesses, let us throw off everything that hinders and the sin that so easily entangles, and let us run with perseverance the race marked out for us. Let us fix our eyes on Jesus, the author and perfecter of our faith.

Hebrews 12:1-2

Probably no other Mennonite endeavor [as MDS] has received as much local and national press coverage all of it favorable. The sight of a host of volunteers in work clothes coming at short notice from distant points to donate time and labor to complete strangers that always makes news. Good news.   *Robert Schrag[1]*

MDS continues to make good news. While guided daily by God s Spirit, MDS is people, in all their humanity, and none of us are perfect. We make mistakes and learn from them, we hope. We take risks, for to take no risks is to risk doing nothing. We must continually evaluate our past, both the good and the not so good, and strive to be more Christlike in our future service. With God s help, we can do good better. [2]

Two Fears of 1975

In *Day of Disaster,* Katie Funk Wiebe verbalized two concerns facing MDS in years to come. The first, Katie cautioned, was that praise may rob the organization of its spirit of servanthood. The second fear was that the trend from charisma toward bureaucracy may cause MDS to become brittle and lose its original vigor and vitality. [3] Twenty-five years later, we need to assess how MDS has faced these fears.

Praise Versus Servanthood

In 1975, in the conclusion to his *Day of Disaster* foreword, Senator Birch Bayh wrote, It may be too soon to call MDS a legend, but the description of the sacrifices of MDS volunteers recorded here can only add to its outstanding reputation. After another quarter-century of service, it is still too early to call MDS a legend. Yet the stories of God s people at work as recorded in these chapters add to the reputation.

Carl Hiebert

Photo, page 158: Are we on the mark and cutting straight? For 50 years, John Burkholder and a multitude of fellow MDS volunteers have given witness to the good news and made good news. Can we do better?

MDS investigators entering an area right after a disaster marvel at how the MDS logo lets them through most roadblocks. Other volunteer or government organizations say, "We'd like the Mennonites to work with us on this project." Wall space in the small Akron office never holds all the awards, plaques, and keys to cities that thankful people have given MDS. This is a reputation each succeeding generation finds hard to live up to. Call it praise; call it respect—MDS still makes good press.

Though MDS leaders have sometimes admitted to being "Mennonite proud" of

A True Blessing: "For this I bless you most; you do much good and know not that you do any."
—Kahlil Gibran[4]

You Need Better Publicity

Many people encourage us to have better publicity. It is interesting to hear the response when we decline publicity and explain that what we do is best done as anonymously as possible. I have come to view the lack of publicity as another peaceful way to lead one's life. —Pam Denlinger

THE DAILY OKLAHOMAN

The State Newspaper Since 1907

FRIDAY, JULY 9, 1999

Faithful Followers of Disaster

The house that love built

Georgians Grateful to MDS for Renewal of Hope

Mennonite volunteers rebuilding houses for local tornado victims

Homes and Lives Rebuilt After Flood

For the first time in my life it was real Christian love for another in action.
— Joanie Tyree

Amidst Shock, Grief and Anger, Tornado Victim Receives Help from MDS 'Angels'

MDS (Make Do Somehow) Has Its Rewards

their recognition by others, our humanity soon splatters in our face, forcing us to acknowledge our need for God's grace and forgiveness. The public may not always note our squabbles and shortcomings, but still they appear.

"Servanthood is one of the hallmarks of Christ's kingdom," Peter J. Dyck reminded MDSers at their 25th anniversary. "Greatness is determined by the willingness to be servant of all." Does the call to serve stand up against unending demands on our time and energy by life swirling around us? MDS can point to thousands of volunteers who have served in recent years and say, "Servanthood is alive and well." But many a contact person has groaned, "I just can't find anyone who will take off a day or a week and serve anymore." It may or may not be praise that robs us of our spirit of servanthood. But whether it is praise, busyness, materialism, or looking out for number one, the challenge of retaining our servant calling is one we face in each generation.

Charisma Versus Bureaucracy

Has MDS become a bureaucracy and lost its charisma, its original vigor and vitality? MDS has made many changes in recent years, as outlined in chapter 11. Does moving from two to three or four staff make a bureaucracy? No. If we are willing to change as the disaster scene changes around us, have we become brittle? Likely not. Thousands of people each year still excitedly serve with MDS, including hundreds of youth. Lost our charisma? Probably not. Still have our original vigor and vitality? Usually 400-700 people show up for our

annual all-unit meeting. This may be a question for more objective historians and each coming generation to answer.

MDS remains a grassroots-oriented organization. The key word continues to be *flexibility*. No two disasters or disaster responses are the same. Yet sometimes one hears from weary leaders, "This isn't the

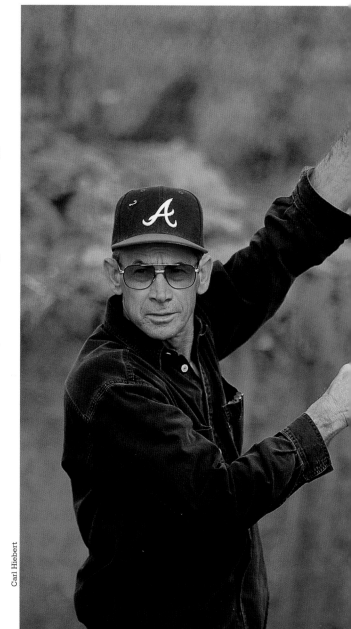

Carl Hiebert

MDS photo

Wilbur Litwiller

way we used to do it," or "Just when you think you understand the situation, what you don't understand is that the situation just changed."

At age 50, MDS has reached a mature middle age. We have learned from the past, yet we know we cannot stay there. We look to the future. Changes may weary us, but we know that much remains to be done. We sense that those fears of 1975 have neither overtaken us nor gone away. New challenges have been added.

Does the Vision from the Past Fit the Future?

One goal of studying history is to learn from that history for the benefit of the future. The questions asked most often during the interviews for this book were "What can we learn from our past?" and "What are the challenges facing MDS in the future?"

The rest of this chapter shares more introspective comments as we ponder our past and hope to gain insights for the future. As a grassroots and constituency-oriented organization, MDS leaders always welcome suggestions from volunteers, supporters, observers, and readers of this book.

Reflections on 12 Years as Executive Coordinator

As author and compiler of this book, I've tried to gather stories of MDS activity during these 50 years in a fairly objective manner. Now I'd like to share the joys and struggles of my 12 years as executive coor-

dinator (1986-98) and reflect on concerns I have for the MDS of the future.

MDS is an incredible organization; no book can do its story full justice. It was a special privilege to be "captain" and to serve the far-reaching grassroots team throughout Canada and the United States. We've circled North America together in project activity: from Maine to Florida, California, Alaska, Alberta, Quebec, and many points between. On behalf of MDS, I've received thanks from former President Jimmy Carter, FEMA Director James Lee Witt, Red Cross President Elizabeth Dole, and hundreds of others MDS volunteers have served. "To God be the glory, great things [God] has done!" (Fanny J. Crosby).

Tough Tasks

People head both the joy and struggle list! When thousands of volunteers come from various backgrounds and perspectives, there are bound to be differences and personality conflicts. How do you "fire" a volunteer? Sending someone home early is likely the most difficult (and thankfully rare) task MDS leaders face. How does one keep working on communication and overcoming misunderstandings, going the second mile? How does one pull together leadership teams for major projects, knowing that different leadership styles folks bring won't always mesh?

MDS volunteers require a spirit of flexibility and service. Some people welcome

Grassroots Readiness

I have been intrigued by the MDS organization and how it has been able to mount such creative and powerful programming with a minimum of structure. I hope we can always have that kind of quick response without big recruiting campaigns. —John A. Lapp

Far left: How do we measure up? Our 50th (golden) anniversary is a good time to take stock and see how we have done.

Top left: Elizabeth Dole, president of American Red Cross (left), congratulates Ann Heinrichs and Lowell Detweiler as they receive the Good Neighbor Award from the ARC on behalf of MDS in 1991.

Bottom left: Mattie Chandler tells the world how pleased she is with her new home, built by MDS volunteers near Birmingham, Ala., in 1998.

the opportunity to try something new. Others complain, "This isn't what I came to do." Project leaders love to hear a volunteer say, "I have this skill, but I'm happy to serve where needed most."

MDSers also need to leave a this-is-the-only-right-way-to-do-this attitude at home. We strive to do each task as we would want it done for ourselves, but there is usually more than one way to achieve it. Quality work is a goal but perfection is not—especially if it means the persons we're working for or the new volunteers can't help because they don't know how to do it just right.

A second tough task involves *unity*. Given our wide diversity, how do we keep people working together, focused on mission rather than differences? We struggle! We listen to the concerns of our board representatives. We develop more respectful guidelines for how we live and work together, guidelines related to dress, lifestyles, and roles of women in leader-

Right: Vic Plessinger (standing, right) receives an award from community representatives after the Lake Blackshear, Ga., flood project. Bev Plessinger (left) records another moment in their long history of involvement with MDS. Standing next to Vic is Lloyd Swartzendruber, MDS Georgia chair.

On Doing Good Better

How does MDS review what has happened in its programs? How much does MDS think about whether doing good is **to** others or **with** others? What ethical sensitivities have arisen regarding when to work side by side with community people, when to accept the leadership of the local community, or when to take over? —Robert Kreider

The Witness of Working Together

We were working on the flood project down at Springfield. We had volunteers coming in to register, from Amish to every branch of Mennonite. The Red Cross workers were standing there, watching men sign in. When they left, one said, "How do you do this? You've got every kind of Mennonite. You've got those with beards and those with wedding bands and some that smoke [not approved in MDS guidelines], and they all just work together."

She said, "That is a real testimony. I wish our Baptist churches would be that way." That struck me—what a testimony our unity in service ministries is. Even though we don't agree on everything in practice, we can work together. —Velma Yoder, Missouri MDS

162

ship. We affirm the gifts each person brings to us, regardless of gender, race, or church. We pray for sensitivity and respect, from each for each.

Nevertheless, some have felt uncomfortable working with MDS, and two other Mennonite organizations also have their own disaster response program. The Church of God in Christ (Mennonite) has long administered its own program. More recently, Christian Aid Ministries has added domestic disaster service to its worldwide program. MDS and these groups communicate with each other on programming and cooperate when possible. Yet our separate programs sometimes confuse recipients and other agencies. I grieve that we have lost some of that special witness that comes from all working together.

Joys

People are the first of my joys. Hundreds of people have blessed my life. They include staff colleagues who helped carry the load, board members who gave wise counsel and encouragement, and project leaders who said yes one more time. I treasure blessings from the thousands of volunteers each year, truly sent by God at just the right time, and the tremendous network at home, sending out spouses and children and praying for MDS work. I remember with appreciation special co-workers like Amos Miller, Dan Bontrager, and Roger Friesen, who now look down from above and whose lives modeled servanthood. With thanks to that *Schekjebenjel* (errand boy, cowboy) poet, Doris Daley, from Calgary, Alberta, I dedicate her poem of blessing to all of you who have enriched my life (poem on page 163).

Concerns for the Future

Like Katie Funk Wiebe in *Day of Disaster*, I have concerns as MDS looks to the future. A key concern is for *project leadership*. No single chronic need in the 50-year history of MDS stands out like the ongoing cry for "project leaders." In 1951 in Kansas, unit leaders asked how they might find persons to stay on project locations longer and provide consistent leadership to rotating crews. With more and larger disasters in today's world, that need is even greater. In recent years, MDS has often responded to six or more major disasters at any given time. Each needs its leadership team, composed variously, according to the size of response.

Project leadership is hard but crucial work. It has usually fallen on the shoulders of older, experienced MDSers who can give more time. Aiding them by taking on significant responsibilities have been younger adults who are part of the long-term team. Both older and younger can be stretched by responsibilities thrust on them; both usually respond with flying colors. But MDS needs more persons like Vic

MDS photo

and Bev Plessinger, who take early retirement and then give significant blocks of time in service, before health and energy can no longer meet leadership demands. MDS needs more people like Lee and Mary Lois Martin, who set aside a block of two years and offer their services in project leadership.

Anyone who has served on an MDS assignment knows the crucial role of the leadership team, and the frustrations that come when things are not organized and ready for volunteers. Whether your gift is construction, office work, cooking, advocacy, or organizing, consider giving time to service. The blessings will be yours.

Whether it's engines or MDS units, we need to keep things tuned up. Bill Mast, MDS Okla. unit leader (left), and Henry Dueck, College Station, Ark., project leader try to keep things running smoothly.

Carl Hiebert

Holding Fast to the Vision: A Spirit of Servanthood

Fifty years ago a group of young men and women had a *vision*. While in CPS camps, they became aware of a larger world and dreamed of how to serve that world in daily life, not only in time of war. I've been touched and challenged as I met and interviewed many of them. They sought a way to keep serving after returning to their home communities. Their vision was for personal faithfulness; little did they imagine the amazing organization their dream would spawn.

Now the draft no longer forces us to participate in alternate service. The typical young Mennonite completes education, gets a job, marries, buys a house, and settles down to raise a family and make money. We know what is happening in the world around us. But when the TV images fade, we turn to the unending tasks of daily life as assigned by our culture.

Like Katie Funk Wiebe 25 years ago, I fear we may lose our vision of servanthood. But it may be apathy we fight to overcome, not praise. It is easy for us to live each day without contact with the hungry, the homeless, the sorrowful, the destitute. Sometime we may have to ask, "Lord, when did we see you hungry?" MDS is one place where our response can provide an "inasmuch as you have done it to one of these" opportunity (Matt. 25). May God keep us faithful.

Bless These Hands

Doris Daley

There's a special pair of hands assigned to do each task,
And to do a job the best we know is about as good as we can ask.
You can try to stand alone, but your world could start to drift
So the good Lord struck a plan and gave each one a special gift.

So God bless the hands that are scarred and brown and rough,
But hands that reach to help you when the trail is looking tough.
Bless young and eager hands that take a challenge in their stride,
And teach us when the chips are down to get back on and ride.

Bless hands that fill the sandbags and hands that scrub the floors,
Hands that paint and clean and do a thousand other chores.
Bless hands that wield the crowbars and hands that pound the nails,
And hands that make do somehow when the first plan sometimes fails.

Hands that make the drywall fit with a little extra shove,
And Cookie's hands that make the meals and serve them up with love.
Bless hands that You've prepared to accept the leader's load,
And bless those hands that buckle down and do the job to code.

Hands that deal with blisters with a smile and a shrug,
And hands that drop their tools when a neighbor needs a hug.
Bless a handshake firm and strong that says, "Howdy, my new friend,
You're not alone, we're here to help, and we're with you till the end."

Bless laborers' hands and tradesmen's hands and each one on the crew,
They're only trying to do their part in a way that honors you.
And if you're feeling generous, Lord, and it's not too much to ask,
Even bless the hands of one like me, who doesn't know a router from a rasp.

God gives each hand a gift, and with his grace we'll stand the test.
Bless each one—we need each one—to do the work of MDS.

Why Wait till Retirement?

I question whether you will have the volunteers we did when we were more rural people. We hear this time and time again, "When I retire, I'm going to do something like you folks are doing." The odds are eight out of ten that they never will. If you don't do something before you retire, generally speaking, you won't once you retire. People are not as adventuresome at 65 as at age 50. That's one reason we said that by the time we were 50, we wanted to be volunteering.
—Vic and Bev Plessinger

A Larger MDS Team

The team approach in our organizational structure has worked well. We've gone a long way toward becoming better prepared to respond, especially to major disasters. We need to continue our training sessions and to keep searching for more project directors.

As we bring more team members into our larger projects, we have to work at ways to get those people to work together more effectively.
—Paul Brubacher

Below: These five have served in MDS for a total of 150 years! Photo taken at the retirement of Ray Hess (seated right) after 42 years of representing the Brethren in Christ on the local unit or the MDS board (29 years): (clockwise from Ray) Landis Hershey, 31 years (17 as Region I director or on the board); Paul Brubacher, 27 years (13 years as Region I director, 14 years on the board, and current board chair); Lowell Detweiler, 14 years (12 as executive coordinator); and Norman Shenk, 36 years on the board (14 as chair).

Chuck Strouse

164

Three Crucial Team Members

All team members are important. Nothing will be accomplished without good volunteers. This book has said much about the importance of the project director. Personnel for three other positions crucial to a good team are often in short supply. If you would consider service in one of these roles, please contact the MDS Akron office.

The construction foreman

A person with good construction experience who can direct an overall reconstruction effort is a necessity on a long-term rebuilding project.

MDS is becoming involved in more projects that involve total rebuilds. A construction foreman works with clients in planning, costing, and ordering materials, and supervising the construction from foundation to completion. The foreman works under the project director. Together they determine priority jobs and select and assign crews.

Bob Bender, Goshen, Indiana, MDS construction foreman on many projects: I'm a contractor, framer, and do a lot of cement work. I like to frame and work with youth. It's good for my patience. It's fun to teach them how to frame something, then see the results in the evening.

A construction foreman needs to be open to listen as well as to give advice. He needs to sit back and let people do their jobs, realizing there are many ways to do things. He

Right: Bob Bender ponders his next move, surrounded by the young folks he loves to put to work.

just needs to make sure the result is right. He needs to be able to organize, to be able to say quickly in the morning where people need to go.

There is real satisfaction in MDS work. To see people in need, and help meet those needs, that's a joy. We have worked for some real appreciative people. They were so pleased and thankful for what we were doing. It gives us a new perspective, once we get home, on how totally wrapped up we get in our work.

The head cook

What can be more important than keeping an MDS crew well-fed and full of energy for work? Feeding 20, 30, or even 50 or more hungry volunteers may seem a daunting task.

MDS kitchens come in all shapes and sizes but usually are fairly well stocked, sometimes with a lot of donated food.

MDS photo

Below: Jean Hampton (right) and Bev Plessinger, hard at work preparing a tasty meal for the next wave of hungry volunteers.

Courtesy of Jean Hampton

MDS photo

Left: Brian Epp (right) consults with FEMA representative Waddy Gonzales, about next steps for rebuilding a house in Puerto Rico.

Planning meals is often a challenge. How many will there be today? Can we talk one or two of the persons (women or men) coming this week into staying and helping in the kitchen?

Jean Hampton, Lancaster, Pennsylvania, one of the busiest MDS cooks around: I went to my first longer-term MDS project in Florida, hoping to work in mental health. They were cutting back on those staff, so I asked if there were other openings.

Oma Smucker grabbed my hand and started for the office. She said, "You're an answer to prayer. Would you be willing to cook?"

That wasn't what I had in mind, but I felt the Lord was leading. So I answered, "If I have good help, I think I can manage." I served two months, took a month off, and went back for another three months. It was really a good experience.

One of the biggest jobs in cooking for MDS is planning meals and buying supplies. Cooks need to start with a good breakfast—workers need something to go on till lunch. As soon as we finish breakfast, we start the noon meal. When we get the noon meal done, we start thinking of the evening meal. Sometimes we get a short break in there. It's a long day.

Cooking is a real need. If I'm available and can do it, I feel like I should. I feel this is where the Lord wants me at this time. I really enjoy being part of the team. What would they do without a cook? At first I thought, *I'm just a cook. Now I think, I am THE COOK.*

The crew leader

When an MDS project has many jobs going, the construction foreman depends heavily on skilled crew leaders to direct the volunteers. Sometimes the crew leader may direct the work at a given project site, or direct special crews doing drywalling, roofing, or painting as they move about from house to house.

Longer-term volunteers, including youth and women who specialize in a given task, often become crew leaders. They can lead crews to jobs and keep them with going with supplies. Crew leaders have the construction foreman or project director for backup.

Brian Epp, Rosthern, Saskatchewan, crew leader with experience from St. Croix to Los Angeles: It's just good to have one person in charge on each job to make decisions and organize people.

You don't need that much experience to be a crew leader; you need to know the basics. Many times I found guys on my crews with more experience than I have. I can learn from them, but they need someone longer-term to get the materials and tools on the job.

I find I get as much as I give. That's something I don't get when I'm working at my job as a truck driver. I always go away feeling better about myself after an MDS term. I have renewed optimism about life.

I've seen God's work firsthand, daily prayers being answered—like when the electrician you need shows up unexpectedly. You sometimes wrestle with shortages of tools or material, struggling to stretch things. But you learn to be resourceful.

MDS is a well-run organization with worthwhile projects. I'll definitely go back again.

Our Volunteers Are Incredible

It amazes me to come to a project like this and see the kinds of things Nick and Iola Thiessen are doing. Leadership, keeping people like them part of MDS on a continuing basis, really makes our organization work. —Jane Kuepfer, board member, after a visit to the MDS project site at Sanford, Florida

The Second Commandment

We need to follow the second greatest commandment, "Love your neighbor as yourself." We need to take time to build our neighbors' house.

That rarely happens at a convenient time. Neither is that time seasonal. We need to respond spring, summer, fall, and winter. Can we imagine having to wait one month, six months, or a year for help?

We're so affluent and independent that we "buy" our help. But we have often failed to follow our Lord's commands. —Mary Lois Martin

Above: What do we see ahead? Will we hold fast to the vision of those who started MDS? Marlin Lehman wonders, Who will take my place?

Right: "When the digging gets tough, the tough get digging." MDSers have perservered through mud, cold, and heat. Will we keep on digging?

Opportunities Ahead

Tom Smucker, MDS Executive Coordinator from May 1998

Growth is one of the issues MDS is already facing. With disasters increasing and more requests coming to us, how much can a small organization do? When do we need to say *no?* What should we do when we cannot find work sites for all the youth groups who want to serve? How do we say no to a small community devastated by a tornado when MDS views each one's loss as important? How do we say no to that young adult or early retired person with limited skills when we do not have construction foremen to oversee them? Since we want to say *yes* instead of no, what direction does MDS need to take?

MDS has truly become a *double-impact organization.* Meeting the needs of the disaster survivors is an obvious goal; MDS assists thousands each year. It is also important to offer church members opportunities to share their faithfulness by giving

MDS photo

time and abilities to help others in a short-term setting. Leaders need to understand disaster survivors *and* volunteers. Both have often noted that their Christian faith has been strengthened through involvement with MDS. We need to keep focusing on our faith and why we are serving.

Many times in MDS settings, *social and racial barriers* have unconsciously been crossed. Volunteers are often in low-income and diverse cultural settings. Yet on the work site, barriers break down when the focus is on a common goal, recovery from disaster. We must continue to identify communities and individuals who have been bypassed because of their position in society. We need to locate our projects by need rather than by media and constituent pressure.

Mitigation, safe rooms, green space, zoning laws, building codes, buyout programs, roadblocks, federal grants—these are terms that affect our operations. People have greatly appreciated MDS for our ability and willingness to stay in a community for an extended period and to work with the unique challenges that come with long-term commitments. This often involves understanding and cooperating with local and federal government programs. If we want to help those who have fallen through the cracks, we must first know how to get them back into the system.

MDS is working to train leaders to understand these regulations so they can help survivors to a more complete recovery. Amid challenges, MDS has provided long-term recovery to many communities. Longevity at a project has provided many opportunities for friendship and lasting

relations. MDS is more than bricks and mortar.

Our highest priority must be to remain faithful to the call of serving our Lord. We need to continue to seek God's leading and direction as MDS looks ahead to the next 50 years.

Courtesy of Lee and Mary Lois Martin

Left: Mary Lois Martin with her friend Arushu on ramp at home in Albany, Ga.

Below left: At the Del City, Okla., disaster scene, with colleagues Joe Steiner (left) and Wilbur Litwiller (right), executive coordinator Tom Smucker points the future direction for MDS. Pray for Tom, the staff team, and the MDS network as they faithfully and creatively lead MDS into the next century.

Keep Your Focus

Congregations want to have direct involvement. Organizations that can't provide that don't have a good future. MDS is better positioned than most in that it has always had a very strong grassroots organization.

Keep focused on your niche—disaster response in the name of Christ—and remain strongly lay-oriented and rooted in our tradition, in our theology, in our congregations. Make adjustments that will make it possible for the people available to serve. If you do these things, I don't see MDS threatened by the changes on the horizon. —Edgar Stoesz

We're All in God's Kingdom

Serving with MDS in places like Haiti; Pine Ridge, South Dakota; and Saragosa, Texas, has been a broadening experience. It has helped me be more accepting of other people. It has made me realize afresh that my first priority is my citizenship in God's kingdom. —Myron Schultz

Between MDS and Mennonite Voluntary Service, I've learned how other people feel who don't have white skin, who don't speak English. I've become more understanding of their life situations. They have feelings of pain and joy like I do. They need God's love just as much. —Phyllis Schultz

167

Courtesy of Carol Rohrer

> *Let us hold unswervingly to the hope we profess, for [God] who promised is faithful. And let us consider how we may spur one another on toward love and good deeds. Let us not give up meeting together, as some are in the habit of doing, but let us encourage one another—and all the more as you see the Day approaching.*
>
> *—Hebrews 10:23-25*

CHAPTER FOURTEEN

Outbursts of Love and Good Deeds

God Is Working His Purpose Out

God is working his purpose out as year succeeds to year.
God is working his purpose out, and the time is drawing near.
Nearer and nearer draws the time, the time that shall surely be,
when the earth shall be filled with the glory of God as the waters cover the sea.

From utmost east to utmost west, where human feet have trod,
by the mouth of many messengers goes forth the voice of God,
"Give ear to me, ye continents, ye isles, give ear to me,
that the earth may be filled with the glory of God as the waters cover the sea."

All we can do is nothing worth unless God blesses the deed.
Vainly we hope for the harvest-tide till God gives life to the seed.
Yet nearer and nearer draws the time, the time that shall surely be,
when the earth shall be filled with the glory of God as the waters cover the sea.

—*Arthur C. Ainger*[1]

While I was writing this book, J. Lorne Peachey's editorial in the April 27, 1999, issue of *The Mennonite* struck me as a gift from above. It was based on Hebrews 10:24 (NLT), "Think of ways to encourage one another to outbursts of love and good deeds." After sharing instances where someone's "outburst of love" was a blessing to him, Peachey gives a final word on "love and good deeds. That is what Jesus brought to us. They are what we have to give others. We would do well to spend much more time thinking of ways to encourage each other to outbursts of both." Amen. The challenge of Hebrews 10:23-25 becomes the outline for this chapter.

Photo, page 168: In 100-degree heat, Becky Rohrer cools off Carey Martin. Their East Chestnut Street youth group of Lancaster, Pa. was helping to build the Mt. Zoar Baptist Church in Ala. in summer 1996.

Right: Tressie keeps looking up as she flies a kite with a neighbor's child. Her husband was killed in the 1997 Ark. tornadoes. She provided sweet potato pie to MDS volunteers and inspired all by her faith and hope.

Below: The April 8, 1998, tornadoes near Birmingham, Ala., destroyed the Open Door Church but did not seriously injure the 70 people there for a prayer meeting.

Let Us Hold Unswervingly to the Hope We Profess

A theme that permeates this book is *hope*. The hope that is in us (1 Pet. 3:15) keeps MDSers slogging through mud and debris from yet another disaster. We are called to restore hope to those who have survived the latest tragedy. Our ultimate purpose is to bear witness to the hope that comes through Christ Jesus.

James Brenneman, pastor of Pasadena Mennonite Church, spoke at the MDS all-unit meeting at Reedley, California, in 1996. Excerpts from his presentation will be used throughout this chapter. He shared a story from his boyhood years, growing up in Tampa, Florida. A hurricane hit one night and sent a huge oak tree through the roof of his sister's bedroom. James and his brother huddled in bed "not sure whether to die right then and there from fright or later from the storm's violent punches. Then an unusual thing happened. Having

grown up Amish, Mama had always been a bit too practical to say much about her faith. But while the rest of us were stone stiff from fright, I could hear Mama singing, 'On Christ the solid rock I stand; all other ground is sinking sand, all other ground is sinking sand.' I shivered there, listening as she sang about the Solid Rock on which our weak, feeble, scared-to-death hearts could stand.

"Would that we all keep singing as we keep on swinging our hammers, 'My hope is built on nothing less, than Jesus' blood and righteousness. I dare not trust the sweetest frame, but wholly lean on Jesus' name. On Christ the solid rock I stand, all other ground is sinking sand.'"[2]

He Who Promised Is Faithful

God's promise to be with us as we go about his kingdom work has been felt by MDSers over these 50 years. MDS records, especially in the early years, are incom-

plete. Even now MDS Akron often does not hear about all the projects handled in the grassroots network. Yet going by the last decade, we can make some estimates of MDS involvement over the years.

During the 1990s, a "slow year" would record the involvement of about 2,000 volunteers. A "big year" would approach

Carl Hiebert

5,000. This includes only those volunteers involved in the major, longer-term projects known to MDS Akron; many more serve in locally sponsored activity. Using a conservative average of 3,000 volunteers per year, times 50 years, likely over 150,000 volunteers have served with MDS.

Some volunteers serve one day, most a week, many one or two months, and a few as long as two years. If one used an average only slightly higher than one week per volunteer, the total days of work contributed by MDS volunteers during these 50 years is approaching *one million*.

To our knowledge, no volunteer has died while on an MDS work assignment. We've had accidents (some serious), heart attacks, and dengue fever. But the Lord and medical teams have brought recovery. Two long-term volunteers serving in Florida in 1998 were caught in an undertow while swimming in the ocean but were saved by lifeguards. Surely the Lord has been with us; "underneath are his everlasting arms."

In the early 1990s, MCC legal advisors described MDS as a high-risk organization. They encouraged a legal separation of organizations to prevent any lawsuits against MDS from reaching MCC resources. This made legal sense. Nevertheless, God's protection and the good common sense of MDS leaders and volunteers have prevented any lawsuit against MDS.

God Gives Life to Another Seed

On any Sunday, you will likely find Hildegard Juell at Community Mennonite Church in Palmer Lake, Colorado. How she found the Mennonites may surprise you.

In 1965, Hildegard and her family were living on a farm near Grand Rapids, Michigan. The April 11 Palm Sunday tornadoes cut a swath three miles long through her community. With no warning of the storm, she barely made it through the trapdoor into the cellar before the tornado devastated their farm, destroying barn, garage, and half the house.

It took a day for the roads to be cleared. Imagine their surprise and thankfulness when a day later a busload of Mennonites came to help in the tremendous cleanup.

In 1996 Hildegard moved to Colorado to be closer to a daughter. She saw a sign for the Mennonite church, remembered the Mennonites from 1965, and visited the church. A friendly welcome and edifying sermons convinced her to stay.

Today she supports with enthusiasm the youth groups and other members who go out in MDS or other service projects. Another seed planted and hope restored.

Sharing the Hope We Profess

I had the opportunity to go to Alaska with MDS. My mother was very ill, so I asked her if I could go to Alaska for two weeks. She said, "If you go and help people rebuild their homes, and through your witness help someone to receive Jesus, you can go."

I phoned our son to tell him I wouldn't be able to help with his construction work for two weeks because I was going to Alaska. He said that was okay; he wasn't very busy. Soon he phoned back to ask if he could go, too. I said, "You're not a Christian. I don't know if they'd allow you to go." I told him I'd ask. After talking with him, local MDS leaders agreed he could go.

In Alaska fellow crew members witnessed to him as they built a new home. One morning the cook asked if they could have a prayer meeting during the day for him. I encouraged that, for he seemed troubled.

A few days later he spoke to me: "Dad, we need to go for a walk. I have to talk to you. . . . I've accepted Jesus, and I'm afraid to go home." (His wife wasn't a Christian.) "I'd like to stay here and work." That wasn't possible since he had to go back to work.

He wasn't home for ten minutes before his wife said, "You're different." She hasn't accepted his new faith. He's having a hard time at home and needs a lot of prayers.

Little was I aware of what would happen on that trip, and I'm sure Mother wasn't. We thank God that MDS gave my son a chance to go and that MDS isn't just about putting houses together but being a living example of our Lord Jesus.
—*An MDS volunteer*

Carl Hiebert

Above: "Bless this house, O Lord, we pray." Dean Denlinger (right), joined by other MDSers, leads in dedicating the house for Rosetta Crenshaw in March 1999 near Birmingham, Ala. MDS gave her a Bible, the keys, and a loaf of bread.

Carl Hiebert

Spurring One Another Toward Love and Good Deeds

Top: Barbara and Roger Friesen rebuilding after the Alaska fire in 1996. Roger and Barbara led many MDS projects before he died in May 1999.

Bottom: J. D. Kuefper (foreground, right) was part of the early response team to St. Thomas after Hurricane Marilyn struck the island in 1995. A tarp over a platform makes a temporary home for a family who has lost everything.

Few public figures have done more to "spur others toward love and good deeds" than former President Jimmy Carter. His own life, especially as demonstrated through his involvement in Habitat for Humanity, is a living testimony of serving others.

In his book, *The Virtues of Aging,* Carter suggests, "There is still a difference between how long we live and how much we enjoy living. With reasonable good health, there are two crucial factors in how happy or successful an older person is: (1) having a purpose in life and (2) maintaining quality relationships with others.[3]

Testimonies of Purpose and Relationships

In this book are many stories showing that involvement in MDS provides those two crucial factors needed for happy liv-ing—*purpose* and *quality relationships.* To encourage you to "outbursts of love and good deeds," note these further testimonies.

Barbara and Roger Friesen, Dinuba, California: MDS has made me see that things are not so important. People and their essential needs, and need for the Lord, have become more important to me. We need to tell about all the wonderful things people are doing out there in MDS. We have made so many friends with so many volunteers. That has widened our horizons and strengthened our faith. I advise anyone who is retired and in good health to pack up and go. It is rewarding to help someone else.

J. D. Kuepfer, Seaforth, Ontario: So many people have such a neat experience with MDS that they just keep coming back. One thing I remember from being in St. Thomas is the gratitude of the people helped. We fixed a roof for an elderly woman who was partly blind, and she was so grateful. She gave us hugs. It's a privilege to be able to serve people.

Beryl Forrester, Salem, Oregon, after serving in St. Croix: The MDS project unit functioned in a way that made me think of what the church ought to be like. It wasn't utopia, just Christian brotherhood and sisterhood at its best. I'm convinced that if our congregations could somehow duplicate what happens in MDS units, the unchurched in our communities would be beating a path to the doors of our churches. There is something irresistible about Christians when they're totally dedicated to ministering in the name of Christ.

Virgil Kauffman, Reed City, Michigan:

Priorities

"We worry too much about something to live on—and too little about something to live for." —Jimmy Townsend, writer and friend of the Carters, quoted in *Virtues of Aging*

Keep on Doing What You're Doing

Throughout our land there is much more work to be done. You've got to be concerned about your brothers and sisters everywhere. I say to you Mennonites, keep on doing what you're doing. There will always be disasters. Unfortunately, they won't all come by tornadoes, hurricanes, and floods. Some will continue to come from evil hearts and hands [such as Mt. Zoar Baptist Church burning]. Be encouraged now, be inspired now; you remember how God has blessed you.
—Pastor Thomas Gilmore, Ensley, Alabama

Courtesy of Barbara Friesen

MDS photo

I still think it's the best way to retire. It's the most satisfying way. How else can you retire and meet so many people and feel like you're serving the Lord? And you go home tired and feel good about it.

A Third Force in Mennonitism

The MDS annual meeting in Morton on February 9-10 grabbed me like a camp meeting, annual church conference, Christian workers retreat, and annual business meeting all rolled into one. There is something about MDS that is elemental, earthy, grassroots, celebrative, loving-accepting, confident, eager, Spirit-filled, and unsophisticated. I had a cleaned, washed feeling in attending the meetings.

It is like a third force in Mennonitism that theologians and church bureaucrats have scarcely recognized. No college or seminary professors were there, and only a few conference leaders. Talk about evangelism, witnessing, and social action—the MDS experiences of 1972 are about the biggest involvement we [the church] have had this year.

There is continuous intrusion of humor in the face of tragedy and weariness. The meeting is one long string of testimonies. One hears no talk about inter-Mennonite cooperation—the ecumenical is implicit, accepted, and cherished.
—*Robert Kreider, after attending the 1973 MDS All-Unit Meeting*

Let Us Not Give Up Meeting Together

The history of the MDS all-unit meeting is fascinating. When MDS came under the umbrella of MCC in 1955, the first meetings of MDS representatives were held at MCC's annual meetings in Chicago hotels (1956-60). In February 1961 the sixth annual MDS representatives meeting was held in Denver, Colorado, with 52 people in attendance. In 1962 it returned to Chicago for the last time. In 1963 the meeting was held in Hillsboro, Kansas, and the following year in Lansdale, Pennsylvania. With the regional structure then in place, the annual meeting began rotating among the five regions, meeting every third year in Canada.

MDS photo

Attendance at the MDS all-unit meetings has continued to grow, demonstrating its grassroots dynamics. In the 1975 meetings in Hesston, Kansas, celebrating the 25th MDS anniversary, about 1,200 people attended the Friday evening banquet. During the last decade, as the meetings have ranged from Vancouver, British Columbia, to Homestead, Florida, attendance has varied from 300 to 850 persons. For the 50th anniversary celebrations, 2,000 or more are expected to gather in Hesston, Kansas, on June 2-4, 2000.

Meetings Highlight Years with MDS

Moving the all-unit meetings around was one thing that really helped MDS grow. They became the backbone of MDS. The stories told were really moving; the reports came alive.

There was such a love shown there among branches of the church that we didn't look at the differences; we looked at the hearts. Close friendships were formed as we worked, shared, cried, and laughed together. The meetings were the highlights of my years with MDS.
—John Jantzi, Region IV director, 1962-83

Courtesy of Egon Hofer

Far left: Syd Reimer greets Barbara Brubacher during a break at an MDS all-unit meeting. Fellowship among MDSers who met on far-flung projects gives spirit to MDS meetings.

Near left: The long and short of it! Mark Lehman (left) from Va. and Waldo Neufeld from Man. added humor to many an MDS meeting.

Let Us Encourage One Another

The work facing disaster survivors and volunteer rebuilders seems endless. MDSers provide a spark that encourages disaster victims as well as other MDSers. Often community people encourage MDSers.

God Works in Awesome Ways!

Ginny Sauder works part-time in the MDS Akron office. Her husband, Jake, is a pastor and feedmill worker. Their oldest child, Jordan, joined Jake, Ginny, and friends Randy Hollinger and his daughter Amber on a weeklong MDS trip to Birmingham in August 1999.

Ginny Sauder: We were looking forward to our week of MDS service, not only to serve with willing hearts and hands, but also for a change of pace, fun, and adventure. We got all that and more!

God works in awesome ways. Because of that trip, lives were changed in Alabama, our church, our family. Jordan and Amber are already talking about "the next trip," and so is Jake. Some highlights:

• Monday evening. Jake and Randy were ready to quit. With no experience, they had been asked to do finish carpentry work. Amber and Jordan didn't have much to do. Why were we there?

• Tuesday evening. Another MDSer worked along with Jake and Randy, encouraging them, helping, and answering their questions. End of day: the guys wore grins; Amber and Jordan wore paint.

• Wednesday. More work done on the Waldrop house. Met Greg, Becky, and the boys. End of day: guys had buttons about to pop on their shirts; Jordan and Amber had paint on their shirts.

• Thursday. Guys were so attached to tool belts and air nailer they could hardly part with them and clean up, knowing the job was done. End of day: Randy and Jake were finish carpenters; Jordan and Amber were finished painting the house.

• Friday. Guys got sweaty on demolition project. They decided the other work was more fun. Amber and Jordan felt important painting without Mom. I painted at Rozelle house and enjoyed visiting with Tonya. End of week: pride in what was accomplished; lots of dirty laundry!

This service week has enriched our lives. We appreciated the challenge of work we weren't qualified to do. With encouragement, the challenge turned into service that honored God.

Top: Finish carpenters—or finished as carpenters? Randy Hollinger (left) and Jake Sauder master new skills as they complete trim work in a house at Birmingham.

Bottom: Jordan Sauder (left) and Amber Hollinger painting trim. They are already talking about their "next MDS trip."

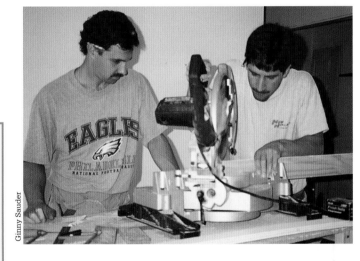

You Have to Pray More

We were serving at Fillmore, California, after the 1994 Northridge earthquake. The head of the Interfaith Committee was a Catholic priest, Father Norman. His church was near the old Fillmore hotel, now our MDS base, so we often worshiped at his church. We learned to love him; he was a real born-again Christian. He would visit us often to offer encouragement and see if we needed anything.

One day he asked the cooks what they needed. Since they were cooking for up to 25 people, they told him a second refrigerator would be welcome. The next day a used one arrived. A few days later, Father Norman came by and asked how things were going. The cooks reported, "The fridge you got us doesn't work." He just nonchalantly replied, "Well, you got to pray more." That's all he said. Then he left.

The next morning when the cooks came to the kitchen, they heard something running. They opened the fridge door. It was working! No one had been there to fix it. We took a lesson on how to pray from Father Norman.

In 1996 when the MDS all-unit meeting was held at Reedley, Calif., Father Norman was a guest speaker. Before his talk, he made a public apology for the persecution Catholics had inflicted on Anabaptists during the Reformation. We learn from, worship with, and are encouraged by Christian sisters and brothers of many denominations as we are drawn together in disaster service. —*Fred Kathler*

All the More as You See the Day Approaching

As you come to him, the living Stone—rejected by men but chosen by God and precious to him—you also, like *living stones*, are being built into a spiritual house to be a holy priesthood, offering spiritual sacrifices acceptable to God through Jesus Christ. —*1 Peter 2:4-5*

MDS photo

MDS photo

Living Stones

James Brenneman, calling MDSers "living stones" in 1996: As living stones, do what comes naturally to who you are as people gathered by God's grace. Don't try to be somebody you're not. Peter says, "Conduct yourselves honorably among the unbelievers, so that they may see your honorable deeds and glorify God when he comes" (1 Pet. 2:12, NRSV, adapted).

Later in his epistle, Peter himself now a "living rock," urges, "Each one of us should use whatever gift [Greek: *charisma*] we have received to serve one another, faithfully administering God's grace in its various forms" (4:10-11, adapted). Each one! Not just a couple of us here and there.

Not just the obviously "charismatic" personality types. If you are Amish, barn raising is a charismatic experience. If you're a carpenter, save people with your hammer and nails. That's charismatic. If all you can do is scrape river mud out of homes in Jesus' name, then you're a charismatic. If you speak well, then preach it, brother; preach it, sister. If you sing, then sing it: "On Christ the solid rock I stand, all other ground is sinking sand" (Edward Mote).

Sometimes we become too spiritual for our good, if not for God's good. We limit God's gifts because we define many gifts God has given us right out of the church. Sometimes you as MDSers may feel you come up short in the charisma department because your gifts are not always recognized as those more flamboyant, spiritually obvious on Sunday morning. Clearing sewers, raising barns, running electrical wire are gifts [charisms] of the highest order.

The church and the world await a movement of God's caring people whose actions of grace match words of hope.

If the rest of the church would begin to practice what many of you already do in practical, concrete ways, we just might experience a true charismatic revival, a renewal of God's grace poured out for all of us to see. The church and the world await a movement of God's caring people whose actions of grace match words of hope.

The world will stop to notice living stones who "love each other deeply enough to cover a multitude of sins" (1 Pet. 4:8). The world stops to notice living stones who "offer hospitality to one another without grumbling" (1 Pet. 4:9). The world stops to inquire of living stones gathered together using "whatever gifts they have to serve others."

Top: "We enjoy sharing our gifts," says the kitchen crew at the Sanford, Fla., project in February 1999.

Bottom: The joy of service comes as we each use our gifts to serve one another.

Use Whatever Gift

The end of all things is near; therefore be serious and discipline yourselves for the sake of your prayers. Above all, maintain constant love for one another, for love covers a multitude of sins. Be hospitable to one another without complaining. Like good stewards of the manifold grace of God, serve one another with whatever gift each of you has received. Whoever speaks must do so as one speaking the very words of God; whoever serves must do so with the strength that God supplies, so that God may be glorified in all things through Jesus Christ. To him belong the glory and the power forever and ever. Amen. —*1 Peter 4:7-11, NRSV*

Appendixes

MDS Time Line

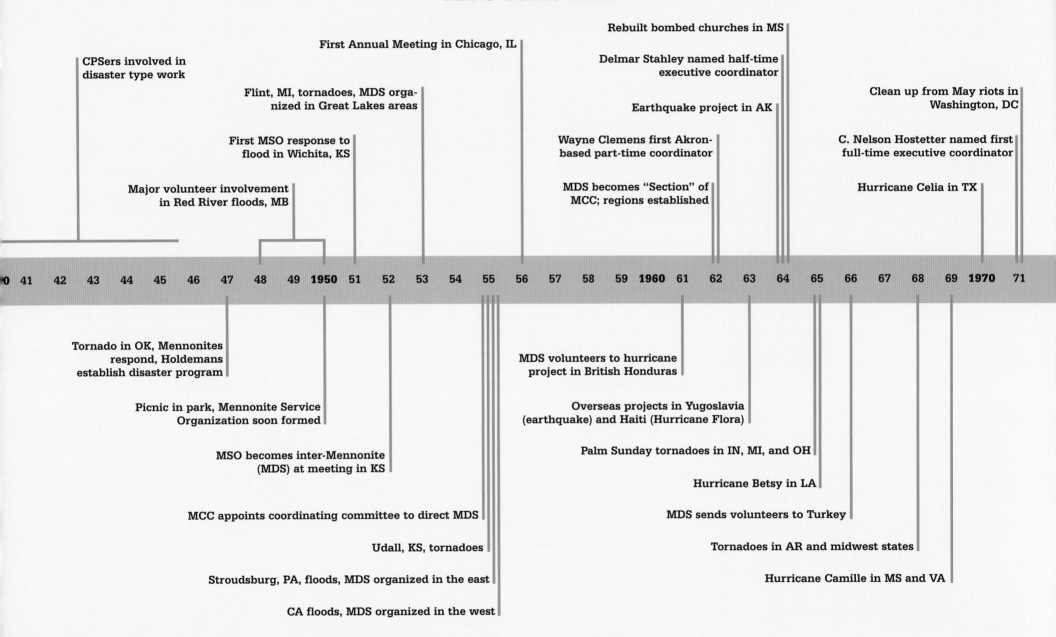

Rebuilt bombed churches in MS

First Annual Meeting in Chicago, IL

Delmar Stahley named half-time executive coordinator

CPSers involved in disaster type work

Clean up from May riots in Washington, DC

Flint, MI, tornadoes, MDS organized in Great Lakes areas

Earthquake project in AK

First MSO response to flood in Wichita, KS

Wayne Clemens first Akron-based part-time coordinator

C. Nelson Hostetter named first full-time executive coordinator

Major volunteer involvement in Red River floods, MB

MDS becomes "Section" of MCC; regions established

Hurricane Celia in TX

0 41 42 43 44 45 46 47 48 49 **1950** 51 52 53 54 55 56 57 58 59 **1960** 61 62 63 64 65 66 67 68 69 **1970** 71

Tornado in OK, Mennonites respond, Holdemans establish disaster program

MDS volunteers to hurricane project in British Honduras

Picnic in park, Mennonite Service Organization soon formed

Overseas projects in Yugoslavia (earthquake) and Haiti (Hurricane Flora)

MSO becomes inter-Mennonite (MDS) at meeting in KS

Palm Sunday tornadoes in IN, MI, and OH

Hurricane Betsy in LA

MCC appoints coordinating committee to direct MDS

MDS sends volunteers to Turkey

Udall, KS, tornadoes

Tornadoes in AR and midwest states

Stroudsburg, PA, floods, MDS organized in the east

Hurricane Camille in MS and VA

CA floods, MDS organized in the west

176

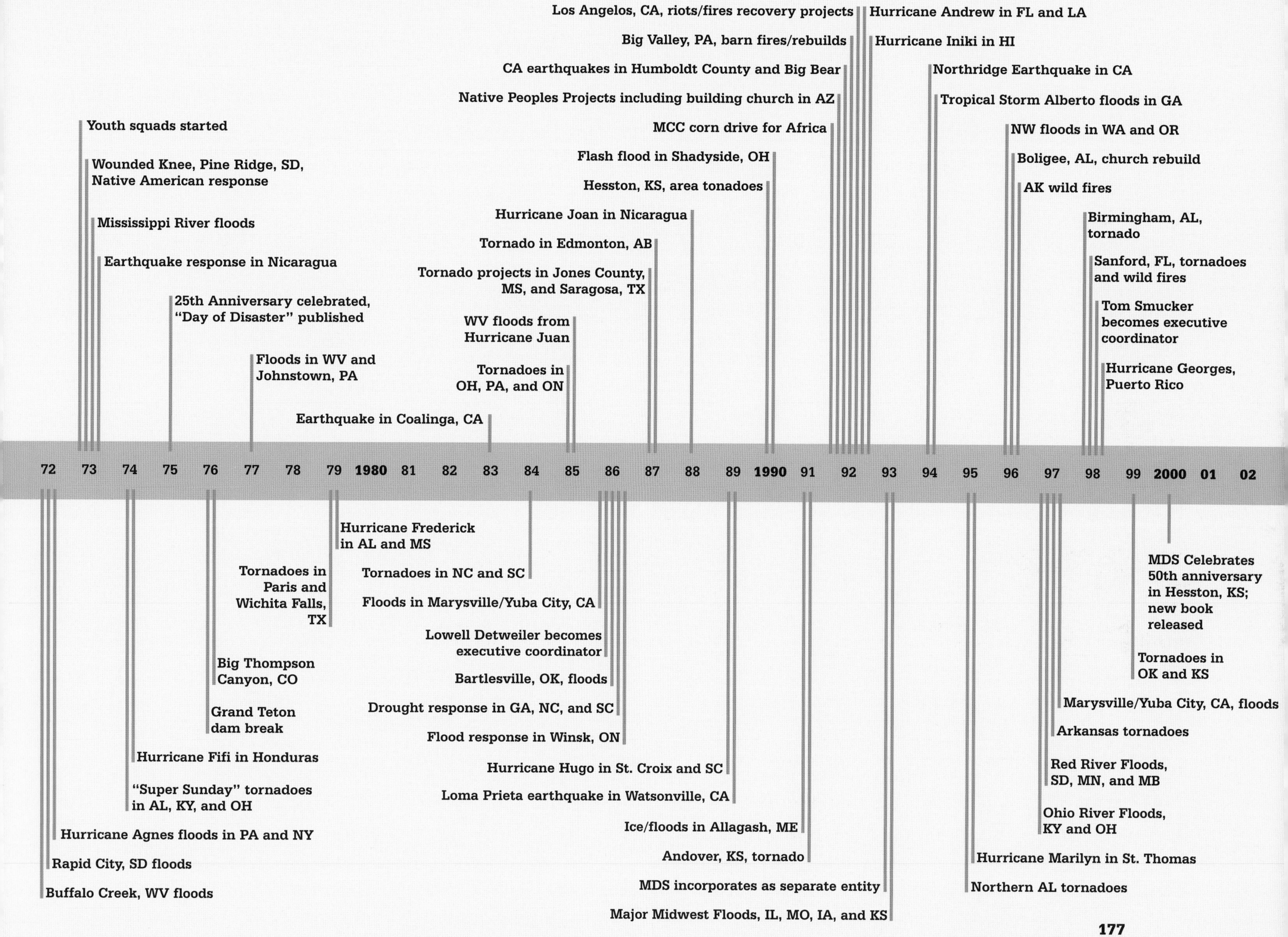

Timeline entries above the axis (top to bottom by label position):

Los Angelos, CA, riots/fires recovery projects

Hurricane Andrew in FL and LA

Big Valley, PA, barn fires/rebuilds

Hurricane Iniki in HI

CA earthquakes in Humboldt County and Big Bear

Northridge Earthquake in CA

Native Peoples Projects including building church in AZ

Tropical Storm Alberto floods in GA

MCC corn drive for Africa

NW floods in WA and OR

Youth squads started

Flash flood in Shadyside, OH

Boligee, AL, church rebuild

Wounded Knee, Pine Ridge, SD,
Native American response

Hesston, KS, area tonadoes

AK wild fires

Mississippi River floods

Hurricane Joan in Nicaragua

Birmingham, AL,
tornado

Earthquake response in Nicaragua

Tornado in Edmonton, AB

Sanford, FL, tornadoes
and wild fires

Tornado projects in Jones County,
MS, and Saragosa, TX

25th Anniversary celebrated,
"Day of Disaster" published

Tom Smucker
becomes executive
coordinator

WV floods from
Hurricane Juan

Floods in WV and
Johnstown, PA

Hurricane Georges,
Puerto Rico

Tornadoes in
OH, PA, and ON

Earthquake in Coalinga, CA

Timeline axis:
72 73 74 75 76 77 78 79 1980 81 82 83 84 85 86 87 88 89 1990 91 92 93 94 95 96 97 98 99 2000 01 02

Timeline entries below the axis:

Hurricane Frederick
in AL and MS

MDS Celebrates
50th anniversary
in Hesston, KS;
new book
released

Tornadoes in
Paris and
Wichita Falls,
TX

Tornadoes in NC and SC

Floods in Marysville/Yuba City, CA

Tornadoes in
OK and KS

Lowell Detweiler becomes
executive coordinator

Big Thompson
Canyon, CO

Bartlesville, OK, floods

Marysville/Yuba City, CA, floods

Grand Teton
dam break

Drought response in GA, NC, and SC

Arkansas tornadoes

Flood response in Winsk, ON

Hurricane Fifi in Honduras

Hurricane Hugo in St. Croix and SC

Red River Floods,
SD, MN, and MB

"Super Sunday" tornadoes
in AL, KY, and OH

Loma Prieta earthquake in Watsonville, CA

Ohio River Floods,
KY and OH

Hurricane Agnes floods in PA and NY

Ice/floods in Allagash, ME

Rapid City, SD floods

Andover, KS, tornado

Hurricane Marilyn in St. Thomas

Buffalo Creek, WV floods

MDS incorporates as separate entity

Northern AL tornadoes

Major Midwest Floods, IL, MO, IA, and KS

177

MDS Organizational Representatives

Organization	1955	1960	1965	1970	1975	1980	1985	1990	1995		
(phases)	56 Coordinating Council →		62 Section →					93 Board →			
MCC Binational/U.S.	56 William Snyder					82 Wilmer Heisey		90 L.Meck	98 B.Wagner		
Mennonite Church	56 B.Nelson	61 Ray Horst		74 John Eby	77 Eldon King						
General Conference	56 E.Ediger	60 H.Martens	65 F.Unruh	68 Walter Neufeld			84 L.Kauffman	91 Irvin Harms			
Evangelical Menn	56 Dale Rufenacht			74 Paul Jorg	79 Carl Nussbaum				96 A.Swartz		
Conservative Menn	56 L.L.Swartzendruber		66 E.Weaver	72 T.Stutzman	76 R.Thomas	80 A.Miller	85 C.Miller	94 A.Miller	98 J.Yoder		
Brethren in Christ	56 P.Martin Jr.	58 Raymond Hess					87 M.Wolgemuth	89 L.Byers	98 Dan Houck		
Lancaster Conf.	58 P.Landis	60 Norman Shenk							96 M.Garrett		
CHPC (Ont)		60 J.B.Martin									
Mennonite Brethren		60 M.A.Kroeker	62 G.Classen	68 D.Wiebe	70 Peter Funk		85 E.Hofer	92 Marvin Toews			
Region I		62 Ivan Martin	69 Landis Hershey				87 Paul Brubacher				
Region II		62 L.Britsch	68 C.Graber	74 Ora Yoder		80 F. Kauffman	83 V. Gingerich	86 A. Miller	92 L.Miller	95 A.Miller	97 O.Mast
Region III		62 A.Ediger	66 W.Unruh	69 M.Hostetler	73 H.Friesen	83 Myron Schultz		89 I.Reimer	95 V.Miller		
Region IV		62 John Jantzi				83 Henry Mast		92 P.Fast	95 W.Leichty		
Region V		62 Eddie Bearinger				80 Syd Reimer		91 Abe Ens			
Region VI		62 W.Loewen									
Church of God in Christ (Menn)			67 Aden Holdeman		79 N.Ensz	83 W.Boehs	86 Stanley Giesel				
Beachy Amish				73 Amos Zook			86 Willis Hochstetler				
MCC Canada				74 Syd Reimer		80 W.Neufeld	87 H.Koslowsky		95 R.Bietz	97 E.Barkman	
Member-at-large (women)					75 Ruby Schmidt		84 V.Weber	91 N.Gingerich	95 P.Schultz		
Member-at-large					75 Evelyn Kaufman			92 A.Miller	96 I.Reimer		
MCCC/Region V							84 Abe Froese				
Member-at-large (youth)							86 A.Yoder	90 R.Stutzman	94 J.Yoder	98 J.Kuepfer	
Mennonite Pilots							89 Rocky Miller				
MennoNet						83 Jacob Swartzendruber		91 Sandy Swartzendruber			
Old Order Amish								94 Emmanual Fisher			
Groffdale Conference								94 David Hoover			
Menn. Health Services								94 S.Kauffman	98 Paul Unruh		
New Order Amish								94 Leroy Stoltzfus			

MDS Board Chairs

	1955	1960	1965	1970	1975	1980	1985	1990	1995
		60 D.Rufenacht	65 I.Martin	66 N.Shenk	74 P.Funk	80 S.Reimer	86 N.Shenk	92 E.King	98 P.Brubacher

MDS Staff

	1955	1960	1965	1970	1975	1980	1985	1990	1995
Coordinator		62 W.Clemmens	64 D.Stahley	71 Nelson Hostetetter			86 Lowell Detweiler		98 Tom Smucker
Other staff			C.Wiebe	71 B.Weaver 72 B.Martin 73 J.Lehman	75 S.Wright 76 P.Horst 78 J.Barkman	80 Sandy Weaver Yoder		92 E.Miller 93 P. Miller 94 T.Smucker 94 R.Augsburger	94 Carla Hunt 95 M.Godshalk 98 M.Doncevic 98 W.Litwiller

History of MDS All-Unit Meetings

The first meetings of MDS representatives were held in Chicago in connection with MCC meetings. They were initially called "MDS representatives meetings," later the "MDS annual meeting," and finally the "MDS all-unit meeting."

Year	Location
1956	Chicago, IL
1957	Chicago, IL
1958	Chicago, IL
1959	Chicago, IL
1960	Chicago, IL
1961	Denver, CO
1962	Chicago, IL
1963	Hillsboro, KS
1964	Lansdale, PA
1965	Kitchener, ON
1966	Fresno, CA
1967	Shipshewana, IN
1968	Kitchener, ON
1969	Kalona, IA
1970	Lancaster, PA

Year	Location
1971	Calgary, AB
1972	Albany, OR
1973	Morton, IL
1974	Altona, MB
1975	Hesston, KS
1976	Sarasota, FL
1977	St. Catharines, ON
1978	Phoenix, AZ
1979	Kidron, OH
1980	Saskatoon, SK
1981	Enid, OK
1982	Newport News, VA
1983	Coaldale, AB
1984	Upland, CA
1985	Archbold, OH

Year	Location
1986	Winnipeg, MB
1987	N. Newton, KS
1988	Hagerstown, MD
1989	Vancouver, BC
1990	Eugene, OR
1991	Shipshewana, IN
1992	Kitchener, ON
1993	Seward, NB
1994	Homestead, FL
1995	Saskatoon, SK
1996	Reedley, CA
1997	Columbus, MS
1998	Calgary, AB
1999	Harrisonburg, VA
2000	Hesston, KS

MDS Largest Projects (as of 12/1999)

MDSers concentrate on getting work done and responding to the needs of persons affected by disaster, not keeping records. The information in this chart is the best available and in many cases not complete. Especially in the earlier years, figures may be estimates and are rounded off. Nevertheless, the chart provides valuable information on the amazing involvement of MDS in many places over the years.

	Project Name	Beginning Date	Ending Date	Number of Volunteers	Days Worked
1	72 Hurricane Agnes (PA and NY)	6/23/72	9/74	8,200	37,000 (first 2 mos.)
2	92 Hurricane Andrew (3 locations, FL and LA)	8/23/92	3/30/94	6,600	42,000
3	89 Hurricane Hugo (SC and St. Croix)	9/20/89	3/31/91	7,100	41,000
4	93 Midwest floods (11 locations—15 million acres flooded)	8/16/93	2/28/95	6,000	22,900
5	65 Palm Sunday tornadoes (report on Indiana only)	4/11/65	12/65		19,000
6	73 Mississippi River floods 12 million acres	3/73	6/74		19,000
7	74 Super Outbreak tornadoes (AL, KY, OH, IN, MI)	4/3/74	8/75		18,000
8	97 Red River floods (MB, ND, MN)	4/25/97	11/01/98	2,100	15,300
9	69 Hurricane Camille	8/20/69	3/15/70	1,800	11,000
10	90 Hesston, KS, tornado	3/13/90	?/90		10,000
11	72 Rapid City, SD, flood	6/10/72	?/72	1,500	7,000
12	94 Tropical Storm Alberto floods, GA (3 locations)	7/16/94	3/29/96	1,250	7,200
13	98 Birmingham, AL, tornado	4/15/98	9/3/99	1,200	6,800
14	99 Oklahoma/Kansas tornadoes/floods	5/4/99	ongoing	1,018+	5,300+
15	98 Florida tornadoes/fires	3/1/98	4/2/99	820	4,960
16	95 Hurricane Marilyn, St. Thomas	9/12/95	7/31/96	250	4,830
17	97 Ohio River floods	3/17/97	9/97	1,300	4,800
18	72 Buffalo Creek, WV	2/26/72	11/72		4,000
19	55 Udall, KS, tornado	5/25/55	?/55	1,100 on one day	?

MDS Unit/Project History

Region	Unit or Area*	Date Started	Largest Disaster Projects in Unit Area
I	Cumberland Valley, PA	1966	72 Hurricane Agnes floods; 85 Potomac River floods; 99 haylift
	Delmarva	1958	Local projects
	Florida	1972	92 Hurricane Andrew; 98 tornadoes/wildfires
	Georgia	1965	86 drought; 94 tropical storm Alberto floods; 94 Jasper tornado; 98 Gainesville tornado
	New England	1978	87 Augusta, ME, floods; 91 Allagsh, ME, floods
	New York	1956	72 Hurricane Agnes; 91 Jefferson County ice storm; 95 microburst; 98 N. N.Y. ice storm
	North Carolina	1974	88 Raleigh area tornadoes; 89 tornadoes; 89 Hurricane Hugo
	Northern Pennsylvania	1996	85 Williamsport area tornado; 96 Williamsport area floods
	Eastern PA and NJ	1955	55 Stroudsburg flood; 72 Hurricane Agnes
	Lancaster Area, PA	1955	72 Hurricane Agnes
	Western PA and MD	1956	77 Johnstown flood; 85 NW tornadoes; 98 Salisbury tornadoes
	Puerto Rico	1978	98 Hurricane Georges
	South Carolina	1974	84 tornadoes; 86 drought response; 89 Hurricane Hugo
	Shenandoah, VA	1957	69 Hurricane Camille, Nelson County, VA, flood; 77 drought; 85 floods; 96 Hurricane Fran
	Tidewater, VA	1965	89 Richmond rehab project for YWAM; 99 Hurricane Floyd
	Washington, DC/Baltimore	1983	71 DC cleanup from May riots; 72 Hurricane Agnes floods; 76 Hurricane Frederick floods; 86 haylift
	US Virgin Islands*		89 Hurricane Hugo, St. Croix; 95 Hurricane Marilyn, St. Thomas
	West Virginia*		72 Buffalo Creek floods; 77 floods; 85 Hurricane Juan floods
II	Alabama	1962	74 Huntsville; 79 Hurricane Frederick; 95 tornadoes; 96 church rebuilding; 98 Birmingham tornado
	Illinois	1956	92 Marion tornado; 93 floods
	Indiana	1955	65 Palm Sunday tornadoes; 74 tornadoes; 97 floods
	Kentucky/Tennessee	1974	74 tornadoes; 97 floods
	Michigan	1966	53 Flint tornadoes; 65 Palm Sunday tornadoes
	Mississippi/Louisiana	1964	64 rebuilding bombed churches; hurricanes: 65 Betsy, 69 Camille, 79 Frederick, 92 Andrew
	Eastern Ohio	1955	85 NW tornadoes; 90 Shadyside flash flood; 97 Ohio River floods
	Western Ohio	1955	65 Palm Sunday tornadoes; 74 Xenia tornado; 97 Ohio River floods
	Wisconsin	1959	76 hay lift; 84 Barnveld tornado
III	Arkansas	1968	68 tornado; 97 tornadoes
	Colorado	1965	76 Big Thompson Canyon flood
	Iowa	1955	93 floods; 98 Washington area tornadoes
	Kansas	1950	Tornadoes: 55 Udall, 90 Hesston, 91 Andover; 93 Midwest floods; 98 Augusta floods
	Minnesota	1956	65 Mankato floods; 68 Tracy tornado; 92 Chandler tornado; 97 Red River floods
	Northern Minnesota	1959	97 Red River floods
	Missouri	1974	75 Macon area tornadoes; 93 floods
	Eastern Montana	1962	64 & 75 Great Falls floods; 84 Bull Mt. fires; 86 & 95 Milk River floods
	Western Montana	1960	64 floods
	Nebraska	1957	53 Hebron tornado; 80 Grand Island tornado
	North Dakota	1960	97 Red River floods
	Oklahoma	1955	47 Woodward tornado; 86 Bartlesville flood; 95 Oklahoma City bombing; 99 tornadoes
	South Dakota	1955	72 Rapid City floods; 92 hailstorm on Rosebud Sioux reservation; 98 Spencer tornado
	Texas	1978	79 Paris & Wichita Falls tornado; 87 Saragosa tornado
	New Mexico*		
	Wyoming*		76 Grand Teton dam break
IV	Arizona	1956	78 floods; 92 Church building Navaho Reservation
	California	1955	55, 86, 97 Marysville/Yuba City floods; earthquakes: 83 Coalinga, 89 Loma Prieta, 94 Northridge
	Idaho	1956	97 Payette flood; Rexburg flood
	Oregon	1959	74 floods; 96 floods
	Washington	1999	96 floods
	Alaska*		64 earthquake; 96 wildfires
	Hawaii*		93 Hurricane Iniki
	Nevada & Utah*		
V	Alberta	1955	87 Edmonton tornado; 97 prairie fires
	Atlantic-Eastern Province	1977	Local projects
	British Columbia	1956	84 Pemberton floods; 95 Princeton floods; 98 Salmon Arm forest fires
	Manitoba	1956	79 Red River floods; 89 forest fires; 97 Red River floods
	Ontario	1958	79 Woodstock tornado; 85 Grand Valley/Barrie tornado; 98 E Ontario ice storm
	Quebec	1997	96 Saguenay floods; 98 ice storms
	Saskatchewan	1959	74 Moose Jaw floods; 96 Osler windstorm; 98 Camp Elim fire

*Italics indicate inclusion in the region but having no organized unit.

Map of MDS Regions

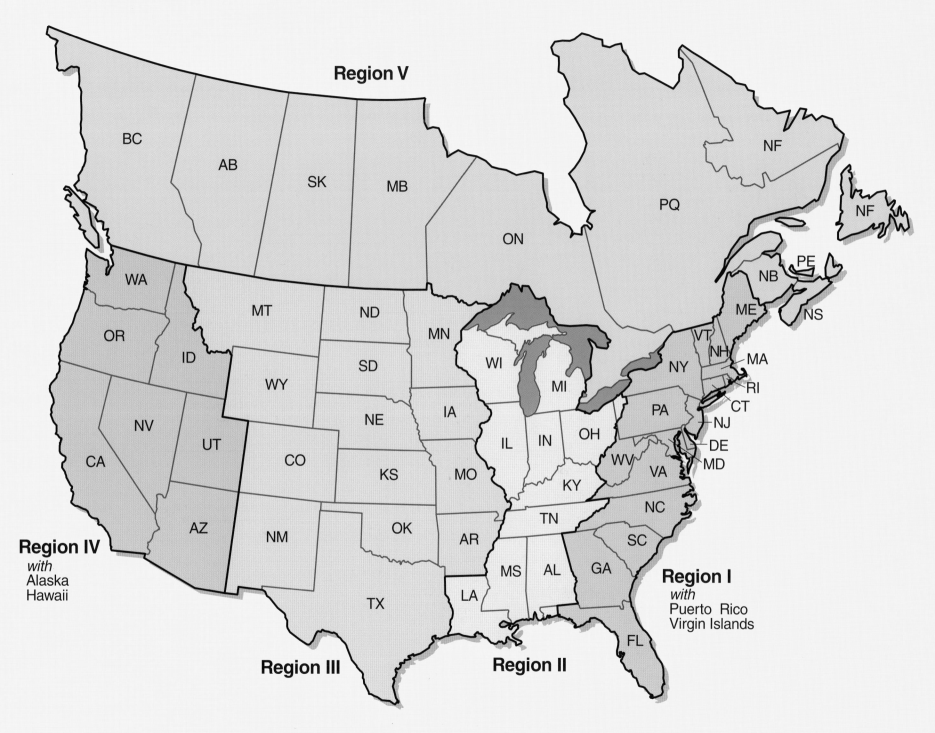

Region V

Region IV
with
Alaska
Hawaii

Region III

Region II

Region I
with
Puerto Rico
Virgin Islands

Notes

1. In the Eye of the Storm

1. Howard Inglish, *Year of the Storms* (Hillsboro, Kan.: Hearth Publishing, 1990).

2. Phil Harrington, *Messenger* (N. Newton, Kan.: South Central Conference, May/June, 1990).

Other printed sources: Evelyn Rouner, *Scrapbook: The Coordinator's Report of the 1990 Hesston Tornado* (Hesston, Kan.: Prestige Printing, 1990); Hesston, Kan., *Record*; *Mennonite Weekly Review*.

Recorded/transcribed interviews in June/July 1998: members of original Sunday school classes: Howard and Anna Ruth Beck, Vernon and Alma Blosser (1997), Allen Diller, Ivan and Doris Diller, Robert and Marcella Diller, Harold Dyck, Lois Hershberger, Daniel Kauffman, Kenneth and Laura Ann King, Milton and Lorraine Miller, Pearl Rodgers, Paul Shenk, Ray Spicher, Gene Weaver, Milford Weaver, Naomi Weaver, Lyle Yost. Others: Kirk and Jean Alliman; Murray Bandy; Dale Hochstetler; Nelson Kilmer; Irvin and Edna Reimer; Evelyn Rouner; John Waltner, Mayor of Hesston; MDS Kansas Leaders Irvin Harms, Marvin Toews, and Homer Wedel.

2. In the Beginning

1. "The Servant Song," by Richard Gillard, © 1972 *Scripture in Song* (a division of Integrity Music, Inc.) ASCAP; all rights reserved; international copyright secured; used by permission.

2. This note, attached to the July 28 entry, was written July 25, 1952; Fred Brenneman diary excerpts as prepared and released by Lawrence Brenneman.

3. Dirk Willems, who became a martyr; reported in Thieleman J. van Braght, *Martyrs Mirror* (Scottdale, Pa.: Herald Press, 1938), 741-742, with illustrative engraving.

4. Albert N. Keim, *The CPS Story: An Illustrated History of Civilian Public Service* (Intercourse, Pa.: Good Books, 1990), 99.

5. John Diller, "Historic Background of Mennonite Service Organization," from collected writings and records of John Diller, in Mennonite Library and Archives at Bethel College, N. Newton, Kan.; and the Archives of the Mennonite Church at Goshen, Indiana.

6. Lawrence Brenneman, "The Story of Mennonite Service Organization," a study paper (1964).

7. John Diller, "The Work of the Co-ordinator of the Mennonite Service Organization" (see note 5).

8. Joseph S. Miller, *Beyond the Mystic Border: A 100-Year History of the Whitestone Mennonite Church* (Hillsboro, Kan.: Multi Business Press, 1985), 135.

Manuscript: Brice Brenneman, "Mennonite Disaster Service—History" (1979).

Recorded/transcribed interviews in June/July, 1998: Members of 1950 Pennsylvania Mennonite Church and Hesston Mennonite Church Sunday school classes (see chap. 1 notes); Marion Bontrager, Don Diller, Peter J. Dyck, Albert Ediger, Ralph and Elizabeth Hernley, Robert Kreider, and Boyd Nelson.

3. Why Are You Here?

1. Excerpted from "Mennonites" from *Sleeping Preacher*, by Julia Kasdorf, © 1992; reprinted by permission of University of Pittsburgh Press.

2. Katie Funk Wiebe, *Day of Disaster* (Scottdale, Pa.: Herald Press, 1976), 94.

3. "About the Mennonite Church: Our Family Can Be Your Family" (Elkhart, Ind., and Harrisonburg, Va.: Mennonite Board of Missions, 1989), brochure.

4. C. Nelson Hostetter, *Anabaptist-Mennonites Nationwide USA* (Morgantown, Pa.: Masthof, 1997).

5. David Augsburger, "The Mennonite Dream" (Elkhart, Ind., and Harrisonburg, Va.: Mennonite Board of Missions, 1970), brochure, MDS reprint.

6. "About the Mennonite Church."

7. See brochure cited in note 3; Harry Loewen with others, *Through Fire and Water: An Overview of Mennonite History* (Scottdale, Pa.: Herald Press, 1996), with reading list on 347-348; C. J. Dyck, *An Introduction to Mennonite History*, 3d ed. (Scottdale, Pa.: Herald Press, 1993); C. Arnold Snyder, *Anabaptist History and Theology*, Rev. Student Ed. (Kitchener, Ont.: Pandora Press, and Scottdale, Pa.: Herald Press, 1997).

8. Excerpts about the Mennonites from www.thirdway.com.

9. John Sobrino, *The Principle of Mercy* (Maryknoll, N.Y.: Orbis, 1994), 17.

10. Menno Simons, "Why I Do Not Cease Teaching and Writing," in *The Complete Writings of Menno Simons*, ed. J. C. Wenger (Scottdale, Pa.: Herald Press, 1956), 307.

11. The 1775 "Declaration to the Colonial Assembly of Pennsylvania," in J. C. Wenger, *History of the Mennonites of the Franconia Conference* (Scottdale, Pa.: Mennonite Publishing House, 1937), 409.

12. John A. Lapp, "God's People Doing God's Work," keynote address at MDS All-Unit Meeting, Seward, Neb., Feb. 1993 (rev. July 9, 1999).

13. Poem by Edgar Albert Guest, 1881-1959, copyright status unknown.

14. Fred Unruh, "Looking at Evangelism in MDS," workshop points, Oct. 9, 1968.

15. Wiebe, *Day of Disaster*, 56-59, adapted.

Transcript of letter from Jeanie Tyson, Apr. 30, 1996. Interviews: Dan Houck, John A. Lapp, Norman Shenk, Ron Mathies.

4. After Seedtime Comes the Harvest

1. Wiebe, *Day of Disaster*.

2. Litany by Archbishop Oscar Romero, copyright status unknown.

3. Birch Bayh, U.S. Senator from Indiana, in Wiebe, *Day of Disaster*, 12, introduction.

4. David Wagler, *The Mighty Whirlwind* (Alymer, Ont.: Pathway, 1966), 85.

5. Wagler, *The Mighty Whirlwind*, 209-213.

6. Wagler, *The Mighty Whirlwind*, 213.

7. David Kniss, devotional, MDS All-Unit Meeting, Columbus, Miss., Feb. 1997, adapted from meeting transcript.

8. For this story, see Wiebe, *Day of Disaster*, chap. 1.

9. For this story, see Wiebe, *Day of Disaster*, chap. 13.

Interviews: C. N. Friesen; Fred Kathler; Oklahoma MDS Unit leaders: Brian Casement, Marvin Dester, Bill Mast, Leroy and Ruth Miller, Melvin Schultz; Leonard Garber; Paul Haarer; persons at Des Alemands, La.: Steve Cheramie, George and Ruby Reno, Robert Zehr; Gulfhaven, Miss., meeting: Ronnie Geil, Warren Miller; Harold Regier; Harold Miller and Community Mennonite Church group of Corning, N.Y.; and by phone with Dick Nickel, pastor of Bible Fellowship Church, Rapid City, S.D.

5. Mending the Torn Land

1. For examples, Hurricane Andrew in chap. 6, and the Red River floods in chap. 7.

2. Barbara Anderson and Sharlynn Wamsley, *Reflections of the Heart: The Big Thompson Canyon Flood* (Loveland, Colo.: Drake Club Press, 1996); available from Linda Hill, 1042 Big Thompson Canyon Rd, Loveland, CO 80537.

3. Mark Twain, pen name for Samuel Langhorne Clemens, original publication unidentified.

Manuscripts: Paul Martin, "Big Thompson." Frank McCoy, "A Peculiar People."

Letters by Addise Capuzzi and Jeanie Tyson.

Big Thompson contacts: Lena and Howard Carman, Indian Village Arts and Crafts, 1348 Big Thompson Canyon, Loveland, CO 80537; Susan Jessup, Sylvan Dale Guest Ranch, 2939 North County Road, 31 D, Loveland, CO 80538.

Interviews: David and Ann Matthews, Moncks Corner, S.C.; Missouri Unit leaders: Irvin and Edith Oberholtzer, William and Miriam Coblentz, Sam and

Corlene Hostetler, Andrew Yoder, Dean L. and Velma Yoder, Richard D. Adams, Elwin D. Yoder, Dan and Martha Miller; Alexandria, Mo., community leader: Willis Kuhns; Keithsburg, Ill., community leaders: Chuck Reynolds, Sharon Reason; Hull, Ill., community leaders: Oliver Friedlein, Paul and Jan Kenady; Lee and Mary Lois Martin; California: Wes and Ann Heinrichs, Ed Ratzlaff, Roger and Barbara Friesen, Eddie and Verona Neufeld, Jim Clymer, John and Wilma Miller, Egon and Naomi Hofer, Carl and Mildred Pankratz; Captain Frank Gordon; Nathan Koslowsky; Irene Mings; Eva Zuniga; Blaine and Myrtle Kizer.

6. Hurricane Andrew: A Shaking and Shaping

Transcripts: Kathleen Hartzler, presentation, MDS All-Unit Meeting, Seward, Neb., Feb. 1993; Program materials, All-Unit Meeting, Homestead, Fla., Feb. 1994.

Interviews at Homestead, Fla.: Walter and Joy Sawatsky, 9/92; others in Jan. 1999: Walter and Joy Sawatsky, in Souderton, Pa.; MDS Fla. unit leaders Atlee Schlabach, Al Kurtz, Nelson Hostetter, and Art Smucker, in Sarasota, Fla.; Lil Worley; Drane Reynolds; Hector and Luisa Vazquez; Chuck Goertz, pastor of HMC; David and Kathleen Hartzler; Gloria Hernandez; Alice Taylor; Pompilio and Gladys Martinez; Nehemiah staff Luis Azan, Marilyn McCready, and Fernando Sandoval.

Interviews in Louisiana in Jan. 1999: at Franklin: Almetra J. Franklin, Linda D. Moreaux, Al Kuhlman, David H. Stiel Jr., Jane Powers, Kate Malloy, Oray P. Rogers, Sam Jones, Ottis Mast; at Des Alemands: Robert Zehr, George and Ruby Reno, Steve Cheramie.

7. The Red River Runs North

1. "No man is an island . . . ," by John Donne, excerpted from *Devotions upon Emergent Occasions* (1624), no. 17, spelling modernized; cf. Paul in Rom. 12.

2. "I bind my soul this day . . . ," by Lauchlan M. Watt, from "I bind my heart this tide," in *The Tryst: A Book of the Soul*, 1907, alt.

Book: *The Red River Valley Echo: A Flood of Images* (Altona, Man.: Interlake Publishing, 1997).

Transcript: Leon and Lea Dorge house dedication.

Interviews: Pete and Marianne Friesen by Marj Heinrichs, Abe Ens, Syd Reimer, Paul Friesen, Gord Friesen, John Geisbrecht, Eddie Bearinger, Harold Koslowsky, Joan Barkman, Abe Froese, Norman Weber, Delmar Zehr, Keith Wagler, Wilmer Leichty.

8. Broadening Our Vision

1. Text © John Oxenham; used by permission of Desmond Dunkerly, 23 Haslemere Rd., Southsea,
Portsmouth, Hants, P04 8BB, England.

2. *Washington Post*, Jan. 23, 1996.

3. Marian E. Buckwalter, letter to Tobin Miller-Shearer, Jan. 26, 1996.

4. Heading and article (adapted) from Rich Preheim, *Mennonite Weekly Review*, Sept. 19, 1996.

5. Wiebe, *Day of Disaster*, 50-51, as told by John Jantzi.

Transcript: Pastor Thomas Gillmore, Ensley, Miss., presentation at MDS All-Unit Meeting, Columbus, Miss., Feb. 7, 1997.

Interviews: Boligee, Ala.: Pastor Arthur Coleman and Deacon Bobby Davis, Mt. Zoar Baptist Church; College Station, Ark.: Tressie B. Robierson, Vera Mae King, Pastor Dr. Hezekiah D. Stewart Jr. of Mt. Nebo AME Church, Emmanual Benton, Kid Henry Williams, Rep. Wilma Walker, Austin Porter Jr., Austin Porter Sr.; MDSers at College Station on March 2, 1998: Linda and Russel Smucker, Henry and Pearl Dueck, Jean Hampton, Mark Ewert, Ryan Hildebrand, Art Toews, Willie Miller.

9. Dear God, It Hurts

Manuscripts: Pam Denlinger, "Stories from Gainesville, Ga." Paul Unruh, "Contributing to the Mental Health of Disaster Survivors."

Interviews: Irvin Harms, Dean and Pam Denlinger, Paul Unruh, Joe Steiner, Tom Smucker, Carla Hunt.

10. Give of the Strength of Your Youth

1. Goshen College *Record*, Oct. 1987; "Students Use Fall Break for Service with MDS."

Manuscripts: Duane Yoder, "Youth Squad Reflections." Dennis Landis, "Letter to MDS Akron." Greg Toews, "[Story of Louisiana Experience]."

Interviews: Dan Bontrager, Joan Barkman, Carla Hunt, Sandy Weaver Yoder; Gulfport, Miss., group including Dave and Sue Weaver, Ashley Swan; Dwight and Luella Unruh; Laws Conservative Mennonite Church Youth, led by Daniel Yutzy, Greenwood, Del.; Pequea Brethren in Christ Youth, led by Dan Houck, Lancaster, Pa.; Virgil and Leola Kauffman, Ralph and Carolyn Metzler, Wilf and Margaret Unrau, Marisa Doncevic, Doug and Rhonda Hartzler, Nathan Koslowsky.

11. New Paradigms: A Changing World

Transcripts: Edgar Stoesz, speech, "The Changing and the Eternal," MDS All-Unit Meeting, Saskatoon, 1995; Monte Sahlin, "Paradigm Shifts," NVOAD Annual Meeting, 1993; Elizabeth Dole, presentation, NVOAD Annual Meeting, 1992.

Interview: Monte Sahlin.

12. When Disaster Strikes, How MDS Works

1. Second verse and refrain, "There Are Many Gifts," text and music © 1977 Patricia Shelly, Box 41, North Newton, KS 67117; used by permission.

2. Drawn from Floyd and Mollie Yoder, *Tornadoes* (Sugarcreek, Ohio: Schlabach Printers, 1998).

Manuscripts: Pam Denlinger, "The Cookie Lady"; Merle Sommers, "MDS Puerto Rico Report"; John Diller, "Writings."

Interviews: Landis Hershey, Bill and Sylvia Mast, Philip Bender, Raymond Yoder, Menno Yoder, Alton Miller, Paul Brubacher, Tom Smucker, Ottis Mast, Pastor Bernice Mahan, Roland Stutzman, Pastor T. L. Lewis, Michael Martin, Paul Unruh, Fan Bailey, Bob and Doreen Rempel, Tim Charles, Jamie Aldefer, Doreen and Jerry Klassen, Carla Hunt, Marisa Doncevic, Julio Vincenty.

13. On Doing Good Better

1. Robert Schrag, editorial, *Mennonite Weekly Review*, quoted in *Day of Disaster*, 108.

2. This chapter title borrows from the book title *Doing Good Better*, by Edgar Stoesz and Chester Raber (Intercourse, Pa.: Good Books, 1994).

3. *Day of Disaster*, 108.

4. Kahlil Gibran, *The Prophet* (New York, N.Y.: Alfred A. Knopf, 1995), 97.

Transcript: Mary Lois Martin, "Georgia Project Report to MDS."

Manuscripts: Doris Daley, poem, "Bless These Hands"; Tom Smucker.

Interviews: Robert Kreider, Velma Yoder, Jane Kuepfer, Vic and Bev Plessinger, Paul Brubacher, Bob Bender, Jean Hampton, Brian Epp, Edgar Stoesz.

14. Outbursts of Love and Good Deeds

1. "God is working his purpose out," by Arthur C. Ainger (1894), *Church Missionary Hymn Book* (1899), alt.

2. Edward Mote, "The Solid Rock" (1834).

3. Jimmy Carter, *The Virtues of Aging*, (New York, N.Y.: Ballantine Publishing Group, 1998), 60-61.

Article: J. Lorne Peachey, editorial, *The Mennonite*, April 27, 1999.

Transcripts: James Brenneman, "A Time to Build," presentation at MDS all-unit meeting, Reedley, Calif., 1996; Pastor Thomas Gillmore, from speeches at Mt. Zoar Baptist Church dedication and at MDS all-unit meeting, Columbus, Miss., 1997.

Manuscripts: Beryl Forester, "Report on Assignment in St. Croix, U.S.V.I."; Robert Kreider, "Reflections on Attending MDS Meeting, 1973"; Ginny Sauder, "Report on Alabama MDS Trip."

Author

Photographer

L owell Detweiler has topped off a lifetime of service with 14 years of involvement with Mennonite Disaster Service. He has early memories of MDS while he was growing up in Fairview, Mich. His father was the local contact person and took crews to work at Flint, Mich., after the 1953 tornado.

Detweiler was trained as a teacher at Goshen College. He and his wife, Ruth (Kauffman), taught in a two-room school in a small Newfoundland fishing village during 1959-61, under Mennonite Central Committee (MCC). After several years of teaching in Ohio public schools, they served in Tanzania under MCC's Teachers Abroad Program in 1968-71, taking along their children, Cheryl and Steve.

Following that assignment, they joined the staff at MCC headquarters in Akron, Pa., where they have lived ever since. Detweiler served as director of the personnel department until 1982, then became the regional director for MCC East Coast. During those years, he learned to know the MDS network as MCC and MDS worked together in several food drives for relief.

In 1986 Detweiler was invited to become the MDS director. In 1998, Tom Smucker followed him as MDS director while Detweiler concentrated on writing this book and leading the planning for the fiftieth anniversary celebration of MDS, in Hesston, Kan., on June 2-4, 2000.

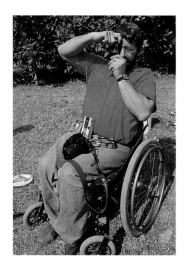

M any photos in this book are by Carl E. Hiebert, who volunteered to photograph MDS project sites. Hiebert has his roots in a Mennonite farming community of southern Ontario and lives in Waterloo. He has traveled around the globe and worked as a salesman, photographer, reporter, technician, public speaker, aerial photographer, flight instructor, and environmentalist.

In 1981, Hiebert's life took a drastic turn when he broke his back in a hanggliding accident. Within two years he opened his own flight school and became Canada's first paraplegic flight instructor.

He has received many awards, such as the Honorary Guild Shield, for enhancing the quality of life for all Canadians; the Vanier Award (1986), given to five outstanding Canadians; and the Paul Tessandier Award, for being the first to fly across Canada in an open-cockpit ultralight aircraft.

Hiebert's writings and photography have been displayed in several books, such as *Us Little People: Mennonite Children; Gift of Wings: An Aerial Celebration of Canada;* and *Paroles et Lumieres—Where Light Speaks: Haiti.*

BENTON MENNONITE
CHURCH LIBRARY